UNTIL SHE WRIT[...]
THIS IS THE BEST [AND ...]
WE'LL HAVE AT THE PHENOMENON
KNOWN AS:

JACKIE O!

HIGHLY ENTERTAINING! . . . Birmingham,
bit by bit, pieces together his answer to the
Jackie riddle. . . . This book is special."
—Pittsburgh Press

"**A FASCINATING CLOSE-UP** . . . the story
of the making of a legend . . . an intimate portrait of a complex, sensitive woman"
—Book-of-the-Month Club News

"The combination of her glamor and Birming-
ham's reputation as chronicler of society's upper
crust is sure to make this book a bestseller. . . .
**HIS TRAVERSAL OF HER LIFE IS THE
MOST DETAILED TO DATE!**"
—San Francisco Examiner

Books by Stephen Birmingham

Jacqueline Bouvier Kennedy Onassis
"Our Crowd" (Wallaby edition)

Published by POCKET BOOKS

Jacqueline
Bouvier Kennedy Onassis

by
Stephen Birmingham

P

PUBLISHED BY POCKET BOOKS NEW YORK

POCKET BOOKS, a Simon & Schuster division of
GULF & WESTERN CORPORATION
1230 Avenue of the Americas, New York, N.Y. 10020

Selection from *The Bouviers* by John H. Davis. Copyright ©
1969 by John H. Davis. (Farrar, Straus & Giroux, Inc.)

Copyright © 1978 by Stephen Birmingham

Published by arrangement with Grosset & Dunlap, Inc.
Library of Congress Catalog Card Number: 77-87799

ISBN: 0-671-82862-2

First Pocket Books printing April, 1979

10 9 8 7 6 5 4 3 2 1

Trademarks registered in the United States and other countries.

Printed in the U.S.A.

For Frances Lindley
May her tribe increase

Foreword

JACQUELINE KENNEDY ONASSIS is not a woman who has caused great events to occur. No wars have been fought over her; she is no Helen of Troy. She is, on the other hand, a woman to whom a number of memorable things have happened and, in the course of being the object of these happenings, she has become the most famous woman in the world—admired, vilified, more argued-about and better known than Helen ever was. Through it all, she has remained an enigma, a riddle. It is in an attempt to unravel the riddle of Mrs. Onassis's elusive, complex character that I have written this book.

This is not an authorized biography. On the contrary. Though Mrs. Onassis issues occasional public statements, and will answer direct questions of fact, when channeled through her secretary, she will grant no interviews—to me or, to my knowledge, any other writer. This apparent shyness, coupled with an amazing amount of self-possession, is one of the facets of her nature I have endeavored to explore. Nor is this the first book to be written about Jacqueline Onassis—nor will it likely be the last. Among the published books which have proved important sources, I would like to acknowledge and thank the authors of *Jacqueline Kennedy: a Biography,* by Gordon Langley Hall; *Jacqueline Bouvier Kennedy,* by Mary Van Rensselaer Thayer; *The Hidden Side of Jacqueline Kennedy,* by George Carpozi; and *Controversy* and *The Death of a President,* by William Manchester. My friend John

H. Davis's book, *The Bouviers,* was a vital source of Bouvier family history.

Since this is a book which has depended on the impressions, recollections, insights and anecdotes of many other people, there are a number whom I would like particularly to thank. I am grateful to Mr. Thomas Guinzburg and Miss Rebecca Singleton of The Viking Press; to Mrs. Henry Brandon of Washington; to Dr. C. E. Lahniers of the University of Cincinnati for psychological insights; to Mr. George Plimpton, Miss Nancy Tuckerman, Miss Letitia Baldridge, Mr. Karl Katz, Mr. Cornell Capa, Miss Helene Gaillet, Miss Liz Smith, Mr. Otto Fenn, and Mr. Louis Auchincloss, all of New York, and to Mr. John Meyer of Palm Beach. I also owe a special word of thanks to the late Mr. Hugh D. Auchincloss and Mrs. Janet Auchincloss of Washington and Newport for past hospitality at Hammersmith Farm.

Though each of these people has contributed enormously to this book, I alone must be accountable for any of its errors or shortcomings.

I would like to thank, too, my friend and agent Carol Brandt, who has guided the project from the start with her usual cool intelligence, and my editor at Grosset & Dunlap, Mr. Robert Markel, who was first to propose that this was a book worth writing.

S.B.

Contents

Contents

Part
One

1

Sleeping in Public

MIDDLE-AGED LADIES who doze off, peacefully, in public places . . .

One thinks of the benches in the Forty-second Street waiting room of Grand Central Station, or at the bus depot, or in the park, each bench with its cuddled occupant, her head resting on her handbag. It takes, one supposes, a certain resigned detachment from life, a certain carelessness about what the world might think, to succumb to sleep in front of others while others are going about their business. Sleep is such a private matter. Most of us dislike being looked at while we sleep. We also feel uncomfortable looking at, or in the presence of, another sleeping person. It seems an intrusion, an embarrassment. We avert our eyes, a little cross that anyone would have the temerity to fall asleep in front of us while we, the waking, have so very much to do.

We had seen her the night before, quite late, in *le Club Privé,* the small, select, members-only drinking and dancing club in the sixteenth *arrondissement* of Paris. That summer in Paris, *le Club Privé* was very much the place to be, and there she was, in a red dress, with her husband, looking more than a little bored—or, more accurately, like a woman doing her pleasant best not to look bored. That was one of their differences, of course: his love of night clubs and late parties, and her distaste for them. They were sitting

3

at a banquette with a group of friends, all of whom seemed to be having a better time than she was, among them jolly, blustery, apple-cheeked Johnny Meyer who handled "personal" public relations for Ari Onassis just as he once did for Howard Hughes. Johnny Meyer, lovable rogue, manipulator, raconteur, friend of kings and Arab potentates, has spent his life swimming powerfully in the wake of one rich man or another for whom he has always managed to perform a valuable service of one or another sort, was one of the members of the Onassis entourage whom his wife cared little for—too many rough edges, perhaps, just visible beneath the manicured and beautifully tailored surface. And the feeling was mutual. Johnny Meyer had little use for her. "I'll last with Onassis longer than she will," he used to say, though he turned out to be wrong about that.

As usual, Onassis, a big, rumpled bear of a man, was holding forth at the table, talking with big gestures, telling stories. His eyes were already giving him a little trouble, and they looked bloodshot beneath the heavy lids, the circles beneath them deeper and darker than ever. But he was in good form and everyone at the table except his wife, separated from him by a couple of people, was laughing. To tease him perhaps she periodically rested her head against the shoulder of the young man seated on her right who put his arm around her gently but protectively. The room was crowded and noisy, but she and her every move were the center of all attention. "Who is *he?*" the room wanted to know about the young man who was behaving in this oddly familiar manner in front of her husband's obviously uncaring eyes. Friends stopped at the table, spoke to the group. She smiled a little wanly, said hello, and shook hands.

The following day, the noon flight on Olympic Airways from Paris to New York was crowded. It had originated in Athens, where many passengers had boarded and were continuing on to New York. The

4

rest of the plane filled up at Orly. Johnny Meyer liked to speak disparagingly of how, for privacy, she liked to have the entire first class section on Olympic flights reserved for herself alone. It is true, she did, but on flights where traffic was light, and where the first class compartment would, have been virtually empty. But she made no such demands on sold-out flights like this one. She did, however, ask for the luxury of two seats for herself. As the rest of the plane filled up, in both the tourist and first class sections, the two front seats on the starboard side of the aircraft remained empty. Flying west, starboard would be the shady side and, in summer, the same rule applies to airplanes that applied to luxury ocean liners: Port Outward, Starboard Home, the acronym of which gave us the word "posh."

There was a brief delay, since she would be driven across the airfield to the plane by limousine and not, as the rest of us had come, by bus. Then her cars, two of them, drew up outside the plane, and there was a collective gasp from within the plane as the most famous woman in the world stepped out of the second car. She was wearing grey slacks, a white blouse, a black sweater over her shoulders, low-heeled shoes and her trademark, the huge dark glasses. She ascended the steps. Four airline officials followed her with a half a dozen pieces of hand luggage, all of it by Louis Vuitton. Out of one casually unzippered bag protruded a bottle of hair-conditioning shampoo. Entering the plane, she recognized the friends from the night before at *le Club Privé,* smiled a little wanly again, said hello again, and again shook hands.

The hand luggage was tucked under and around her two front seats. A flight attendant hovered. "Can I get you anything, Mrs. Onassis? The captain has opened the bar." Just a glass of water, she replied in that curiously whispery, and yet audibly distinctive speaking voice. Of the men who escorted her aboard she asked, "Did you cable George to meet me in New York?"

Yes, she was assured, George had been cabled. The glass of water arrived, the escorts urged her to have a pleasant flight, and departed. The plane door closed, the steps were wheeled away, and the plane made its slow turn to taxi toward the runway.

In the air, this was a woman who had several things to do. She arranged several little airline pillows against the armrest of her chair. She requested, and received, a light blanket. She slipped off her shoes, revealing bare feet—a bit thin and bony, like her hands, and not her best feature. She removed her dark glasses, lowered her window shade, and, from her purse, removed two pale grey sleep masks and placed them, one on top of the other, over her eyes. Then, under the gaze of the entire first class compartment, the most famous woman in the world nestled her head against her pillows, arranged the blanket across her knees, and fell asleep. Her sleep seemed dreamless and peaceful: a sleep that took no one else into account, a sleep that belied some of the nightmarish things that had happened in her life (a husband's shattered skull had been cradled in this woman's lap), and a sleep that lasted her across the North Atlantic. Just as we began our slow descent into the airport named in memory of that dead husband, she awoke easily, as if alerted by an inner clock, to remove her sleep masks, to return her dark glasses to their place, to fluff her hair, to prepare to be met, to be taken off the plane ahead of the other passengers, to be whisked through a special door in order to avoid the rigors of Customs. At the door, we waved good-bye.

During that Atlantic passage, there were certainly more than the usual number of trips to the forward lavatories by passengers who merely wanted to view the sleeping cargo, to study the sleeping face. Once or twice during the trip she snored lightly; once or twice she stirred, shifted her position, raked a hand across her forehead to brush back a stray and tickling lock of hair. Each sound, each move was observed and commented upon by each of her thirty-odd fellow passengers in first class. The whispers were in English, in French, in Italian, in Greek. Her sleeping presence added something almost electric to the air, a sense that we were in the presence of History, of something earthshaking and galactic, even though all she was doing was—sleeping.

Sleeping on an airplane is difficult, at best, for most people. To sleep and to know that you will be watched as you sleep is an even more unsettling sensation. To sleep, and to be a giant public figure knowing (as surely you must know) that you will sleep under the intense scrutiny of a public whose names and faces you will never know—could be a terrifying impossibility. After all, among that public there lurk hostile hearts and erratic minds capable of great, irrational crimes. Asleep and vulnerable in a more or less public place; a woman traveling alone. Who knows from what direction an enemy might approach? Sleep could be risky for the famous, the controversial, the envied, the adored, the hated. To curl up in public, cover your eyes, and sleep would, it might seem, be something you would never dare to attempt to do if you were this particular woman. And yet, as in everything else she has ever done, Jacqueline Bouvier Kennedy Onassis brought it off. She closed her eyes, and *slept*.

2

Daughter
of Illusion

JACQUELINE BOUVIER WAS born on July 8, 1929 in East Hampton, Long Island. She was a plump baby weighing eight pounds. The outward circumstances could not have seemed more auspicious for the child and her parents, John Vernou Bouvier III and Janet Lee Bouvier. It was a glorious summer in East Hampton, and it was a giddy time for Americans everywhere. When Herbert C. Hoover had taken the oath of Presidential office four months earlier, the country was basking in the sunny glow of the "Coolidge Boom," and Hoover had been elected on a campaign that had assured Americans that they were on "a permanent plateau of prosperity," and that there would be "a chicken in every pot and a car in every garage." Perpetual prosperity had been the Hoover theme, and in his acceptance speech he had declared, "We in America today are nearer to the final triumph over poverty than ever before in the history of the land," adding that "the poorhouse is vanishing from among us." The stock market had never been higher, and even the shoeshine boys in barber shops boasted of how well their stocks were doing.

On the surface, things seemed even rosier for the Jack Bouviers and their firstborn daughter. There was more than one chicken in their pot and more than one automobile in their garage. The Bouvier family estate in East Hampton, Lasata, was one of Long Island's great showplaces, with extravagant gardens and full time gardeners to attend them, with a chauffeur, two maids, a cook, and a stable of jumping horses for amusement. For winter, there was the huge family apartment in Manhattan at 765 Park Avenue. Jack Bouvier's father was rich and, on paper at least, Jack himself had made a fortune which he estimated at $7,500,000—all in the stock market. Janet Lee Bouvier's family were far from poor, either. Her father, James T. Lee, was considered one of the most remarkable self-made men of the century who, after working his way through City College and Columbia, had practiced law for a while, speculated in real estate successfully, become a vice president of the Chase National Bank and, eventually, president and chairman of the board of the New York Central Savings Bank, amassing a multimillion-dollar fortune in the process. Grandfather Lee, too, maintained an estate, Avery Place, in East Hampton on Lily Pond Lane. Money had hovered all around Jack and Janet Bouvier at their wedding, a year before their daughter's birth, at East Hampton's St. Philomena's Roman Catholic Church. Afterward, five hundred guests had gathered for the reception in the hedge-enclosed garden of Avery Place. Meyer Davis's orchestra had played and, after spending their wedding night at the Savoy-Plaza, the newlyweds sailed the following day aboard the *Aquitania* for an extended European honeymoon, characters in an American fairy-tale dream come true.

And they were such a *beautiful* couple, as everyone pointed out—Jack Bouvier in particular, "drippingly handsome," as a contemporary society reporter gushed at the time. Columnists wrote of his "dark, Latin looks," his slim Roman nose, his wide forehead, flashing dark eyes, sensuous mouth, and trim figure. Jack Bouvier's handsomeness was of a movie star's quality, and he knew it, and was appropriately vain. (In later years, because of the remarkable resemblance, he would enjoy being mistaken for Clark Gable and having fans accost him on the street for autographs.) In the late 1920s, he wore his hair in the Rudolph Valentino style, slicked down with pomade and parted in the middle, and added to the Latin look with a pencil-thin moustache. In New York, he was famous as a clotheshorse. His suits were custom-made by Bell, and his shirts were made to measure by Tripler and Sulka. His custom shoes were made by Peel in London, his cravats by Turnbull & Asser. A bright silk handkerchief blossomed from his breast pocket, and just the right amount of linen shot out from his jacket sleeves. He was, in short, a dandy.

Jack Bouvier had waited until fairly late (he was thirty-seven) to marry and, in his bachelor years, had gained a wide reputation as a heartbreaker and a Casanova. Before finally settling down with Janet, he had been engaged to, and then broken off with, a number of beautiful society ladies, and had affairs and more casual relationships with scores of others. His romantic path was strewn with women upon whom he had bestowed brief favors and then cast aside—or so, at least, he liked to boast. Even his indulgent mother liked to speak fondly of his "naughty French streak." And so, when Jack Bouvier and Janet Norton Lee announced their engagement in 1928, New York society reacted with some surprise, and a certain skepticism.

To begin with, Janet was not as beautiful as Jack Bouvier was handsome, nor did she have the kind of showgirl prettiness that Jack had seemed to favor in his other women. Though she was petite and animated— "coquettish," some called her—her nose was a shade too long and her chin a shade too pointed. Her eyes were her best feature, and she had an interesting, one-sided smile and perfect teeth. For Janet Lee, fifteen years younger than Jack, to have captured and married one of New York's most glamorous and successful bachelors, it was considered quite a catch. And when their first daughter was born, it was happily noted—at least on the Bouvier side of the family— that little Jackie looked like Jack, after whom she had been named.

Beneath the glitter of the marriage, meanwhile, and the luxury of the surroundings in which the young Bouviers moved, there were some troubling undertones. There was, for instance, the "problem" of Janet's social background and credentials. Though the Bouviers had had money and social position for several generations, the Lees were *nouveaux riches*. Janet, in fact, had been branded a "social climber" who, having befriended Jack Bouvier's twin cousins, Maude and Michelle, had ruthlessly and relentlessly clawed her way up to marriage into the clan. These were the days, of course, when being "of good family" mattered far more to Americans than it does today. In what passed for American society in the early 1900s, it had become almost an obsession. These were the days when Americans, having no true aristocracy of their own, turned almost desperately to Europe and England for models, and created abject copies of European social institutions on these shores—private schools (with "grades" designated as "forms"), and debutantes shipped annually to London to be presented at court. It was an era when the daughters of rich Americans were sent to Europe specifically in order to return as countesses and duchesses, no matter how impoverished the titles or how thin the bloodlines they married might be. Society, and who was in and who was out, was taken so seriously that the New York Sunday *News* could report in 1933, about the opening of Belle's Hampton Country Club, operated by Belle Livingston between East Hampton and Southampton:

The social respectability and acceptability of Belle's newest supper club was established once and for all with the arrival of Mr. and Mrs. John

11

Vernou Bouvier, pillars of the East Hampton summer colony. . . .

These Bouviers were Jack Bouvier's parents. No one, in that era, would have written anything like that about Janet Lee's parents. It was very simple. The Bouviers were in society, and the Lees were not. The difference in social class manifested itself unpleasantly even on Jack's and Janet's wedding day when, at the reception, Jack got into a violent argument with his new father-in-law—the first of many. The subject of the quarrel was the Lees' social aspirations and the Bouviers' sense of social superiority.

There is no question that Janet Lee Bouvier was then, and would remain, a woman extremely conscious of social status. In later years, she would take to referring to her family as "the Lees of Maryland," as though her antecedents were somehow connected with the redoubtable Lees of Virginia. The fact is that there are no Lees of Maryland. James T. Lee's father (Janet's grandfather) had been a New York doctor with a modest practice, and he and his wife, Mary, had both been children of humble Irish immigrants who had made their way to these shores, possibly by way of Maryland, to escape the Great Potato Famine in the 1850s. Janet, in fact, was rather embarrassed by her Grandmother Lee, and disliked being seen with her in public, since Grandmother Lee still spoke with a brogue. The sense of unease over differences in lineage and social caste was quite apparent on both sides of the aisle at the wedding. These differences would continue to be felt, and painfully, throughout the marriage.

Things, meanwhile, were not quite as rosy as they might have seemed within the family-proud House of Bouvier. While guests sipped champagne and danced to Meyer Davis's music at Jack's and Janet's reception, tongues clicked about an ongoing Bouvier scandal that showed no signs of playing itself out. It involved Jack

Bouvier's younger brother, William Sergeant Bouvier, known in the family as Bud. Bud Bouvier had become unquestionably the family's black sheep and showed every indication of retaining that distinction. At the wedding, Bud served as his brother's best man and, throughout the ceremony, more eyes were on Bud than on the bride and groom because no one was sure that Bud would be able to "carry it off." He had been "not well" for a number of weeks prior to the occasion. To everyone's relief, however, Bud carried it off. He seemed sober.

Bud Bouvier had served as a major during World War I in Europe, and had been severely gassed. He tended to blame his gassing for his problem, but the fact was that Bud Bouvier had been a heavy drinker at Yale, long before the Army experience. One factor that may have led to Bud's drinking was his intense jealousy of his older (by two years) brother. Bud was good-looking, but not in Jack's dashing, swash-buckling way. Bud was "good old Bud," but Jack was nicknamed "the Sheik" and "Black Jack" for his swarthy complexion, which he regularly assisted with a sun lamp. Bud copied Jack's slicked-down hair style and moustache, but Jack was a Don Juan with women and Bud was not. Though Bud considered himself brighter than Jack, he could not seem to match Jack's dazzling success in Wall Street. Where stocks and bonds were concerned, Jack Bouvier seemed to have a Midas touch, and Jack was earning $75,000 a year in commissions before he was thirty-five. Bud, meanwhile, had gone through a number of jobs. His drinking had cost him the presidency of the Independent Oil and Gas Company. At the time of Jack's wedding, he was unemployed, living, on and off, at the Yale Club on rapidly dwindling capital. He had visited sanitariums in New York, Connecticut, and White Sulphur Springs. He had tried sedation, night nurses and psychiatrists. Nothing had helped. His family had despaired of him.

13

He had married, in 1917, a young woman named Emma Louise Stone after a three-day courtship, and had a young son, Michel. By 1925, because of his prolonged drinking bouts, his wife was divorcing him, and Emma Louise was awarded $800 a month alimony plus custody of the child. The Bouviers were not particularly devout Catholics, but Catholics they were on such matters as divorce, and one of Bud Bouvier's aunts, Louise Bouvier, had been a nun. There had never been a divorce in the family until then, and the Bouviers were devastated. Two years after the divorce, in 1927, the family had to endure the humiliation of a story published in the *New York Times* to the effect that Mrs. Emma Louise Bouvier was suing her former husband for non-payment of alimony, and that W. Sergeant Bouvier was pleading that he was without funds or resources to care for her or their child. All these untidy matters were very much in the air at Jack's and Janet's wedding in the summer of 1928 and, in a sense, it was courageous of Jack to ask Bud to perform the duties of his best man, since by then it was well known by everyone in New York society that Bud Bouvier was seldom able to survive social situations without collapsing in a drunken stupor. After the reception, everyone agreed that it was a miracle that Bud had been able to carry out the assignment as well as he had.

After Jack's marriage, however, Bud's drinking went from bad to much, much worse. It was as though the brilliance of the occasion, the brightness of the auspices of the day, the enthusiastic society-page coverage of the affair with its emphasis on the rich, sunny good fortune of the young pair reminded him all the more cruelly of his own failures, financial and matrimonial. Bud had often said that if only he could find some quiet place to live in the country, away from the pressures of city life, he could cure himself. In the summer of 1929, he announced that he had found such a place in the town of Los Olivos, California, in the

14

Santa Ynez Valley, not far from Santa Barbara. He had been permitted a month's visitation period with his young son each summer, and it was to Los Olivos that he and little Michel repaired that July, just a few days before Bud's niece, Jacqueline, was born. They put up at an old stagecoach inn called Mattei's Tavern which, as the name implied, was famous for its bar.

Still, while Michel was with him in Los Olivos, Bud did well, from all reports. But when, in August, it was time for Michel to be returned to his mother in the East, Bud stayed on at Mattei's Tavern alone. On October 7, Bud Bouvier went riding, then had dinner and, after dinner, went into the bar. At one point during the evening—it was past midnight in the East —he telephoned his former wife and asked her if she would take him back if he stopped drinking. Later, Emma Lou insisted that she had assured him that she would, on that condition. But whatever assurances he may or may not have received during that conversation, he returned to the bar and, early in the morning, had to be carried to his room. A doctor was summoned, but Bud Bouvier died in an alcoholic coma a few hours later. Jacqueline Bouvier was less than three months old when this happened. For years, in order to protect the illusion of a happy, tight-knit family, Jackie was told nothing of her Uncle Bud's harrowing story, even though she and Bud's son, Michel, grew up to be extremely close—she thought of him almost as an older brother. Whenever she happened upon Bud's yellowing photograph in one of the many family scrapbooks, and asked who he was, she was told, "An uncle, Major Bouvier, who died."

The Bouvier family was also being supported, throughout this period—supported and suffused with a sense of *hubris*—by an even more alluring piece of fiction. Jack Bouvier's father, John Vernou Bouvier, Jr., had graduated Phi Beta Kappa from Columbia in 1886. The following year, he received his master's degree from that university in political science. From there, he went on to Columbia Law School and passed his New York State bar examinations with flying colors in 1888. He was immediately taken into the prestigious law firm of Hoadly, Lauterbach and Johnson, where he soon became a specialist in trial work. By 1899, at the age of thirty-four, he had gained a sufficient reputation in his field to form his own law firm, Bouvier & Warren, with offices at 31 Nassau Street in downtown Manhattan.

He was considered a brilliant lawyer. Benjamin N. Cardozo, later Associate Justice of the Supreme Court of the United States, wrote of him: "Mr. Bouvier is one of the ablest and most brilliant lawyers in the State of New York. He is a man of wide experience, of fine training and of broad culture. I cannot think of anyone more admirably suited for the position he seeks," the position being that of Major Judge Advocate for the Army after America's entry into World War I, and to which he was duly commissioned. After this, he, too, enjoyed being known as "Major Bouvier."

But whatever his skills as a trial lawyer and judge might have been, his greatest interest and most devoted efforts involved establishing the Bouviers, once and for all, in New York society. If the family had managed to acquire, by 1929, a gilded social image it was J. V. Bouvier, Jr.'s, doing. Previous American generations had been concerned mostly with making money, but the Major's concern was that the money become polished with the luster of style and class. He accomplished this, to begin with, by joining every prestigious club that New York and its environs offered. He joined the Union Club, the Racquet Club, and the Sons of the Revolution in Manhattan. On Long Island, he joined the Maidstone Club and the Piping Rock Club. In Washington, he joined the Society of the Cincinnati. In Florida, he joined the Jupiter Island Club at Hobe Sound and, for good measure, he joined the Havana Country Club in Cuba. In his pince-nez and with his twirled walrus moustache, he both looked and acted the archetype clubman. Like his son Jack, he was a meticulous dresser, favoring English tweeds and spats. He was also careful to see to it that, as his social position and image improved, so did his address. In 1914, he abandoned suburban Nutley, New Jersey, to 247 Fifth Avenue, then to 521 Park Avenue, then 935 Park Avenue, and finally 765 Park Avenue, a choice location just off 72nd Street. By the early 1920s he had established himself as a summer resident of fashionable East Hampton in a house called Wildmoor on Apaquogue Road; by 1926 he had moved to sumptuous Lasata on Further Lane.

It was an era, too, when wealthy Americans, longing for an aristocracy of their own, often searched backward in their family trees for some trace of nobility in the past, and when genealogical "experts" were happy, for a fee, to unearth ancient thrones, honors, and titles for their happy clients. But what is curious is that John V. Bouvier, Jr., a lawyer who was professionally so concerned with the truth in his clients' cases, should have, in his family's case, personally created ancestors that he must have known were bogus. His slender volume, *Our Forebears,* was first published in 1925 when its author was sixty. His researches, he concluded, proved beyond doubt that the Bouviers were descended from ancient French nobility. The Bouvier family he described as "an ancient house of Fontaine, near Grenoble." He described one Bouvier as "a counsellor in Parliament in 1553," and another as "a celebrated lawyer in Parliament about 1620" who "was ennobled in 1609." He described the noble Bouvier crest and coat of arms, while failing to note that the Bouviers he was talking about came from the province of Dauphiné, whereas his ancestors actually originated in Savoy. *Our Forebears* is riddled with other examples of illogic, inaccuracy, and

17

simple fabrication, all designed to "prove" that the Bouviers were descended from French princes and courtiers. In fact, Major Bouvier's great-great-grandfather had kept a small hardware shop which specialized in kitchen utensils. Other French relatives had been drapers, tailors, glovers, farmers, and in at least one case a domestic servant to a "Counsellor in Parliament."

Major Bouvier even falsified the history of his own grandfather, Michel Bouvier, the first Bouvier to come to America and the founder of the American branch of the family. He pointed out that Michel Bouvier had prospered as a manufacturer of veneers, as an importer of marble and mahogany, and as a real-estate operator, without mentioning the fact that Michel had started out as a poor, uneducated cabinetmaker in Philadelphia. Major Bouvier also spoke with pride of Michel Bouvier's close friendship with Joseph Bonaparte, while the fact was that Bonaparte had bought a couple of chests of drawers from Mr. Bouvier's little shop. And Major Bouvier went into even more fulsome detail on the family history of the Vernous, saying, "The family of Vernou is one of the most illustrious and ancient of the Province of Poitou . . . it has been in existence since 1086 . . . confirmed in its nobility of ancient extraction by two Royal decrees . . . secretary to Charles V, King of France, William de Vernou. . . ." On and on *Our Forebears* went, listing Vernous who were counts, barons, marquises—all of it either totally false or without foundation.

Still, people believe what they want to believe, and when Major Bouvier's family genealogy book came out—he had it published himself, of course—and when he distributed it to all the members of his family, the Bouviers were overwhelmed with excitement and pride. The book proved, after all, what they longed to believe—that Bouviers had been at the top of the heap since the beginning of time. Major Bouvier updated his book several times over the years, each time adding new "data" and "research." He sent copies of the book to historical societies and to the Library of Congress so that his researches could become a part of public record permanently and, as each new edition went to press, new titled Bouviers and Vernous were added. It occurred to no one in the family to question the Major's work or to doubt the distinguished jurist's authenticity, or to suspect that the search for noble antecedents may have, in some way, warped his mind. *Our Forebears* was accepted as gospel truth.

It was within this myth of huge genetic superiority that little Jacqueline Bouvier was born, and it was with it that she grew up. No one, certainly not she, ever supposed that Grandpa Bouvier could have made it all up, that *Our Forebears* was, at best, a work of massive self-deception. She grew up surrounded by assurances that the blood of princes coursed in her veins —there on the nightstand was Grandpa's book to prove it.

Her belief in Grandpa's book followed her into the White House. There, with the spotlight of a nation turned upon her, it was inevitable that *Our Forebears* should share the spotlight and, as a result, come under the scrutiny of true historians and scholars. The first to question the book was Francis J. Dallett, former director of the Philadelphia Athenaeum. Rather than attack the veracity of the book, Mr. Dallett, out of courtesy to the First Lady, merely commented in an article in *Antiques* magazine that the book was "so full of errors that it should be checked against other sources."

It was not long thereafter that other scholars were checking other sources, and had come to the irrefutable conclusion that Grandpa Bouvier's book was nothing more than a work of the imagination.

To a family that had set its sights by the book for the better part of forty years, it came as something of a blow.

3

Money, Money, Everywhere

THE ORIGINAL BOUVIER money had been made by Jack Bouvier's great-grandfather, Michel Bouvier, who arrived in America in 1815 at the age of twenty-three from the village of Pont-Saint Esprit on the Rhone in southern France. Today, most Americans like to think that their immigrant ancestors came to these shores because America had come to symbolize "the land of golden opportunity," but the fact is that many immigrants came for more stern and practical reasons. Some came to avoid taxation, persecution, or jail. Some came to avoid military service. In Michel Bouvier's case, he had been an infantryman in Napoleon's army at Waterloo, and, in the weeks following that celebrated defeat, royalist forces in Paris were demanding the arrest, torture, and execution of all who had participated in the Hundred Days. Feelings ran particularly strong in the Midi, and to be a veteran of Waterloo meant death. There was little for Michel Bouvier to do but get to Bordeaux as quickly as possible and book himself on the next boat for New York.

From New York, he made his way to Philadelphia, where there was already a French-speaking colony and where he was able to find work as a handyman. In France, before his military stint, he had been apprenticed to his cabinetmaker father, and gradually he began to pick up jobs as a carpenter and furniture maker. He was a slight, solemn-faced young man, but he must have been industrious and he must have been thrifty because the first record of any financial transaction involving him shows that, in 1817, he was able to deposit $536 in the Girard Bank of Philadelphia—the equivalent today of several thousand dollars.

By no coincidence, Napoleon Bonaparte's older brother, Joseph, also was required to leave Europe in the wake of Napoleon's defeat at Waterloo and he, too, decided to spend his exile in Philadelphia. The arrival of the ex-King of Naples and the ex-King of Spain created a predictable stir in Philadelphia society and the Comte de Suvilliers, as he now called himself, was welcomed with a series of galas, balls, and receptions on an imperial scale. Joseph Bonaparte had brought with him trunksful of Imperial jewels and paintings, and was able to buy himself a huge estate called Point Breeze on the New Jersey banks of the Delaware River, which he proceeded to fit out in lavish style. Michel Bouvier, uneducated though he was, must surely have been aware of his distinguished countryman's presence in the city, and he may have actively tried to ingratiate himself with Joseph Bonaparte. If so, it would have been very un-French of him. The French have a rigid sense of class and the barriers that divide classes, and it is usually unthinkable for a member of the *bourgeoisie* to attempt to mingle with the nobility. On the other hand, by 1818 Philadelphia had become the center of an American movement to rescue Napoleon from Saint Helena, bring him to the United States, and to collect funds and forces to return him to the French throne. As a Waterloo veteran Michel Bouvier, even though he had been only an ordinary foot soldier, would certainly have been qualified to take part in such a movement. In any case, by 1818, Michel had begun doing odd bits of carpentry jobs for Joseph Bonaparte at Point Breeze, and, when Bonaparte decided to erect a cot-

21

tage for one of his daughters on the estate, Michel was put in charge of that project.

Michel's first real good fortune, however, occurred in 1820 and in the form of a disaster. Bonaparte's Point Breeze burned to the ground and, obviously pleased with the young man's work, Bonaparte appointed Michel to supervise the reconstruction. This was an assignment that lasted three years and earned Michel his first real money. Bonaparte was an important customer to have, and soon Michel was able to collect another—the millionaire Philadelphia banker and financier, Stephen Girard, who also happened to have been born in France. Girard and Bonaparte, in fact, vied with each other to see who could create the grandest residence, and Michel Bouvier happily abetted their competitiveness. Gradually, Michel was becoming known as the carpenter for the wealthy, and other well-off Philadelphians started coming to him with jobs. He continued, however, to do humble chores. His 1828 ledger shows that he billed Girard $20 for "furnishing cloth and silk for tables;" in 1829, he received one dollar from Girard for "polishing dining room table," and fifty cents for "taking down and putting up bed." He was, in other words, an interior decorator.

By 1837, however, Michel was beginning to make the transition from a maker of hand-made custom furniture to a manufacturer of mass-produced items. He installed a steam-driven saw in his shop, and began turning out marble tops for tables and dressers, marble mantels, and veneers for all kinds of furniture. He began importing mahogany and marble, and, by 1839, he no longer listed himself in the Philadelphia business directory as a "cabinet and sofa warehouse" but as a "manufacturer of veneers and dealer in marble and mahogany."

Two years later, he made his first step into real estate. He bought a tenement on South Front Street, and a small lot on North Broad Street. Thirteen years

later, he had sold the Front Street property at a
healthy profit, bought a decaying mansion on Third
Street, torn it down and built three brownstones in its
place. He then sold them, bought more Broad Street
property, built a big house on that, bought several
other choice pieces of Philadelphia business property
and—most important—had bought a vast amount of
land in West Virginia. At one point, he owned a total
of 157,000 acres of West Virginia land, for which he
had paid as little as thirty-five cents an acre. What
prompted him to buy so much West Virginia land is
unclear, but it was what lifted him permanently into
the ranks of the American rich. Railroads were opening up the country, moving westward. Michel Bouvier's West Virginia land was covered with valuable
timber, which he knew, and beneath it lay rich beds
of coal, which he could not have known. When he
sold his West Virginia acreage—at more than three
times what he had paid for it—he made a profit of
about $100,000 (half a million dollars in today's
money).

Michel Bouvier built a huge mansion for himself
at 1240 North Broad Street, then Philadelphia's choic-
est address—a three-and-a-half-storey residence topped
with a square cupola, in the Italian Renaissance
style. It had more than twenty-five rooms, including
a private chapel, and there were adjoining stables,
greenhouses, and a "grapery." The entire house
was surrounded by a fenced garden filled with Italian-
ate fountains, sculpture, and topiary. An imposing
flight of curved stone steps led up to the great entrance.
The house was all the advertisement that was needed
to tell Philadelphia that Michel Bouvier had "arrived."
Michel had, meanwhile, married a woman named
Sarah Pearson who had died after giving him a son
and a daughter. He had then married a French woman
named Louise Vernou. She and Michel had seven
daughters and, of their three sons, only two—John

Vernou Bouvier and Michel Charles Bouvier—lived to maturity.

Michel and Louise's children were the most devout of any Bouvier generation. One daughter became a nun and, of the six others, only one married. The others remained spinsters and spent a great deal of time with their beads and their missals as "house nuns." The boys, armed with trust funds and comfortable bank accounts, headed for New York and Wall Street.

At the time, the reason given for the move was that the financial capital of America was no longer Philadelphia; it was New York. New York was where the money was. But there were other, stronger motivations. Michel's big, garish castle on Broad Street offended the sensibilities of Philadelphia society. He had come up from nothing at all too rapidly to flaunt his success so flashily. The backbone of Philadelphia society was then, and is now, composed of families who trace their presence in the city to before the American Revolution. "Who *were* these Bouviers, anyway?" people asked themselves. Socially, the Bouviers had everything against them. Michel Bouvier was self-made, *nouveau,* uneducated. He was a Roman Catholic, and a foreigner. Worse than that, he was "in trade" and, even more shocking than that, a man who had worked with his hands. For any one of those reasons, the Bouviers would not have been invited to the Assembly, or to join the Philadelphia Club, much less the Fish House or the Rabbit Club. Just as, a couple of generations later, Boston would make it clear that it would never accept the Kennedys, Philadelphia had made it clear that it would not accept the Bouviers. They were not "Philadelphians." It was that simple.

Emma Bouvier, the only one of the seven sisters to marry, had made a good choice. She had married Francis A. Drexel of the Philadelphia banking family. Frank Drexel gave Emma's two brothers, John and Michel, a leg up in the financial community. John joined Drexel, Winthrop & Company in New York, and Michel, after working for a while with Drexel & Company in Philadelphia, asked to be transferred to that firm's New York office. Soon both young men branched off on their own and bought seats on the New York Stock Exchange. Michel Bouvier formed the brokerage firm of Bouvier & Wallace, and John set himself up as John V. Bouvier, Banker & Broker. Soon the brothers were cooperating in railroad deals with J. P. Morgan, the Vanderbilts, E. H. Harriman, and other Wall Street barons of the era. Actually, Michel Bouvier did better on Wall Street than his brother John: he increased his personal wealth by half a million dollars before he was thirty-five. But it didn't matter, really. Both young men were comfortably rich. Michel Sr.'s death in 1874 made them even richer. The income from old Michel's properties in downtown Philadelphia alone assured them of lives of ease forever—or so it seemed. When the New York *Social Register* was first published in 1889, the Bouvier brothers went sailing into it—a thing that would never have happened in Philadelphia.

When young "Black Jack" Bouvier—Jack the Sheik —marched down to Wall Street following World War I, he was following the jaunty footsteps of his grandfather and great uncle. It was, in those days, what one did, especially if one had no particular ability to do anything else. Hundreds of well-dressed young men, fresh out of Yale and Princeton, flocked to the "Street" after graduation. In their bowlers and Panamas, the Street was like an extension of college. On weekends, they climbed into roadsters and drove out to Long Island. On the Street, the hours were easy and flexible. If a party ran on all night, you could go down to the Street in white tie and tails, place a few orders and go back to your office and sleep off the night before. Wall Street in those days was anyone's game. The rules were few and simple, and even a novice could play. "Inside" information could be passed clubbily from broker to broker, who would then buy for their own accounts, forcing up stock prices; the customer came last. Through a device such as selling short, money could be made in a falling as well as in a rising market, and markets could be made to rise and fall at Wall Street's whim. No real talent was required to succeed.

And Jack Bouvier had no real talent other than a talent to charm. At Yale, Class of '14, he had been a mediocre student, much to his Phi Beta Kappa father's disappointment, and spent most of his time on his social life—a playboy before the term became current. On the Street, it went without saying, he would be a whiz. In *The Bouviers* John H. Davis details his financial career.

For three years Jack worked as a floor broker for Henry Hentz & Company. Then he left the firm to work on his own as a "specialist," a broker who trades for other brokers in a specialized list of stocks. The stocks Jack chose to specialize in were Kennecott Copper, Texas Gulf Sulphur, Kress Department Stores, Colorado Fuel and Power, Baldwin Locomotive, and Holland Furnace. Throughout the early Twenties, these stocks did so well and Jack traded them so nimbly that, by the time he married Janet, Jack had increased his personal wealth by almost a million dollars and was earning $100,000 a year in commissions alone. The future seemed limitlessly bright. By the late summer of 1929, however, when Jack's and Janet's daughter was still a baby, a number of Wall Street investors had grown wary of the steadily booming market and were beginning to suspect that there would be an inevitable reaction. One of these canny fellows was Joseph P. Kennedy. Another was Jack's great-uncle, Michel C. Bouvier, who converted his stock position into several millions of dollars' worth of cash, gold, and Liberty Bonds.

Bud Bouvier was buried on October 15, 1929, a dark day for the family. Four days later, there was an even darker one. Stock prices dropped sharply, the first tremor of the great crash that was to come. When the Exchange reopened the following Monday, October 21, prices dropped sharply again and the word "panic" made its first appearance in the newspapers. On Tuesday, there was talk of recovery but, by Wednesday, all hopes were shattered. There was a deluge of selling, the tape ran 104 minutes late, and the *New York Times* composite index showed an 18.74-point loss. Thursday was "Black Thursday"— 12,880,000 shares were sold—and the New York Stock Exchange registered the greatest decline in its entire history. By Friday, a bankers' pool had managed to raise prices somewhat but, on Monday, October 28, the market was even worse than Black Thursday, setting another record. And by Tuesday, everyone had stopped talking about Black Thursday. It was the blackest day of all. Still another record had been set: 16,410,000 shares liquidated. It was Tuesday, October 29, when speculators started leaping to their deaths from office windows across the country. After leaving his office that day, Jack Bouvier went out to East Hampton to spend the night with his father. Jacqueline Bouvier, just three months old, remained with her mother in a shattered and terrified New York.

Interestingly, Jack appeared to have made money during the month of October. At the close of the day's trading on that terrible Tuesday, he had made, on paper at least, a profit of $100,000 by selling short on the crash. But when, in November, the market declined even more steeply, that paper profit was completely wiped out. In the early spring of 1930, stock analysts talked hopefully of an "inevitable upturn," but no upturn came, and on June 18, stock prices hit a new low. It was then that it was reported that one out of four factory workers in America was out of work. The breadlines formed, and the apple-sellers appeared on the streets.

During this grim period, however, the Bouviers decided that, no matter what reversals they might have endured, there was no reason to alter their splendid style of life. Jack Bouvier's father continued to maintain Lasata, with the gardener, the cook, the maids, and the chauffeur. Jack, Janet, and little Jackie continued in style on Park Avenue, with a governess for the baby. Jack kept his stable of jumpers in the country. In 1930, Jack contributed an expensive marble altar in memory of his brother to one of the Catholic institutions where he had sought help in the last months of his life, and there was an elaborate dedication ceremony. The stock market would rebound soon, Jack seemed to feel, and, in the meantime, one could live on capital. In 1931, Jacqueline Bouvier celebrated her second birthday with a family trip to the dog show, and this was reported in the society columns.

Behind this fragile and elaborate facade, however, there were some harsh realities which no one talked about. At the time of the crash, Jack had gone to the richest relative he had, his great-uncle Michel, and asked to borrow money. Michel, then in his eighties and a bachelor, had foreseen the crash. He had gotten out of the market $1,600,000 ahead, and was now worth about $7,000,000. Jack had hoped for a loan of at least $100,000. The old man, however, was not in a generous mood, and was willing to lend his nephew only $25,000.

Jack then turned, in humiliation, to his father-in-law, a man with whom he had never got along, and asked for money. James T. Lee was a crusty Irishman who had made every penny he had by himself, and who deplored and derided the kind of "high sassiety life," as he called it, that Jack led. He put his son-in-law on the carpet and lectured to him for the better part of four hours. It was a triumphant moment for Big Jim Lee—the self-made tycoon being asked for alms by the profligate aristocrat. He ordered Jack to cut down on his extravagant style of living—specifically to divest himself of a number of expensive club memberships. Then, though he would lend Jack no money, Jim Lee said that he would help out by letting Jack, Janet, and Jackie live, rent free, in a large duplex apartment in a luxury building Lee owned at 740 Park Avenue. Meekly, Jack accepted this largesse. From then on, he was under the thumb of his father-in-law, who did not let him forget it. "Remember, you're living in my house," he would remind Jack, whenever he came to visit his little granddaughter.

Franklin D. Roosevelt swept into office in 1933 and, though Roosevelt was anathema to Wall Street, there was a surge of optimism in the country and something of a rally in the stock market. In anticipation of the repeal of Prohibition, Jack Bouvier had bought some liquor-company stocks, and these had begun to rise. This was enough to make Jack decide to celebrate his fifth wedding anniversary as though the Depression did not exist—with a large party at the Long Island place. It was to be a summer of parties reminiscent of the great balls that went on in Vienna even as troops marched through the city and, all over Europe, the lights went out. Beggars and panhandlers might be crowding the streets and the suburbs might be sprouting shanty towns, but Jack and Janet Bouvier had their party. Three weeks later, Grandfather Lee tossed a huge birthday party for little Jacqueline's fourth birthday. The following day at St. Philomena's, her baby sister, born earlier that year, was christened Caroline Lee Bouvier in an obeisant gesture to her grandfather. Afterwards, Jack and Janet gave a garden party for two hundred guests, and everyone drank to the fact that the Depression was over.

But the Depression was not over. In September, 1933, the stock market slumped again, wiping out any advances that had been made during Roosevelt's first months. Still, there were brief bright spots for Jack Bouvier. In the summer of 1933 he had made a profit of $2,000,000 from his liquor stocks. At his father-in-law's advice, he sold them and deposited the money in father-in-law's Chase National Bank, swearing that the money would stay there, drawing interest, until the day he died. But the temptation to speculate was too great. Auburn Motors, he was told, looked good (the company was to go out of business within the decade). He withdrew the two million in cash and, just before the September nosedive, plowed it all into Auburn. By the following January, all that was left of the two million was $195,211.94.

Roosevelt had appointed former stockbroker Joseph P. Kennedy to head the newly created Securities and Exchange Commission, an organization designed to police the Stock Exchange and prevent the unchecked speculation of the 1920s from happening again. At first, Wall Street interpreted this as a conciliatory gesture in Wall Street's behalf. After all, Wall Street knew Joe Kennedy as "one of us" and, perhaps, an even greater scoundrel than any of them when it came to speculating. But when Joe Kennedy turned around and began imposing all sorts of rules and regulations designed to hamstring his old cronies and bridle their familiar, carefree practices, there were cries of dismay. Kennedy was called a traitor to his class, and a great many worse things than that. Kennedy was blackballed by every exclusive club in the country—even ones which he had no desire to join. To Jack Bouvier, the name Kennedy was enough to make his entire face clench and, if anyone had told him in 1934 that his daughter would one day marry Joe Kennedy's son, he would have knocked that person to the floor and kicked him. When Jacqueline Bouvier was learning to read and write, one of the first things she learned was that Kennedy was a dirty word around the house.

Nineteen thirty-four was, meanwhile, an even worse year for Jack Bouvier. That year he earned a mere $4,683.75 in dividends, and $2,188.44 in brokerage commissions. At the same time, he suffered a trading loss of $43,000. Nor had his cost of living diminished. To maintain himself, his wife, two daughters, the 740 Park Avenue duplex, the summer place in East Hampton, two servants, a chauffeur, and, of course, the stable of seven hunters, cost him $38,894.81 that year. Where was the money coming from? From a steadily diminishing supply of capital. To a five-and-a-half-year-old daughter, just beginning to form impressions of the world, being taken for strolls in the park with her crisply uniformed nanny, kissing Daddy good-bye as he rolled off for the office in a big chauffeur-driven car, it must have seemed a very secure world, and that she had a lucky place in it. "You're a very fortunate little girl," her nurse would remind her.

In 1935, however, something nice happened. Old Uncle Michel Bouvier died, the day after Jacqueline's sixth birthday. He was eighty-eight, was the richest of the Bouviers, had never married, had no direct heirs, and it seemed about time. Everyone waited excitedly to see what his or her slice of Uncle Michel's pie might amount to. It turned out that Uncle Michel wasn't quite as rich as everyone thought. His estate amounted to only about $3,250,000. State and Federal taxes took about $600,000. His brother John, Jack's father, got roughly $1,300,000. Charities got $145,000. Jack himself, of whom his great-uncle never really approved, got $5,000. But in addition to this token bequest, Jack Bouvier did inherit the "mantle" of his uncle's brokerage business, along with such intangibles as the firm's prestige and good will.

With this he quickly formed the firm of Bouvier, Bishop & Co., which, on its letterhead, proclaimed itself "Successors to M. C. Bouvier & Co." In 1935, things began to seem brighter for Jack. That year he earned $32,444.20 from commissions plus $3,442.11 from trading—a nice jump from the $2,000-plus he had made from commissions and the $43,000 trading loss he had taken the previous year. Still, his living expenses had climbed to $39,692.25, so it was clear that he was far from breaking even. And at the same time his marriage was coming apart. Nineteen thirty-four, Jack's worst financial year, had placed obvious strains on the marriage. Though prospects looked better in 1935, Jack's and Janet's relationship did not improve. Jack's indebtedness to Janet's father, of which he was daily reminded, did not help. Jack had begun to say—and his friends agreed—that he was just "not cut out for" marriage. He had been a happy-go-lucky bachelor too long, had enjoyed his bachelorhood too much, to be pinned down to a wife and children. By 1936, the couple had agreed to an ominous "trial separation." Lawyers worked on the financial arrangements.

What should have been clear to everyone was that Jack and Janet Bouvier were ill-suited to each other from the beginning. Their temperaments, and goals, were quite different. Jack was a frivolous man, a jolly soul, spoiled by indulgent parents, a man born for good times, not bad. When times were good he was an affectionate man, good fun to be with, generous with his time and his money, a doting father. When times were bad, however, he simply could not understand them. Also, Jack was a man not meant for middle age. He was a youth at heart, a Yalie who had never—because he had never had to—grown up. In 1936, Jack Bouvier was forty-five. Fifty loomed. The famous trim figure had begun to paunch, and the ministrations of the sun lamp could not prevent the famous square jawline from developing jowls. The dark, pomaded hair had held, but there was greying at the temples. Adonis was growing old.

Janet was, and is, another matter. Beneath a smiling surface of bright chatter and social charm was a serious woman of steely toughness and determination. If Jack was a dreamer, Janet was a realist. She had grown up watching her father go from poor to rich. She knew what poor was like and that rich was better. She had, as they say, "improved" herself by marrying

Jack Bouvier, but watching the alarming seesawing of Jack's finances during the early Thirties had caused her to wonder what had happened to the improvements, and what further improvements, if any, might lie in store for the family in the future. Janet Bouvier was not an extravagant woman who craved for expensive clothes, furs, and jewels. She did, on the other hand, very definitely like nice things. She had learned to appreciate, and need, the luxury of servants, and a household that worked like clockwork under her orders. She liked breakfast in bed, and linen sheets with deep embroidered hems that extended halfway down the length of the bed. She liked imported French soaps in her bathroom. She was a perfectionist who knew that perfection was expensive and that, without money, there is no point in being a perfectionist. When Janet Bouvier wanted climbing roses planted against a trellis, she wanted roses planted that would reach to the trellis's top. She was not content with a young plant that would take years to grow to the height she had in mind. Once, to a gardener who was explaining to her that full-grown roses were not available locally, she waved her hand impatiently and said, "Then have some flown in from somewhere else." That was Janet. She liked things just so. With Jack, by 1936, it was clear that things were not just so at all. This was nothing compared with what her father said.

And so the dreary terms of the separation were worked out. Janet would have custody of the two little girls, with Jack given "reasonable" visitation rights. Jack would pay all Janet's bills accumulated prior to October 1, 1936, at which date he would begin paying monthly payments of $1,050 for his wife's and children's maintenance and support. In addition, he would pay the children's medical and dental bills, and for their education. Needless to say, Janet could remain indefinitely in the Park Avenue duplex in the building her father owned. Jack, however, was reduced to taking a room at the Westbury Hotel.

Throughout the year of 1936, financial troubles continued to plague him. He had had a reasonably good year in terms of income, earning nearly $49,000. But everyone, it seemed, was after him for money. Janet wanted $12,600 a year for support payments. Doctor and tuition bills for the girls poured in. Michel C. Bouvier's estate was after him for repayment of the $25,000 loan his great-uncle had extended him in 1930. The Federal Government was claiming that he owed over $16,000 in back taxes, and an additional $23,000 income-tax claim was pending disposition in the court. By the end of 1936, the once-millionaire's net worth was calculated by his accountant at slightly more than $56,000. Soon, it began to seem, he might not even be able to afford the Westbury.

The Bouviers' divorce became final in 1938. To Lee, who was only five, all the rancor and bitterness and angry money talk between her parents and their respective lawyers meant little. But Jackie, who was nine, had listened to it all and had understood it all too well.

4

Daddy
versus
Mummy

WITH THE SEPARATION and the divorce there began between Jack and Janet Bouvier a pattern of exchange that is all too familiar between divorced parents: an endless tug-of-war for the affection of the children. In this angry competitiveness, each parent

trying to outdo the other, Jack was the easy victor—
a situation that did not ease Janet's bitterness toward
her former husband.

To begin with, Jack had the girls on weekends, and
weekends were for fun and games. Jack managed to
see to it that every weekend was a gala. There were
pony rides in the park, trips to the zoo, lunches at
expensive restaurants, skating at Rockefeller Plaza,
trips to the theater and to movies—an endless round,
with Daddy, of interesting and pleasant things to do.
In his tiny digs at the Westbury, the girls were given
the run of the place. Though he could ill afford to do
so, the girls' Daddy lavished them with expensive gifts
and clothes. His aim, of course, was obvious. When
they returned to Mummy's house on Sunday nights, it
was a letdown. Their faces were long. Weekdays, after all, were for schoolwork, piano lessons, and other
dreary chores. When his daughters complained that
they hated going home to Mummy's, their Daddy
couldn't have liked it more.

Janet, needless to say, disapproved of all this. Jack,
she said, was spoiling his daughters just the way he
himself had been spoiled. Anything they asked for he
gave them. At home, with her, it was not like that at
all. Janet, who liked order, tidiness, and manners, was
the strict parent, Jack the permissive one. To Janet,
the complaint "But Daddy lets us do it!" became a
familiar one. Well, they couldn't do it *here,* she reminded them sternly, and soon "here" began to seem
to Jackie and Lee like a very boring and restricted
place. Also, Janet bitterly resented the gifts Jack
bought the girls. On this score she simply couldn't compete with him nor, for that matter, with her father,
who also liked to shower his granddaughters with
costly presents. Janet, after all, was now having to live
on a fixed income of $12,600 a year—a comfortable
enough sum compared with what other households
were living on in the Depression, and she was far
from the poorhouse. Still, out of this sum she had to

feed and clothe herself and her children. Though she had a luxurious apartment, rent-free, at a splendid address, there were expenses involved in the maintenance of the big place that she had to bear. With Jim Lee alive she had not as yet received any inheritance. Her father was generous, presenting her with checks from time to time, but one could never be certain when these bursts of generosity might strike him, and so one could not count on them. For the first time in her life, Janet Bouvier was having to live on a budget. And so life at 740 Park Avenue was Spartan, frugal, and disciplined, whereas life with Father was gay, madcap, devil-may-care.

As a woman named Berthe Kimmerle, who was the girls' governess during 1937 and 1938, testified at the Bouviers' final divorce proceedings, "There were very sorry weeping little girls when Mr. Bouvier's custody would come to an end and they were compelled to return to their mother." Painful as this fact was to Janet, she knew that it was true, and there was nothing she could do about it.

The children, meanwhile, quickly learned how to turn their parents' competition for their hearts to their advantage. They recognized a situation in which both parents wanted their daughters' love badly—each wanted it exclusively, in fact—and so the extent of each parent's affection could be regularly tested in little ways, and result in little concessions. "You don't love me as much as Daddy does" would usually extract something from Mummy, and vice versa. Or, complaint to Daddy about Mummy's strictness would usually result in something by way of compensation from Daddy. Sometimes the reverse would work. A glowing comment to Mummy about the marvelous time that was had with Daddy would usually get Mummy to let up on her discipline a little. In some ways, though constantly being pulled this way and that by Jack and Janet, the girls managed to have a better time of it than when their parents had been married to each other.

Jack, of course, used his time with the girls to disparage the *nouveaux-riches* upstart Lees, and Janet could not prevent herself from running down the effete and wastrel Bouviers. These comments, carried faithfully back to the eagerly waiting ears of two sets of wealthy grandparents, also produced favorable results in terms of gifts, privileges, concessions.

Jack Bouvier, an experienced ladies' man, had a particular interest in women's clothes. He liked fashions that were New York chic, but to which some individualistic, theatrical touch had been added—a bright scarf, say, or an unusual piece of jewelry. When, on his weekends, he trooped his daughters through Saks Fifth Avenue, Bonwit Teller, Bergdorf Goodman, and the old De Pinna, he lectured to the girls on what was currently in fashion, what he considered in good taste and what was not. Pointing to a mannequin in a Fifth Avenue window, he might say, "Hideous dress. It might work if it were belted," or, "Now there's a beautiful outfit if it were worn by the right woman." How interesting—indeed how very French—that the great grandson of Michel Bouvier, who had been so concerned with French veneers, surfaces, table tops, and who had made a fortune at it, should similarly have been so concerned with appearances and polish.

Early on he labored to instill in his daughters a sense of fashion. Needless to say, he often disapproved of the way their mother dressed them. "Now let's go out and get you something pretty to wear," he would say. But when they wore something he liked—and usually it was something he had bought—he complimented them and praised them. Naturally, the girls tried to dress to please their father. In their growing-up years, Lee was considered the prettier of the two girls, with a heart-shaped face and delicate, perfect features. Jackie was the brainy one—quieter, more introspective, a little shy. Even in her early teens she carried a bit of baby fat, and she had inherited her mother's almost too-sharp chin. She had naturally curly, almost kinky hair which was difficult to do much with other than to pull it back tightly with a ribbon. But her eyes—dark and widely spaced and large like her father's—were extraordinary, her best feature. Still, her father stressed, a woman's looks were less important than how she dressed. If she dressed well, even a plain woman would stand out in a crowd.

Jack Bouvier also had definite theories about what made a woman attractive to a man, and these he also imparted to his daughters. In addition to dressing well, he said, it was important that a woman create an aura around herself of *reserve,* or inaccessibility. In dealing with the opposite sex it was important that a woman maintain a certain aloofness, that she not seem too open or available. If a woman could create the impression with a man that she was withholding a little something, that she was not offering of herself as much as she could give, this drove a man wild. The more inaccessible a woman seemed, the more untouchable, the more madly a man yearned to know her better, to see her more often. The mating dance that Jack Bouvier described involved a woman offering a man a little something, then withdrawing it, then offering him something else, and then withdrawing that. The most attractive boy at the party, he explained, the one you most wanted to dance with, would be more fascinated by you if, when he approached, you merely smiled faintly and moved away. Tease a little. Be mysterious. Never be aggressive. Never let a man know quite what you are thinking. Remember La Gioconda and her strange, disturbing, eternally provocative smile.

Stand out in a crowd. It was important that a woman know how to enter a room: smiling, chin up, eyes straight ahead, not darting this way and that to see who else might be there, moving slowly but purposefully to the center of the stage. Never appear to be too available, too eager; that would scare men off. Be selective about which invitations you accept. Be "too busy" to go to certain parties, even if you're really not. That way, when you do accept an invitation, the person giving the party will consider himself particularly honored that you're there.

Jack was able to give his daughters practical examples which proved that his formula for being an enticing, alluring woman really worked. On weekends in the Hamptons, Jack and his daughters kept pretty much to themselves. Cousins, grandparents, aunts and uncles frequently asked them to drop by, but they were seldom available. At large family gatherings, there was always some doubt as to whether Jack and the girls would be able to make it. "We'll try," their father would say. Then, all at once, in the middle of the party, Jack and the girls would make their smiling entrance. Everyone would say, "Isn't it wonderful that Jack and the girls were able to come!"

Jackie Bouvier, always the better student than her sister Lee, learned her father's lessons well. Even as a young teenager there was something baffling and confusing about her that made one wonder what it was, exactly, that made her tick. She seemed to have not one personality but two distinctive and conflicting ones. When one was alone in a room with her, she seemed not only distant but painfully shy, uncomfortable, and hesitant. She lowered her eyes as she spoke, and there was that little-girl whispery voice. She seemed as unsure of herself as her mother must have been when she first entered the charmed circle of the Bouviers. One felt touched by her, sorry for her, this girl from a broken home who seemed to want to unburden herself of some troublesome secret and yet who, for intensely private reasons of her own, could not quite bring herself to do so. And yet, when she entered a party, exquisitely dressed in something her father had chosen for her, all the shyness vanished. She was smiling, poised, serenely confident. She moved among crowds of people, kissing relatives, shaking hands, like a princess from some exotic land. She had more than charm. She glowed. Was this the same withdrawn and seemingly worried girl? Yes, apparently it was. Which was the *real* Jackie, people wondered. Or were both the facades she presented simply roles she was playing, roles she had been drilled in by her father? Beneath the facades, perhaps, was buried a secret third Jackie, protected, private, that no one in the world would ever get to see or really know.

About who her sister was there was no question. She was the typically happy second child, not in competition with her parents. Pretty, vivacious, and full of mischief, Lee was always up to something. Her sudden whims came and went like summer showers. Every day, it seemed, she had some new enthusiasm, some new passion. She considered herself a crusader for civic and social causes and, at one point, spent several weeks in lively correspondence with Mayor La Guardia, telling him what was wrong with New York City and what she, Lee Bouvier, felt should be done to set things right. One afternoon, Jackie walked into Lee's bedroom to find Lee on the phone busily telephoning orphanages. She had, that morning, become concerned about orphans and the plight of the parentless. She was telephoning orphanages to recruit a group of orphans whom she wanted to take with her to the theater.

Jackie was the opposite. She was not particularly gregarious, and enjoyed her own company. She was happy to spend hours alone in her room, not daydreaming but reading and listening to music. She read so much that, during her adolescence, her mother worried that she might be going to have a "bluestocking" on her hands. She sketched with pencils and watercolors —pictures of faces, mostly, her own, sketched from her mirror, her sister's, her mother's, her father's. She pasted the sketches carefully in scrapbooks. She wrote bits of poetry. She wrote a sad little story about a girl who lost her horse.

But she also had, her family noticed, an extraordinary power over people, a strange ability to get people to do what she wanted, to go with her where she wanted to go, to play the games she wanted to play. "Guess the name of the song I'm thinking of," she said to a group of friends one morning in East Hampton. All day long the friends sat around her, guessing and guessing, trying to come up with the name of the song—for Jackie.

5

Revenge

"THERE ARE NO rich Auchinclosses," people used to say. But then one would always have to add, "Except Hughdie."

The Auchincloss family, while not rich, has always been, as the author in the family, Louis Auchincloss likes to put it, "respectably prosperous." Respectability, in the family, has always been equated with prosperity. Poverty is the eighth deadly sin. Nowhere better than in the novels of Louis Auchincloss have been delineated the manners and mores of the small group of families which, whether we like to admit it or not, compose America's ruling class—and the Auchinclosses are one of these families. Though not rich, the Auchinclosses have been prominent in society for more than seven generations. In the late 1960s for example, nearly two full pages of the New York *Social Register* were devoted to listing members of the Auchincloss family: forty-seven separate listings, compared with forty-two for the Rockefellers, eight for the Vanderbilts, a mere two for the Astors.

Though not rich, Auchinclosses have always married well—which lifted them early out of the disgraceful ranks of the impecunious, and into the ranks of the respectably prosperous. The first Hugh Auchincloss arrived in the United States from Greenock, Scotland, in 1803, and from him all Auchinclosses descend. He married a Philadelphia girl of Scottish descent named Ann Anthony Stuart and one of their grandsons, John Winthrop, decided that his grandmother's maiden name was sufficient to permit him to have the crest of the Royal House of Stuart engraved on his silverware. Auchinclosses claim a great deal of royalty in their family tree. The late Charles C. Auchincloss, when his doctor advised him to give up drinking, took up genealogy for something to do and his family charts—considerably more elaborate and thorough than Major Bouvier's—show how the Auchinclosses are connected with William the Conqueror, and the kings of England, Scotland, and France, by way of the French Philippe II.

In America, the Auchincloss connections are even more faithfully chronicled. They became thread merchants through marriage into the Coats thread-making family and, over the years, Auchinclosses have acquired family ties, via marriage, with such imposing American names as the Vanderbilts, Rockefellers, Sloans, Winthrops, Saltonstalls, Cuttings, Van Rensselaers, Reids, du Ponts, Grosvenors, Truslows, Tiffanys, Bundys, Adamses, Rutherfurds, Ingrahams, Goodsells, Russells, Burdens, and a great many others. The "only rich" Auchincloss, Hughdie, as Mr. Hugh D. Auchincloss is affectionately called, came into his money as the result of a marriage when his father married Emma Brewster Jennings, the daughter of Oliver B. Jennings who, along with John D. and William Rockefeller, put together the Standard Oil Company. The wealthy Emma Jennings Auchincloss was, as the family puts it, "always very nice to her Auchincloss relatives," though, since they were for the most part less well off than she, she regarded them with a certain amount of condescension. Nonetheless, when Emma died, most of her vast fortune passed to her son, Hughdie. He had used this inheritance to open the Washington-based stock brokerage firm of Auchincloss, Parker & Redpath. With the advent of World War II, which finally pulled America out of the Depression, Hughdie's firm began to prosper.

When, after her divorce, Janet Bouvier began to be seen around town on the arm of Hughdie Auchincloss, tongues wagged. You had to hand it to Janet, people said, she was doing it again. Here, furthermore, was not only a man who had unquestionable position in New York society but who was also imposingly wealthy. In addition to a New York apartment, Hughdie was master of a huge estate called Merrywood in McLean, Virginia, and another enormous place, Hammersmith Farm in Newport. In appearance, Hughdie Auchincloss was the antithesis of Jack Bouvier. Hughdie was tall, powerfully built, ruddy-cheeked—a commanding figure next to Janet's slightness. He had, to be sure, a poor track record at the altar, as many much-married and much-divorced Auchinclosses have had. Hughdie had been married and divorced twice. His first wife was Maria Chrapovitsky, the daughter of a Russian naval officer, his second was Nina Gore Vidal, the daughter of T. B. Gore, the blind senator from Oklahoma, and the mother of writer Gore Vidal. Hughdie had a son by his first wife, and a son and daughter by his second. And yet, from a money standpoint, he was admirably equipped to offer Janet what she liked to refer to as "security." Janet and Hughdie became engaged in 1942, barely four years after her divorce, and were married in June of that year.

Jack Bouvier, needless to say, took this news badly. Though Janet's remarriage relieved him of the burden of alimony, it did little to relieve him of his feelings of inconsequence and failure. Janet's new husband was not only much richer and more successful than he, but he was also nearly ten years younger. Jack took Janet's marriage to Hughdie as an insult, a personal slap. She had married, he felt, out of spite, as though to say, "So much for you. Just see what I am today." Of course, some motive of revenge on Janet's part could not be ruled out. Janet was not the sort of woman who, the second time around, would have settled for anyone *less* successful than Jack. And, if revenge was one of her motivations, she got back at Jack in ways that even she might not have anticipated. Because, in marrying Hughdie, she was able to turn the tide of the girls' affection away from Jack, and back to her and her new husband.

To begin with, it was impossible *not* to like Hughdie Auchincloss. He was easygoing and cheerful and hardly ever lost his temper—unlike the mercurial Jack. And there was so much that he could offer Janet's daughters that Jack could not—Rolls Royces, servants, stables of horses, and two big country estates, one for summer and one for winter. Jack could not compete with any of that. Hughdie Auchincloss loved Janet's pretty daughters, and they quickly loved "Uncle Hugh," as they decided to call him. With Hughdie and Janet dividing their time between Virginia and Newport, there was simply less chance for Jack, in New York, to spend those gay weekends with Jackie and Lee. And Jack was bitter. In Wall Street, to try to get back at Hughdie, Jack made a weak joke and said that the slogan of Hughdie's brokerage firm should be "take a loss with Auchincloss." Unfortunately, the phrase stuck, much to the displeasure of Auchincloss, Parker & Redpath.

But, to Jack Bouvier, the Auchinclosses were no joking matter. In the months following Janet's remarriage, they became an obsession, almost to the point of paranoia. He became convinced that Janet and Hughdie had entered into a conspiracy to take his daughters away from him permanently. Jackie, for example, was now thirteen, and was beginning to be invited to sub-debutante parties in New York. Jack was delighted. That meant that she could stay with him, in the four-room apartment he now maintained at 125 East 74th Street. But often as not, schoolwork meant that she had to turn down these invitations and remain in Washington. When that happened Jack was devastated, convinced that the Auchincloss influence was behind it. When Janet sent Jackie to a dentist in Washington, and then forwarded the bill to Jack to be paid, he stormily announced that he would pay no bills for Washington dentists. If she needed dentistry she could come to New York—and stay with him.

At the same time, when she did come to visit him, there were nearly always quarrels. Any mention of the grand scale on which the Auchincloses lived—a remark about a party by the swimming pool, for instance—would send him into a towering rage, and he would fume about "those snobs," "those phonies," and "those members of so-called society." When Jackie would tease him about the number and variety of Jack's lady friends—in middle age he had developed a taste for girls who were not entirely ripe for inclusion in the *Social Register*—he was certain that some disparaging Auchincloss remark was behind it and, when she tried to laugh him out of these suspicions, he flew into another rage. At the same time, he had begun drinking heavily.

He was constantly begging her to come and stay at his apartment and use it as a base for attending "the parties you ought to be going to." Yet, when she did, often arriving late at night after a party, and departing early the next morning, he accused her of "using" him as a convenient hotel, a place to dash into to freshen her makeup and then dash away from. Jackie, having learned about fashion from her father, had now developed her own taste in clothes and was exercising it—though now, of course, the Auchincloses were paying for most of what she wore. He hated what she wore, and told her so. Again and again he threatened to do the only thing he could think of to get her to pay more attention to him, spend more time with him— cut off her allowance. He must have realized, of course, that cutting off her allowance could only have the effect of making her more dependent on the Auchinclosses. And so, though he threatened hundreds of times to do so, he never cut off her allowance. It seemed the only thing he had left to give her.

There were more Auchinclosses involved in what Jack saw as the Auchincloss plot to seduce his daughters away from him than just Janet and Hughdie. There were Hughdie Auchincloss's three children by his former wives, who spent much of their time with their father. There was young Hugh, nicknamed "Yusha" because of his Russian mother, and there were Nina and Tommy, by Hughdie's second wife. The Auchincloss children were close to the Bouvier girls in age, and the girls got along well with their stepbrothers and stepsister—a fact that infuriated Jack Bouvier. They were a part of the conspiracy too. Then, in 1945, Janet and Hughdie had a daughter of their own, whom they named Janet Jennings Auchincloss. In 1947, James Lee Auchincloss was born. That gave Jackie and Lee a half-brother and half-sister to cuddle, and two more Auchinclosses to contend with in his battle for his daughters' love, two more reasons why the girls would prefer spending time at Merrywood or Hammersmith Farm than on East 74th Street, with Jack. Most damnably insulting of all was the fact that Janet had named her new daughter after Jennings, the scoundrel who was responsible for Hughdie's millions to begin with, and she had named her new son after old man Lee whom Jack had never been able to stand. The villainy Janet had committed against him seemed complete.

Poor, luckless suitor for the hearts of his daughters, he could not accept the fact that the girls were growing up, that they were growing away, inevitably, from their father's passion. Pony rides in the park no longer allured them, they had grown weary of the bitter tug-of-war between Mummy and Daddy, they were now striking out for something else—such as lives of their own.

When Jackie told her father that she had decided to go to Miss Porter's School, he was furious—as he was, those days, about almost anything she told him. The Auchinclosses were behind the selection of Miss Porter's, he was sure. It was part of the plot to steal Jackie. Miss Porter's was where Auchinclosses *always* went. It was a tradition. It was in Auchincloss country, and an Auchincloss cousin, Mrs. Wilmarth S. Lewis, lived just down the street from the school. There was only one consolation for Jack. Farmington, Connecticut, was closer to New York than Washington, D.C. Perhaps, with Jackie at Farmington, he would be able to see more of her, he said. Perhaps.

6

Farmington

FARMINGTON, CONNECTICUT, is proud to be considered one of New England's most beautiful towns. Technically, Farmington is a suburb of Hartford and yet, in mood and attitude, Farmington is aloof and distant. West Hartford, which Farmington abuts is regarded as "suburban." Farmington, next door, is "country." Farmington's white church and the village green which it addresses are picture-book New England Colonial.

For years, its stately Main Street was lined with traditional elms which, one by one, have succumbed to Dutch elm disease, a loss which the town feels deeply. By mutual agreement, all the large Colonial houses which face Main Street are painted white, with black shutters, and woe betide the Farmingtonian who does not keep his white paint fresh and sparkling. Interspersed among these comfortable and well-kept residences are the white-painted, black-shuttered school buildings and dormitories of Miss Porter's School for Girls.

It is difficult for the uninitiated to tell which Main Street houses are private homes and which are the eighteen buildings which comprise the school, which is just as Farmington prefers things to be. A private boarding school in its midst is always something of a mixed blessing to a New England town. Adolescent children are, after all, adolescent children, no matter how illustrious their pedigree. They can be noisy, active, mischievous, and run up bills at local shops which even the wealthiest parents may refuse to pay. And yet, by integrating itself architecturally with the surrounding village—camouflaging itself, in fact—the school has managed to ingratiate itself with the town, and to become accepted by it. No loud bells ring along Main Street to announce the beginning and the end of classes, and no noisy shouts from hockey fields disturb the quiet lives of Farmington residents. Perhaps the fact that school and town get on so well—while always maintaining a polite distance from one another, as good neighbors are expected to—explains why students and alumnae of Miss Porter's most commonly refer to the school as "Farmington."

Also, the school has a long and ingratiatingly cozy history in the town. It was founded in 1843 by Miss Sarah Porter, spinster sister of President Porter of Yale, who had "educational theories advanced for her age": in particular, a theory that young women deserved some sort of education. For years, Miss Porter's was run as strictly a Porter family affair. Following Miss Sarah Porter's retirement and death, the school was taken over by her nephew, Robert Porter Keep, and, following his death, his widow became headmistress. Following her death, her son and daughter-in-law took over the school. It was not until Jackie Bouvier's generation of young ladies that an "outsider," Mr. Ward Johnson, had been brought in to serve as the school's headmaster.

For years, Miss Porter's was run as a "finishing school." Literally, a young woman finished her education there, and hardly any of the early Porter graduates went on to college. At the same time, at Farmington, a young woman was expected to be "finished" in the finer arts of womanhood—to have learned good manners and good morals, the art of polite conversation, of needlework, along with a bit of French, a bit of history and, perhaps, piano. A Farmington girl was prepared for what her future role was presumed to be—wife, mother, mistress of a well-run house and staff. It was not until well into the twentieth century that Miss Porter's began to think of itself seriously as a college preparatory school, and to compete with other, newer private girls' schools to place its graduates in the best New England women's colleges.

Miss Porter's has always been small, and it has always been expensive. (Today, the student body numbers only three hundred, and the tuition is $5,200 a year.) Among exclusive girls' boarding schools, Farmington has often been compared with Foxcroft in Middleburg, Virginia, but this is unfair. Though both schools educate the daughters of the rich, Foxcroft is both more pretentious and less ambitious than Farmington. Foxcroft stresses equestrian ability, for one thing. At Farmington, though there are bridle trails among the wooded acres behind the school and along the Farmington River, riding is not a preoccupation. Under the idiosyncratic rule of Miss Charlotte Noland, who founded Foxcroft in 1914, the school developed

49

some unusual theories and practices. High heels, for example, were forbidden because, according to Miss Noland, "high heels tip a girl's uterus." Military drill, in uniforms, was also part of a Foxcroft girl's regimen. Still, in a society sense, Foxcroft has risen to the top of the heap. Farmington, in its quiet New England way, is also a "social" school, but it has never carried —or wanted to carry—the perfumed cachet of Foxcroft. Instead, as the school states, it tried to offer "a healthy balance between intellectual activities and physical exercise."

Jacqueline Bouvier might easily have chosen to go to Foxcroft. Many of her friends went there. The school was only a few short miles from the Auchinclosses' Merrywood, and all the pleasures that offered themselves there. But she did not choose social Foxcroft. She was athletic and an excellent rider, and she was also developing an intellectual side. Like her grandfather Bouvier, she was a straight-A student and ambitious to succeed at whatever she undertook—to be a success, possibly, to compensate in some way for the desperately bitter failure of her parents' marriage and the continuing bitterness between Jack and Janet. She was also beginning to try to relieve herself of her dependency on the Auchinclosses, and on her father, it would turn out as well. So she chose correct, traditional Farmington—far from Virginia and Newport, and not all that handy, after all, to New York.

Farmington has been called a stuffy town—a town of wealthy retired New Yorkers and men from Hartford's business and banking community, reserved, conservative, Republican. And Miss Porter's School has also been called a stuffy place—still redolent, in the 1940s, of the old Yankee Porter-Keep regime. But at least the stuffiness of the community and the stuffiness of the school were independent of one another. The school didn't try to tell the town what to do, and the town let the school go about its quiet business. An unwritten rule at Miss Porter's School was "keep to yourself." The school still stressed Victorian good manners—it was still important to curtsey on certain occasions—and Victorian morality was also emphasized. In a sense, the school had not quite entered the twentieth century—which it would do, abruptly and unpleasantly in 1977 when the unwanted baby of a Miss Porter's girl was found in a garbage can. In the 1940s, one could still make the distinction between a man and a "gentleman," a woman and a "lady," and not be laughed out of the room. In all, when Jackie entered Miss Porter's in 1943, it was a very pleasant place to be.

Among the values with which Farmington attempted to imbue its young ladies was the importance of being able to rise to occasions. When something had to be done, you did it, and you did it yourself without running to someone else for help. When the chips were down, you faced the situation squarely and took on the task of piling the chips up again. Two good New England words, heard often in sermons at Farmington Sunday chapel services, were "guts" and "gumption." A perfect example of the guts and gumption and sense of duty that Farmington managed, somehow, to instill in its women was the case of Jackie's cousin by marriage, Mrs. Lewis, the former Annie Burr Auchincloss (through another auspicious Auchincloss marriage, Mrs. Lewis was a collateral descendant of Aaron Burr). Mrs. Lewis, a Farmington alumna, had spent most of her life doing needlepoint and collecting eighteenth-century prints. When World War II was declared, however, she put down her needle and her art catalogues and went to work for the Red Cross and other wartime agencies. No previous education or training had prepared her for this—no provisional year, even, with the Junior League doing volunteer work. She simply *was* prepared, and did what needed to be done, providing, in the process, leadership for others. Since Mrs. Lewis also happened to live in Farmington, her example was often cited to Farmington girls during the war years when Jackie attended the school.

When Jacqueline Bouvier arrived at Farmington, every Farmington girl, it seemed, owned and wore a "junior cut" mink coat for winter. It was the style. Jackie, however, did not have a junior cut mink coat. Her cold-weather coat was sheared beaver. In warmer weather, all the girls wore white poplin raincoats, whether it was raining or not. Jackie did not wear a white poplin raincoat. Her own sense of nonconformity, and her father's lessons in fashion, prevailed and she would not succumb to any standard. She did not dress outlandishly, of course, but quietly and carefully and always somehow individualistically. She fit no pattern.

At Farmington, in those days, there were no black girls. There was only a tiny handful of Jewish girls, and Jewish girls were presumed to be not interested in schools like Farmington where, it was assumed, there was a quota, written or unwritten. No one noticed ethnic imbalances in those days in terms of student populations; it would take World War II to focus national attention on such matters. But Jackie sensed the situation, and made note of it, and would take steps to remedy it later on, as a Farmington alumna. At Farmington, she did not have as much spending money as many of her classmates had. Her father's allowance was $50 a month. Janet, who disapproved of largesse being handed out to young people, carefully restricted her gifts of money to special occasions, such as birthdays and Christmas. Hughdie respected Janet's wishes in this regard. Also, he was a Scotsman who, though he liked to live luxuriously, had never been particularly openhanded with his money. Life for Jackie at Farmington was reasonably Spartan. Still, she stood out.

It was during the years at Farmington that Jackie Bouvier began to become a legend. She was becoming a legend, to be sure, only within the comparatively small world of Eastern Seaboard society, but she was becoming one nonetheless. She was different. There was something about her that you couldn't put your finger on. She was 'pretty, yes, but not the delicate, classic beauty that her sister Lee was. Her dark hair was still uncontrollably curly, her jaw was a little too sharp, her nose a little too snubbed, her eyes a little too far apart. But she was special. At Farmington, her headmaster, Ward Johnson, had begun to talk about her as "this extraordinary girl"—not only of her high academic marks but of her unusual ability and appreciation of the arts, and of her sense of history. Soon Johnson was pointing her out as *the* outstanding Farmington girl. She took such praise politely.

Though she was obviously bright, she also displayed a charming modesty about this fact—a lesson she had learned from those New York weekends with her father. If a young man she was with moaned that he had just flunked his math exam, she would match his glum look with a worried look of her own and say, "Oh, I'm just terrible at math, too!" even though she was excellent at it. Soon the word about Jackie Bouvier had passed, through the prep school grapevine, to every boys' campus in the East. Invitations poured in to dances and parties at Hotchkiss, Choate, St. Paul's, St. George's, Exeter, Andover and Groton. As her father had instructed her, she was selective about these. She would use, as excuses, a "boring" term paper that she had to write, or a "stupid" exam that she had to study for. Last minute "blind dates" were always ruled out. As a result, the prep school youth who could truthfully say that he had taken out Jackie Bouvier had something to boast about. And the legend grew.

In 1947, society columnist Igor Cassini, who billed himself as "Cholly Knickerbocker," voted Jacqueline Bouvier Debutante of the Year, noting her enormous popularity with Eastern prep school and college men, and adding that, because she never pushed herself at men—always held herself at a white-gloved arm's length from them—she was also enormously popular with the girls who were her contemporaries. That summer, the Auchinclosses tossed a huge dinner dance for her at the Clambake Club in Newport, as a coming-out party. She looked radiant, the stag line perspired and panted for her, and her relatives all commented on how Jackie had all at once "come out of her shell," that shell of distance, uncertainty, and shyness. But she hadn't come out of any shell at all. The shell was there, perhaps more impervious to prying than ever before. On the night of her coming-out party, she was the heroine of the evening, knew it, rose to the occasion, and acted her part to perfection, without missing a line. But behind the performance, within the intricate contours of the shell, lay a secret person only she was on speaking terms with, a person whose exact nature would perplex and baffle friends and acquaintances—and eventually the world—forever.

Jack Bouvier, who might have been watching the triumphs of his successful pupil with delight, was actually in a state of despair. During Jackie's Farmington years, she had made far fewer visits to East 74th Street than he had hoped for, far fewer telephone calls. Reaching her on the dormitory phone at school was maddeningly difficult, almost impossible. She answered his imploring letters with hasty notes. She put him off, just as she put off her prep school swains, with excuses —exams to cram for, term papers to write. Of course Jack blamed Janet—vicious, vengeful Janet who, having made him eat crow once, was forcing him to devour that bird again and again, never satisfied until she had completely divested him of every shred of pride, of manhood, of fatherhood—who would not be happy until she had turned his beloved daughter into a casual friend who dropped in now and then between other engagements. To the few friends who would still listen, he railed against Janet and her Auchincloss co-conspirators. "Those so-called blue-blood Newport snobs!" he would rant. On the subject of Janet, he could become quite irrational, especially after he had had a few drinks. Janet, he would say, close to tears, was the cause of all his woes—marital, paternal, financial. "My whole life has been ruined by that bitch," he would say. "I should have stood up to her from the beginning. I should never have let her throw me out of that apartment." The few friends would smile and try to look sympathetic. They would not remind him of what they all knew. They would not say, "But, Jack, you had to move out of the apartment. It belonged to her father."

The coming-out party at the Clambake Club, to which he had not been invited, and the surrounding publicity about the Debutante of the Year were the cause of even more grief. The damned Auchinclosses were at it again, taking over his daughter, presenting her to society as though she were an Auchincloss property and not his very own. When he complained to Janet about the party, Janet coolly reminded him that he could, if he wished, give another coming-out party for Jackie in New York at which she, Janet, would refrain from appearing. This was common practice among divorced parents. But of course she must have known that Jack could never have afforded such an extravagance. He could simply not compete with the Auchinclosses.

Nor should he have ever tried. What he could not seem to grasp, during the growing-up Farmington years, was that Jackie was now beginning to learn to run her own show. It was to be a show independent of any particular backers. It was not that she loved her mother, or Hughdie Auchincloss, any more. She was merely becoming her own woman and, as such, needed both parents less. In a sense, both parents had let her down. She would not let herself down. If she was running her own show, it would be quite a show. And, more than becoming her own woman, she was becoming a force—a woman to be reckoned with.

7

A Word
about Janet

"AT LEAST," PEOPLE said, "she's made Hughdie very happy."

That was more than could be said for his other two wives—the Russian, who had once had the misfortune of being injured when she accidentally walked into a whirling airplane propellor, and Mrs. Gore, who had brought Gore Vidal into the family. (He had occupied, briefly, the same position in the household that was later taken by Jackie Bouvier, and would always resent her for having "usurped" it.) There were a lot of other nice things one could say about Janet. She was slender, attractive, an excellent organizer, good at detail, a good mother. She was an excellent bridge player, she spoke fluent French. She loved animals, horses, dogs, all furry creatures. Every summer, at Hammersmith Farm, the Auchinclosses rented a large herd of Black Angus cattle from a local breeder, and let the cattle graze in the broad fields that rolled down to Narragansett Bay because both Janet and Hughdie "liked to look out on animals." Janet had a quick wit, and an excited, enthusiastic way of speaking that was quite charming. She had a bright laugh. With men, she was something of a flirt. When Hughdie displeased her, she had a mocking, teasing way of letting him know it that he clearly found attractive. "Hughdie, *Hughdie!*" she would exclaim.

But what Janet's detractors—and these were mostly

56

people who had taken Jack's side at the time of the divorce—said about her was that she was what people called a "climber." They said that she was money-mad, that she had married Jack for his money and then, when that had turned out not to amount to much, she had cast Jack aside and married another man for his money. True or not, no one could say, now that she had married Hughdie, that she had not been an attentive and caring wife. She pampered him and fussed over him and, when he became ill with emphysema, she worried over him and nursed him and ran little errands for him, always careful to see that he did not overexert himself. Though Hughdie's was a much less demonstrative nature than hers, it was clear that he adored her. And if, at one point in the past, she had been a climber, it was also clear that now, married to Hughdie, she had need to climb no more. In social situations she was poised and confident.

As a parent, she was cool and sensible. Once, when Lee was about ten years old, Janet caught Lee telling a fib. She sat her daughter down and began telling her the Parson Weems Fable about George Washington and the cherry tree. When she got to the part in which George Washington's father asked his son who had chopped down the tree, Janet paused and asked her daughter, "Now what do you suppose George Washington told his father?" Lee quickly replied, "He said, 'I don't have any idea who cut it down, Daddy.' " "But, Lee," said her mother, "that would have been a *lie*. What George Washington said was, 'Father, I cannot tell a lie. I did it with my little hatchet.' " Lee thought a moment and then said, "Well, I think that was an awfully stupid thing for him to say when his father was so mad at him."

As the *chatelaine* of two large estates, it had to be admitted that Janet ran a tight ship—or, rather, two tight ships. When she became mistress of Hammersmith Farm, for example, it was wartime, and there were all sorts of restrictions and inconveniences. Janet's mother-in-law had employed fourteen full-time gardeners just to groom and tend the big place. Old Mrs. Auchincloss was from a grand Newport era when it was fashionable to locate the garden some distance from the house and it was part of a daily ritual: one strolled to the garden after lunch and, when there, arranged oneself in the shade of pergolas to be served tea brought out on a wagon by the "second man." In wartime Newport, it was impossible to find so much as a first man, and the fourteen gardeners were a quaint and distant memory.

It would have been simpler to get rid of the old place, but Hughdie had a sentimental attachment to it. He had been born there and, he said cheerfully, he intended to die there. So Janet put her daughters to work—pruning rose bushes and fruit trees, clipping hedges and cutting grass. It was very nearly a hopeless task—there were five hot houses full of growing things to tend. Gradually, under Janet's supervision, the scale of the gardening operation was reduced. The huge old gardens were carefully photographed for posterity, then plowed under. A smaller garden was built next to the main house, considerably shortening the hike to the garden that used to be required. Wartime restrictions, meanwhile, meant that there could be only one telephone in the house, and so the children were assigned tours of telephone duty, which meant staying within earshot of the ring. Cooks and maids were hard to find, and so the children learned the techniques and disciplines of cooking and housework.

After the war, of course, everything changed, and Hammersmith Farm returned to its former opulence. Everyone had to admit that Janet managed the transition beautifully. In fact, Janet managed *every* transition beautifully. What her detractors failed to grasp, in fact, was that one of the secrets of her success—the secret of her climb, if one wanted to call it that—was that she was as skillful at role-playing as her older daughter. Society in America involves a certain amount of play-acting, and Janet had mastered all the rules. She could put on one face for one occasion, and a different face for another. As situations changed she changed. In running a place like Hammersmith Farm, which was built for entertaining, she was involved in a kind of show business, and if she had chosen the stage instead of society as her career, she doubtless would have been a consummate actress.

When a guest arrived at Hammersmith Farm, he was met at the door by a butler, and his luggage was whisked upstairs to one of the guest rooms where his things were unpacked and put away in closets and dressers. If dinner was to be black tie, his suit would be taken downstairs to be pressed. A maid would appear at his bedroom door to say, "My name is Maria. May I draw your bath? If you need anything, just ring this bell twice." On his bedroom desk would be letter paper, envelopes, post cards (picturing the old gardens), even stamps, and a printed breakfast menu, with choices to be circled the night before. In his bathroom would be all sorts of lovely scents from colognes, shaving lotions, and Janet's French soaps. Her thick white towels with her blue monogram, J.L.A., would hang in absorbent profusion.

Downstairs, on this particular occasion, a summer day in 1966, Janet waited to take her house guest on a tour of old Newport, to look at the restorations of the historic houses. She had a new car, a Jaguar that Hughdie had just bought her as a present, and which had reclining seats. She thought the reclining seats a little silly. "Who would want to lie down while driving a car?" And she was complaining about the size of the monogram, J.L.A., that had just been hand-painted, in Old English script, on the front door. "It's too large. It looks vulgar. I told him I wanted a *tiny* monogram. He'll just have to come back and do it again," she said.

Off in the car with her guest, Janet chatted about Newport. "I'm really still an East Hampton person. I still miss it. But I've managed to *put up with* Hammersmith. I guess I'll just go on putting up with it," she said. She pointed out historic sights as they appeared. Auchinclosses have been coming to Newport since the mid-nineteenth century, and she pointed out the cemetery where a number of Auchinclosses repose—"They're in an *older* part, of course, and on a hill." The cemetery was on Farewell Street. "Isn't that an appropriate address for a cemetery?" she asked.

"The original Auchincloss house is still standing," she explained. "It's on Washington Street, which is not a very good part of town anymore. It's become a Catholic retreat house. It's an ugly, dark old Victorian place—hideous, really, but I'll take you to see it if you'd like." Her guest said he would like.

The Stella Maris retreat house on Washington Street did indeed seem unprepossessing, as dark and ugly as Janet had described it. "They've let it run down terribly," she said as she pulled up in front of the house. "Do you want to see the inside? I'm sure that if you go up and ring the doorbell, and explain why you're interested, they'll let you take a quick peek around." The house guest said that he would like a quick look, got out of the car, and went up to the front door.

The doorbell was answered by an elderly, spectacled nun, who said that yes, this was the old Auchincloss place and, rather shyly, she led him through a dark-paneled entrance hall into two even darker front rooms, the original parlors of the house. In the gloom, it was still possible to see the monastic furnishings: straight-backed chairs, a crucifix on one wall, an icon of the Blessed Virgin on another. The guest thanked the sister, and said that he had to leave; Mrs. Auchincloss was waiting in the car.

At the mention of the name, the little nun became transfixed. She clutched at her beads as though she had seen a Holy Vision. "Mrs. *Auchincloss?*" she cried. "You mean Jackie Kennedy's *mother?* She's

outside—here? Oh, please, please ask her to come in!
I know the Mother Superior would so want to meet
her!"

Back at the car, Janet was not pleased with this
newest development. "Oh, for heavens' sakes," she
said crossly. "It's quarter of one, lunch is at one, and I
have guests coming. Do I really *have* to go in there?
Well, I suppose it'll seem rude if I don't. Come on,
let's go."

Now, at the front door of the retreat house, the
original nun, and her plump Mother Superior, were
wringing their hands with delight and anticipation. Now
Janet Auchincloss, all smiles and graciousness and
charm, was presenting herself to them. Janet had
never been a particularly devout Catholic. She had
married Jack Bouvier, to be sure, in a Catholic nuptial
mass. But she had divorced him, had married
Hughdie, a Presbyterian, and had, at that point, been
living publicly out of the Church for some twenty-five
years. Still, she entered the dark house full of enthusiasm and eager questions about the sisters and their
mission. There then proceeded a much more ex-
haustive tour of the house. Janet and her guest were
taken down plaster-chipped hallways, into dark little
devotional recesses, and were even shown two of the
bleak little cells where the people on retreat stayed:
each was furnished with a narrow iron cot, a Bible, a
crucifix, nothing more. At each turn in the house,
Janet murmured, "Beautiful . . . simply beautiful.
Such a sense of peace . . . serenity. Oh, this is so
lovely what you're doing here." Then, suddenly, she
said, "Would it be possible for *me,* a civilian, to come
here and make a retreat?" Almost overcome at the
prospect, the Mother Superior replied that yes, indeed
it would be possible. The house would be honored. "I
would love to do it!" cried Janet. "I want to."

The tour ended, appropriately, in the chapel and,
entering it, Janet seized the railing of the nearest pew
and fell to her knees, crossing herself. Her head fell to

her chest. The others knelt also. For several minutes all prayed in silence. Then, crossing herself again, Janet rose, and the others rose as well. At the door she said, "Thank you so much. It's all just so beautiful."

The Mother Superior said, "Mrs. Auchincloss, whenever you want to come here—for a long stay, or even for just a few days—you will always be welcome with us."

"Oh, thank you," said Janet.

Mother Superior then added tentatively, nervously, "And Mrs. Auchincloss, I just want to tell you, I just want you to know, that we all love your daughter. We all love Jackie Kennedy."

Smiling, holding out her hand, Janet said, "Thank you, Mother. So do we."

Back at the new Jaguar, Janet was cross again. "See?" she said, pointing to her watch, "I knew it. We're going to be late for lunch. I knew we shouldn't have got involved with that silly business."

She drove back to Hammersmith Farm rather fast.

8

College Days

IN THE FALL of 1947, Jackie entered Vassar, and once more her father was pleased with her choice of schools. Not so much because Poughkeepsie was an easy distance from New York, but because, geographically, Vassar placed Jackie farther away from the hated Auchinclosses. For a while, Jack's expectations were fulfilled. That autumn, he visited her several times at college, and she proudly showed off her handsome father, taking him to lunch and dinner in the main dining hall. For the round of fall and winter debutante teas and dances, she used the 74th Street apartment as her base. But it wasn't long before Jack was complaining again, in a familiar vein, that her New York visits had nothing to do with him; his apartment was merely a convenience. She cared little whether he was there or not, as long as she had a key.

Then, by the winter of that year, it was clear that Jack Bouvier's father was dying of cancer. Old Major Bouvier was eighty-two, and the family gathered at or near Lasata to ease his final days. His traditional Christmas family dinner was cancelled and, on January 14, 1948, when it was clear that he would not last the night, a priest was called to administer last rites, while the Major's daughter, who had flown home from Rio de Janiero, held his hand.

Jack had been a disappointment to his father, and knew it. Nevertheless, during his father's last months, Jack had solicitously called on his father nearly every day, hoping that his father's displeasure with him might be forgotten before he drew up his final will. While, once again, all the Bouviers did their best to conceal their enthusiastic avarice and waited to see who would get what, Jack was confident that his father had remembered him. He would once again be rich. After all, the Major had inherited $1,300,000 from his bachelor brother just a dozen years earlier, and he had been a man, everyone supposed, of sizable personal resources of his own. At least he had always *lived* like one. But alas, when the vault was opened, something seemed to have happened. All the lawyers could uncover of the Major's assets amounted to only $824,000. Where had all the money gone? "Lost" was the answer given. "Spent" would have been a more exact word. State and federal taxes took more than a quarter of the estate. Jack received $100,000 tax free, and was forgiven a debt of fifty thousand dollars that he had borrowed from his father. Servants, secretaries, and charities received some small bequests. Each grandchild received $3,000. It was Jacqueline Bouvier's first inheritance, and it was a small one.

In order to disperse the bequests in Major Bouvier's will, Lasata had to be sold. It has since—considerably altered and expensively redecorated—become the summer home of Mr. and Mrs. Joseph Meehan, another irony. Joseph Meehan is the son of the notorious Mike Meehan, a Wall Street trader of the ilk and era —indeed, they were cronies—of Joseph P. Kennedy. Mike Meehan had started out as a theater ticket broker, and had specialized in getting choice seats for hit Broadway shows for Wall Street bankers and their wives. When he came up with the idea of placing brokerage offices on the decks of ocean liners, the bankers decided that Meehan was a bright lad. His greatest coup in the stock market was bull-trading RCA stock up from a 1928 low of 85¼ to an unprecedented 549 in 1929—even though RCA had paid no dividends whatever in the period. When Meehan sold "Radio" just before the crash, he became a multi-millionaire. The passage of Lasata from the hands of the effete Bouviers to those of the upstart Meehans symbolized a takeover of wealth and power by a younger and tougher generation.

Lasata had been Jack Bouvier's trump card for luring his daughters to spend their summers with him in East Hampton. Now all he could afford was a small rented summer cottage, some distance from the sea. Needless to say, Hammersmith Farm on the sea at Newport offered far more attractions to the girls. Still, Jack kept Jackie's favorite horse, Danseuse, stabled in East Hampton and refused to allow the animal to be shipped to Newport. Surely, he hoped, Jackie would spend at least *some* of her summer time with him, if for no other reason than to ride Danseuse. In the summer of 1948, however, he was disappointed again. Jackie announced that she wanted to spend the months of July and August touring Europe with three other girls, and she had her $3,000 from her grandfather to pay for the trip. Jack was immediately suspicious that Janet was behind the trip, and opposed the scheme vigorously. But Jackie, by now, knew how to get around her father and, in the end, she prevailed. Furthermore, Jack paid for her European tour, and Jackie took off for France, Switzerland, and England with her friends.

By her sophomore year, Jackie had begun to lose her taste for Vassar. She found the all-woman atmosphere of the place oppressive, and she complained to her father about it. By now, Jack's advice was nearly always negative. Don't do this, don't do that. "If you do, I'll cut off your allowance"—the threat echoed through her life. Don't, he admonished her, leave Vassar. But, on her own, she applied for admission to the Smith College's Junior Year in France program, to be undertaken the following academic year. When she was accepted, Jack, for a change, was delighted. A year in France would take her away from him but it would also, more important, take her away from Janet. The more he heard that Janet opposed the idea, the more thoroughly he endorsed it. And, as was becoming usual, it was Jackie who prevailed. As a concession to her father she spent two weeks with him in East Hampton in July, 1949, then sailed for Europe in August.

The Smith program called for two months of intensive French lessons at the University of Grenoble, followed by the remainder of the school year in Paris, where Jackie was to study French literature and history at the Sorbonne. Oddly enough, Jack would later tell friends that during that year abroad he felt closer to his favorite daughter than at any other time of his life. True, she was three thousand miles away, but she was *there,* where he had put her, where he was paying for it all, where she was clearly having a wonderful time, where she was no longer subject to a *choice* of being with him or with her mother, and where she might choose the latter. In Paris, she seemed—psychologically, at least—in his possession.

At Vassar, meanwhile, the legend of Jackie Bouvier had continued to grow. Now the invitations flooded in from Yale, Princeton, Harvard, and Williams—invitations to college proms and fraternity parties—and, as usual, she picked and chose. As a date, she continued to be aloof, withdrawn, mysterious—even a little frightening. She had, for example, that exotic, non-standard beauty. She was known to be smart. She was also a member of a very wealthy family and so, most college boys thought, she was apt to be an expensive date. Not that Jackie asked to be taken to expensive places; she was far too bright to do that. It was just that the expensive aura around her suggested that she *expected* to be treated expensively. With her, the wealthiest college boys were assumed to have the edge. Poorer boys could only look on hopelessly, from a distance, and yearn. To them, she seemed totally inaccessible.

Then there was a disconcerting little habit she had. When talking with a boy, or dancing with him, her gaze would wander to some spot in a middle distance just beyond his shoulder. Her eyes would travel to the others in the room, creating the unpleasant impression that she was more interested in others than in the man she happened to be with. "Who is that?" she would ask as a new youth entered the party. "Is he in your class? Is he a friend of yours?" This habit infuriated men—but it excited them too, and made them try all the harder to please and entertain her. And when Jackie Bouvier departed for her year in France, there was a sense of loss felt throughout much of the male college population in the East.

For Jackie, meanwhile, the year in France meant freedom: freedom from the endless bickering between her mother and her father over her affection and her whereabouts. She had grown more than a little weary of it all. To friends she confided that what she would really like to do would be to remain in Paris permanently and never come home to either parent. One thing was certain: she was not going back to Vassar. For her senior year, she wanted a coeducational college. And she wanted it to be in an important city, where things happened, not in a little Hudson River town like Poughkeepsie. When she came home from Europe in the summer of 1950, she informed her father that she had applied to, and been accepted by, George Washington University in Washington, D.C. That was the summer of her twenty-first birthday, and she was beginning to assert herself.

Jack, of course, was devastated. Washington was Auchincloss country, and surely treacherous Janet had had a hand in this decision. No, Jackie assured him, the decision had been her own—though naturally he didn't believe her. While Jack ranted, Jackie remained cool. She knew that he had no choice but to go along with what she wanted. The terms of the divorce agreement specified that he had to pay for her college education at whatever college she might choose. In the end, he asked her for just one concession. After graduation, would she come to work for him in his office? He would pay her fifty dollars a week. She said she would think about this.

Actually, Jackie's senior year at George Washington turned out to be a happy one for Jack. She had begun seeing a young stockbroker, just out of Yale, named John Husted and during the Washington year she made a number of trips up to New York for dates with Husted, always staying with her father when she came. Husted came from a proper *Social Register* background, and had parents properly based in northern Westchester. Jack thoroughly approved of young Husted. The two men had Yale in common, the brokerage business in common, and New York in common. When Jackie and John Husted announced their engagement early in 1951, Jack Bouvier was delighted. When Jackie married Husted, she would settle in New York, and Jack would have her to himself again. A few months later, however, Jack's hopes were dashed again when the Bouvier-Husted engagement was formally broken, "by mutual consent," as the papers announced. Actually, Jackie had begun to find John Husted and his line of work a bit too tame and predictable for her taste. She called John Husted "immature," a word young people used a great deal in the 1950s. But Jackie's friends had begun to notice that she seemed to have a preference for men who were older than she.

Meanwhile, the wretched Auchinclosses had, behind Jack Bouvier's back, been concocting schemes of their own for Jackie's post-college career. In 1951, without consulting anyone, Jackie had entered *Vogue* magazine's Prix de Paris contest. Contestants were asked to write four technical papers on various aspects of *haute couture,* plus an essay on "People I Wish I Had Known." Jackie had chosen three exotic types—Oscar Wilde, Charles Baudelaire, and Sergei Diaghilev. There were 1,280 entrants in the contest, and Jacqueline Bouvier won first prize—six months in France with *Vogue*'s Paris office, followed by six months in the New York office of the magazine.

Her father was delighted. With Jackie out of her mother's range, he could continue his wistful long-distance flirtation with his daughter. Janet, on the other hand, was less pleased. Jackie, she argued, had spent altogether too much time out of the country in recent years. She was becoming such a Francophile that she was in danger of expatriating herself entirely, Janet said. In Janet's mind, there was something a little undignified about accepting the *Vogue* prize. It was like accepting a scholarship and that was something that poor people did. She urged Jackie to turn down the prize.

In many ways, 1951 was a troubling year for Jackie, a time of painful choices. She had transferred from a fashionable Eastern women's college to a large, impersonal university whose diploma carried no particular prestige. She had toyed with the idea of marriage, and had had the on-and-off engagement to John Husted. During her year in France there had been not one but two men, both Frenchmen, with whom she had had attachments, and whom she sometimes thought she would like to see again but, at other times, was less certain about. Now college was behind her, and so was her twenty-first birthday. She was legally an adult, a voter. "Life" loomed ahead, full of uncertain prospects and possibilities. She was weary of being pulled this way and that by a mother and a father who never agreed on anything, and she was eager to be independent of them. And yet independence, now that it was a clear possibility, seemed a little frightening. In some ways, she seemed to need her parents' advice and guidance more than ever, even though nothing that she did would ever please them both. And so, uncharacteristically, she wavered, vacillated, on the question of the *Vogue* prize—with her father begging her to accept it and her mother urging her strongly to turn it down.

It was one of several moments in her life when her two very different heritages seemed to be at war with one another—the effete French elegance of the veneer-maker and designer of ornamental marbles on one side, and the tough, hard-headed Irishness of Grandpa Lee on the other. She dangled uncertainly in between.

She had worked hard on her contest entry. To have won first prize seemed too good to be true. The prize itself—travel to two exciting cities, work in a field she cared about for the most prestigious fashion magazine in the world—seemed almost incredibly glamorous, something that most girls her age would give anything to have. Perhaps that was it: success suddenly seemed to be coming too fast, too easily. She felt unready for it. The *Vogue* prize carried with it a challenge, but what if she were unable to meet the challenge? What if she failed at *Vogue?* After her promised year, *Vogue* would simply bid her *adieu.* Perhaps she was already a failure, and her mind swarmed with the black self-doubts that assail every college graduate. Whether Janet realized it or not, she was pressing her case during a particularly vulnerable moment in her daughter's life. And so, in the end, it seemed simpler to do as her mother said, to turn down the prize, and let it pass to some more "deserving" person. Once more, Jack's hopes were crushed.

He reminded her, however, of his offer to come to work for him in his office for $50 a week. But, in the meantime, Hughdie Auchincloss had also been working on his stepdaughter's career future, and for something that would compensate her for the *Vogue* disappointment. The *Vogue* prize had suggested a talent for journalism and, through his friend Arthur Krock of the *New York Times* Washington bureau, he had arranged an interview for Jackie with Frank Waldrop of the *Washington Times-Herald.* Waldrop, interested, offered her a job as inquiring photographer for the paper. The pay was only $42.50 a week, but the work was certainly more interesting than a clerical job in a stockbroker's office and, to her father's further chagrin, she accepted it.

She went to work for the *Times-Herald* in the late autumn of 1951 and, at first, the inquiring photographer's stories were unsigned. Within four months, however, the byline of Jacqueline Bouvier had made its appearance and the columnist had been given a small raise. Her questions were bright and amusing. Outside a Washington dental clinic, she asked, "Are men braver than women in the dentist's chair?" Of women shoppers along Connecticut Avenue she asked, "Can you spot a married man?" Of a series of antique dealers she asked, "If you could keep one thing in your shop, what would it be?" From downtown businessmen she wanted to know, "Are men as inclined to fall for a line as girls are?" This sort of newspaper work might not carry the cachet of working for an international magazine like *Vogue*—to compare *Vogue* with the now-defunct *Times-Herald* would be like comparing Vassar with George Washington University —but Jackie's first steps into the world were still tentative, still shy and uncertain.

The job got her around town, and Jackie managed to give the column a spark and gaiety of her own and soon she was being given more demanding assignments. When Dwight D. Eisenhower defeated Adlai Stevenson in 1952, Jackie was asked to interview various members of Truman's outgoing cabinet and staff about their future plans after the inauguration. She interviewed the Treasurer of the United States, the Secretary of State, and the Attorney General. She also interviewed Washington hostess Perle Mesta, who had been one of the pets of the Truman administration. Would Mrs. Mesta continue to rule the social seas of Washington under Eisenhower? Mrs. Mesta replied that she would do her best. After the inauguration, Jackie interviewed the workmen who were taking down the parade grandstands in front of the White House. Had they received any complaints from the new residents of the mansion because of the racket they were making with their hammers?

As a newspaperwoman one of the men she met in Washington was Yale man Charles Bartlett, the Washington correspondent for the *Chattanooga Times*. On the evening of May 8, 1952, Jackie was invited to a small dinner at Charles and Martha Bartlett's house. At the dinner was Congressman John F. Kennedy from Massachusetts, who was just beginning his campaign for election to the United States Senate, and whose campaign manager had said of the handsome Irishman, "Every woman wants to mother him or marry him." Jackie Bouvier was then twenty-two. Jack Kennedy was within weeks of his thirty-fifth birthday, so confirmed a bachelor that it seemed to many that he was likely to remain one.

At the Bartletts' dinner, there was no indication that Jackie Bouvier wanted either to mother or marry Representative Kennedy. In fact, they seemed to make no particular impression on one another that evening, and it was several months before they saw each other again.

Part
Two

9

Two
Weddings

IN APRIL, 1953, Jack Bouvier was forced to undergo an ordeal of considerable proportions. His younger daughter Lee had studied briefly at Sarah Lawrence, had studied art briefly in Italy, had worked, again briefly, for *Harper's Bazaar* in New York, and was now marrying young Michael Canfield, the son of publisher Cass Canfield, whom she had dated on and off since her debutante days. Lee's marriage to Canfield would also turn out to be brief. Lee's mercurial nature was such that her enthusiasms came and went with speed. At the time, however, it was considered an auspicious marriage. The Casses and the Canfields were old New York families. Michael had an interesting diplomatic job with the American Embassy in London. And then there was something very different about Michael Canfield—a mystery. It was said that he had royal blood. He had been adopted by the Canfields during a period when the family was living in London, and the senior Mr. Canfield had been head of the British division of Harper & Brothers. The rumor persisted that Michael was the illegitimate result of a union between a highly placed, titled, and married Englishwoman and none other than the Duke of Kent, the younger brother of the King, to whose own legitimate son Michael Canfield bore a striking resemblance. The Canfields had stepped in to take the baby, it was claimed, in order to prevent a scandal that would have rocked the British Royal Family on an even higher level of the Richter scale than the one created by Mrs. Simpson. Throughout his lifetime, Cass Canfield, the only person who could know the truth of Michael's origins, has steadfastly maintained a stony silence on the subject.

Lee's and Michael's wedding took place at Merrywood, and Lee had asked her father to give her away. This meant that Jack would have to spend a day in hated Auchincloss country. It meant that he would have to be civil to Janet, to Hughdie Auchincloss, and to his former father-in-law, James T. Lee, as well as to other members of the large Auchincloss clan. None of this would be easy to do and, to his credit, he was determined not to fortify himself for the occasion with alcohol. He arrived at Merrywood for the ceremony, greeted Janet and Hughdie as politely as he could, and was taken on a quick tour of the house and grounds of the estate. To his sorrow, he could see how the huge Georgian house, the rolling acres of green hills and the distant view of the Potomac had managed to appeal to his daughters more than his small apartment or his rented cottage in East Hampton. Cruelly, the contrast between what he had been able to give his daughters and what Hughdie Auchincloss had been able to provide was brought home to him. Yes, he admitted, Merrywood was even more beautiful than Lasata had been. Still he bore up well, and, chin high, walked with his daughter, who was just twenty, down the aisle and presented her to the hand of his new son-in-law.

Lee's wedding, at which Jackie was maid of honor, may have had an effect on Jackie's own plans. For the past several months, she had been seeing Jack Kennedy and more and more frequently. He had suddenly, out of the blue, called her and reminded her of their meeting at the Bartletts', and asked to take her out. Now Kennedy was the exciting junior Senator, and their appearances together were being noted by the gossip columnists. In January, he had escorted her to Eisenhower's inaugural ball. More and more of her newspaper assignments took her to Capitol Hill and, when they did, she would drop in on him at his Senate office. At Lee's wedding, however, when friends and family asked her if there was anything in the published reports about a romance with Kennedy, Jackie dismissed the questions as ridiculous. "He wants to be President," she said with a laugh, implying that to be President was the only serious thing he wanted. It may not have occurred to her that, if he did want to be President, he surely also wanted to run for that office with an attractive wife at his side. Presidents, to most Americans' way of thinking, are supposed to be family men. At the same time, the marriage of her younger sister may have set Jackie's thoughts in motion in that direction.

In May, the *Times-Herald* gave Jackie her first foreign assignment: to London, to cover the coronation of Elizabeth II. While she was there, there were a number of trans-Atlantic telephone calls from Jack Kennedy and, in one of these, he asked her to marry him. She returned in June to give him her answer. Their formal engagement was announced June 25, 1953. Actually, she had told her family and a few close friends of the engagement several days earlier, but had sworn them to secrecy "because it wouldn't be fair to the *Saturday Evening Post*." The *Post*, it seemed, was preparing a story with the title, "Jack Kennedy—The Senate's Gay Young Bachelor."

Remembering that, as a girl, mention of the name Kennedy had been sufficient to provoke banishment from the dinner table, Jackie was a little nervous about how her father would react to her fiancé. Actually, Jack Bouvier and Jack Kennedy hit it off quite well. In addition to having the same name, both men liked to think of themselves as worldly sophisticates and liked nothing better than a good, off-color joke. Also, they discovered that they shared an ailment—back troubles—and they spent a good amount of time discussing exercise and therapy. The subject of Joseph P. Kennedy was carefully skirted. Underneath the goodfellowship, however, it was clear that Jack Bouvier was sad to lose his daughter to another man, and to realize that she would now be living more or less permanently in Washington. Janet was less sanguine than her former husband about their daughter's choice. To her, the Kennedys were *nouveaux*. As Jack Kennedy wrote to his friend Red Fay, asking him to be an usher in the wedding, "The bride's mother . . . has a tendency to think I am not good enough for her daughter."

For Janet, meanwhile, putting together two large weddings within a six-months' span was not too much at all. It was just the sort of challenge to her organizational abilities that she welcomed. The wedding was scheduled for September 12, and it was decided that this time it would take place at Hammersmith Farm, when Newport would be at its autumn best. The garden would be tented. As, during the summer, plans progressed, it was soon being billed by the press as "the wedding of the year." A few days before the wedding some of Janet's worst fears about her future son-in-law were being realized. Across the road from Hammersmith Farm lay the golf course of the Newport Country Club, an exclusive, members-only club. In his brash, cavalier way, Jack Kennedy and two of his ushers marched into the clubhouse with their golf clubs and, though none were members, announced that they wanted to play nine quick holes, and asked for a couple of caddies. Though the party sensed an undercurrent of tension among the club's staff, they were given what they wanted. Later in the afternoon, when word of the episode got back to Hammersmith Farm, Janet was horrified. One of the club's strictest rules had been breezily defied and broken. The upstart Boston Irish were invading stately Newport.

Once again, Jack Bouvier would give away the bride. It was no secret that Jackie was his favorite daughter. His passion for her verged on the incestuous and was the cause of all their battles, all the emotional stress between them, all the tender greetings and the often stormy partings. Sentimentally, after he had had a few drinks, he would sometimes refer to her as "all things holy," and it was no wonder that they often quarreled under the pressure of so much love. All summer long, her father underwent a self-improvement program in preparation for her wedding. He lay for hours on the beach at East Hampton to deepen and even his famous tan. He dieted and exercised and went to a masseur to trim his figure. He assembled, at no small expense, a wardrobe for the wedding: a custom-made cutaway, striped trousers; custom-made shirt, vest, and grey suede shoes. He assembled his jewelry: the pearl stickpin, the cufflinks, the studs. He supervised the ironing of the underwear and the silk socks that he planned to wear. Of course, the wedding would mean another difficult encounter with the Auchinclosses and Janet's father, and he would be called upon to admire yet another great Auchincloss estate at Hammersmith Farm, and have to bear the knowledge that Jackie's lavish wedding was being paid for by the Auchinclosses, and not by him. Still, hard though all these facts might be to swallow, Jack assured his friends that he was up to it, and would look his handsome best, and would make Jackie proud of him.

On the afternoon of the eleventh, Jack Bouvier checked into Newport's Viking Hotel. Already the town was filling up with press and Jack suddenly found himself a celebrity, the father of the bride in the wedding of the year. Reporters showered him with questions and, in his room, the phone rang constantly. Room Service answered his every beck and call, delivering champagne, fruit, cheese and crackers, ice for his drinks. When he entered the hotel dining room that night for dinner, all eyes were on him and guests whispered excitedly to each other, "That's her father!"

After dinner, back in his room, his evening progressed. Room Service came obediently again and again. Early the following morning, he began making telephone calls—to Bouvier relatives at a nearby hotel, to Jackie at Hammersmith Farm. He tried repeatedly to reach his future son-in-law, and the telephone calls became increasingly incoherent. By ten o'clock, while Jackie worried, it was clear that her father was in no condition to participate in the noon services. A hasty family conference was held. Something had to be done. Janet took over. The wedding must proceed on schedule. Two Bouvier cousins were dispatched to the Viking Hotel to care for Jack, who had passed out in his room, and the bridal party entered their limousines and headed for St. Mary's.

It was indeed a dazzling wedding. Archbishop Cushing of Boston officiated, bringing the blessing of Pope Pius XII on the young couple. Lee had come from London to be matron of honor, and she and the bridesmaids were in pink taffeta with crimson sashes. Robert Kennedy was best man for his brother. The church was filled with Kennedys, Bouviers, and Auchinclosses. When the bride appeared, not in traditional white but wearing a dress of cream taffeta faille and a yellow veil set with fresh orange blossoms, she looked so beautiful that hardly anyone noticed that she was not on her father's arm but on the arm of her stepfather, Hughdie Auchincloss.

In fact, it was not until the reception, and at the receiving line, where some 1200 guests milled about the tented garden, sipping champagne and dancing to Meyer Davis's orchestra, that Jack Bouvier's absence was noted, and the gossip began to circulate, and the whispers, "Too drunk . . . passed out in his hotel . . . too drunk . . ."

And, in the way that gossip has, it was not many more hours before the word had reached all the fashionable enclaves of the Eastern Seaboard. Disgraced, humiliated, Jack Bouvier returned to New York and his 74th Street apartment, and bolted the door. For days, he would not come out, or answer his telephone. Only his housemaid was admitted. The days turned into weeks. He spent his time sitting in his sunless sitting room, drinking and weeping until, late at night, he would collapse across his bed. His father, once, in an angry mood, had told him that he would one day bring shame and dishonor upon the family. Now, it seemed quite clear, he finally had.

Jack and Jackie Kennedy, meanwhile, were off on their honeymoon in Acapulco. From Acapulco, Jackie wrote a letter to her father. The contents of the letter have never been disclosed, but Jack Bouvier's partner, John Carrere, to whom Jack once showed the letter, remembers it for its compassion, its forgiveness.

10

Hard
Times

DESPITE THE FUSS in the society columns that surrounded her marriage to Senator Kennedy, Jacqueline Bouvier Kennedy was not, in 1953, by any means a household name in America. Her photograph appeared on no magazine covers. No photographers stalked her. Her appearance, on the street, in a restaurant, or at a party caused no stir of excitement or recognition. She was not written about, talked about, speculated about. To most Americans in 1953, the name "Jackie"—which now has universal meaning—had no connotations whatsoever. If an inquiring photographer had polled Americans in 1953 and asked whether Senator John F. Kennedy was married or

single, most would have answered that they had read
that he had married recently. But almost none would
have remembered the lady's name. In fact, the *National Social Directory* (not to be confused with the
Social Register, which is usually very accurate) continued until 1956 to list "Bouvier, Miss Jacqueline"
under the Hugh D. Auchinclosses' name, and to give
her addresses as Merrywood, and Hammersmith
Farm.

In Washington, she was merely another Senate
wife—and a quiet, soft-spoken, not particularly visible
one at that. True, Senate wives were not, as a group,
noted for their beauty, and, for that, Jack Kennedy's
wife stood out. But otherwise she was merely "Jack
Kennedy's wife" and she melted quietly into the
politics-as-usual background of the city, accompanying her husband on the required rounds of Washington
cocktail parties and dinner parties, being pleasant to
important people, who were mostly men, and listening
to what the important people, who did most of the
talking, had to say.

In their new house in Georgetown, the Kennedys
gave the required number of little dinners and cocktail
parties of their own, and it was remarked that Mrs.
Kennedy served excellent food (something of a rarity
in Washington) but not much else was singular about
her, except that she seemed to have nice taste in
clothes. A Senate wife. That was the role she played,
the role, in fact, that her husband both expected and
demanded of her. Conversation, at her dinner table,
revolved around the Senator, the Senator's opinions,
the Senator's long-range views, the Senator's appraisals of situations, the Senator's forecasts. Not that this
particular Senator was a pompous man. He was jolly,
good company, liked a good joke. But still, in the
middle of the levity at the Senator's dinner table, the
Senator could not resist becoming serious for a moment and coming forth with an appraisal, an opinion,
or a long-range view. Politics, like society, is a game

with certain rules, and one of the rules is that the seriously ambitious politician cannot be all fun and sport.

And Jackie had discovered, early on, that her husband was seriously ambitious. He really *did* want to be President. She had married a man with energy, drive, and an enormous—and growing—ego. It was something all the Kennedys seemed to have in bewildering abundance. Kennedys did not like to be contradicted. They did not like to have their instructions disregarded, or their opinions and long-range views ridiculed. Kennedys had another disconcerting habit: they never apologized. They did outrageous things and expected to get away with them—and did. At a party, a Kennedy could push you in the swimming pool in your new Yves St. Laurent, and you were expected to take the destruction of your dress as a jolly good joke. Jack Kennedy's sisters, Jean Smith and Eunice Shriver, could accidentally tip over a table laden with drinks, crockery, and flaming candles into the lap of a guest at one of Stewart Alsop's parties, and could simply walk away from the mess. They had, it seemed, been doing such things all their lives.

Yes, Jackie had to admit during the first Washington months, she had married a difficult man, and into a difficult family. He told her what to do and what to wear, what to talk about with whom, whom to be particularly charming to, whom to ignore. There were parties given by people she and her husband actively disliked but which, for political reasons, he insisted they attend. To her family and friends she complained privately about "all these boring politicians," saying that she would much more prefer the company of artists, writers, photographers—the circle she had moved in as a newspaperwoman. Still, as a Senate wife, she must do her duty. Senate wives are expected to help their husbands win elections; it was rule number one. So she dutifully shook hands, and smiled, and tried to be nice to all the bores.

And, of course, there were certain compensations for doing her husband's bidding. Janet and Hughdie Auchincloss had never believed in lavishing large sums of money on their children, and Jackie, in terms of cash, had never had much spending money. It had amounted to $56.75 a week, which had been her final salary at the *Times-Herald,* plus the $50 a month allowance that her father faithfully sent her. Beyond that, in terms of cash, there had been only occasional gifts from parents and grandparents. (Grandpa Lee, at seventy-seven, was still going strong as president of the Central Savings Bank, and was showing no signs of making her an heiress.) Of course, there were fringe benefits which had come from living with the Auchinclosses: houses staffed with servants, automobiles at her disposal, horses to ride. Now, however, it was all quite different. She had married into a family richer than any she had been associated with before, including the Auchinclosses. The Kennedys, furthermore, were a family which considered conspicuous spending rather fun. From the beginning—from the square-cut emerald and diamond engagement ring to the diamond bracelet he gave her as a wedding present—Jack Kennedy had made it clear that, where money was concerned, the sky was virtually the limit. The duties of a Senate wife might be boring, demanding, and repetitious, and the duties of a wife of a man whose primary ambition was himself might mean that she was often left out of things, but at least there was the consolation of having no money worries.

After returning from their Mexican honeymoon, Jack and Jackie Kennedy lived at Merrywood for several months, while house-hunting, and Jackie went back to school—a winter course in American History at Georgetown University. Again, it was something she felt she must do for her husband—he seemed to know so much and care so much about American history, and she had known and cared so little (her real enthusiasm was European history). But there were soon problems that strained the marriage. Kennedy's bad back—a problem caused by a college football accident, when he had presumably ruptured a disk, and later aggravated by the famous wartime incident in which the PT boat he commanded was sliced in half by a Japanese destroyer, and he was hurled to the deck—was getting worse. He was subject to spasms of excruciating pain and, by the summer of 1954, had had to resort to crutches in order to get around. Furthermore, he was mysteriously losing weight, and had dropped to an alarming 140 pounds. In October, 1954, Jackie accompanied her husband to New York's Hospital for Special Surgery, where a lumbar spine operation was attempted. The operation failed, an infection set in, and on midnight of October 21 the family was alerted that Senator Kennedy was near death, and last rites were administered. He rallied, however, and six weeks later the operation was performed again, this time successfully. Throughout these illnesses and convalescences, Jackie remained dutifully at his side.

During the first year and a half of their marriage, the Kennedys' existence was, of necessity, somewhat peripatetic. They lived at borrowed family places in New York or Virginia or Hyannis Port, or at a series of rented flats and houses in Washington. During John Kennedy's healthy periods, there were the inevitable speech-making tours to be conducted and, on nearly all these engagements, Jackie went along. He insisted on it. He needed her, he said. But what, she might have begun to wonder, did he need her for? Had he wanted a wife mostly as decoration? Surely that was part of it. As his wife, she had also endowed him with an elusive quality—a touch of class, that social background, that entrée into the world of Old Guard Eastern society that the Kennedys had always wanted, but had never quite been able to achieve.

At Miss Porter's, Jackie had once said, "I'm sure no

one will ever marry me and I'll end up being a house mother at Farmington." Now, very much married, she was discovering that being married to a man of John Kennedy's ilk was going to be an arduous task. She longed to have a baby. In 1955, she discovered that she was pregnant and it was decided that the Kennedys must now have some permanent home. For $125,000 Jack Kennedy purchased Hickory Hill in McLean, not far from Merrywood, and very similar in scale. Like the Auchinclosses' place, the centerpiece of Hickory Hill was a fine old Georgian house, and Jackie set about redecorating it. Then, a few months into the pregnancy, she suffered a miscarriage.

By the spring of 1956, Jackie was pregnant again, and one of her projects became the creation of an elaborate nursery at Hickory Hill. As usual, cost was no object. Jack Kennedy was, meanwhile, consumed with plans for the 1956 Democratic convention where he hoped to receive the Vice-Presidential nomination, but he insisted that Jackie keep him informed on the progress of the nursery. At the August convention, Jackie saw her husband lose—though only by a handful of votes—the nomination to Estes Kefauver, and watched him as he stood and asked the convention to make the Kefauver nomination unanimous.

During the convention, Jack Kennedy had gone without sleep for three days. In its disappointing aftermath, it was decided that he should go to his father's home in Val-sur-Mer on the French Riviera for a few weeks' rest, and that Jackie would go for a similar rest at Hammersmith Farm with her mother. Separate vacations seemed called for. They parted. On August 23rd, Jackie was rushed to Newport Hospital, where an emergency Caesarean was performed and Jackie was delivered of a stillborn child one month prematurely. Naturally, the strains of the convention, all the travel and campaigning and speech-making were blamed, and for several hours after her dead baby was born Jackie's own condition was listed as critical. Once more, a priest was summoned.

All this bad news was telephoned to Val-sur-Mer but Kennedy, at the time, was cruising on a yacht in the Mediterranean and could not be reached. He did not learn of his baby's death and his wife's near-death until several days later. He flew home immediately.

When Jackie had recovered sufficiently to return to Hickory Hill, the place seemed to smell of defeat and death. The beautiful nursery, now completed to the last luxurious detail, reminded her only of unhappy things. Jack Kennedy sold Hickory Hill to his brother Bobby, for the same price that he had paid for it, and the John F. Kennedys moved again, to another rented house in Georgetown. To friends, Jackie Kennedy began to confess that she suspected she was incapable of childbearing.

Early the following year, however, she was pregnant again—with the healthy baby that would become Caroline Kennedy, born the day after Thanksgiving, 1957. The baby would have to be born by Caesarean section, and a date for surgery was set. Jackie was frightened but, for her husband's sake as much as for her own, she wanted a baby. A baby would tie him to her, perhaps, this driving and driven man who had set his sights on the highest office in the land, and who would be impossible to live with until he achieved it —and possibly more impossible to live with after he did.

Once more, full of hope, the Kennedys set out in search for a permanent residence. This time they settled for a Georgetown mansion, in the slant-set Federal style, at 3307 N Street. They moved into the house when Caroline Kennedy was three weeks old.

Jack Bouvier, meanwhile, had become a virtual recluse in New York. He was seen at none of his old haunts, and was no longer a familiar figure at East Hampton, stretched out on the beach and working on his tan. In 1950, he had sold his seat on the New

York Stock Exchange for a mere $90,000. In 1929, a seat could have been sold for as much as $625,000 and, by 1968, would be worth as much as $515,000. He had retired on a small capital of $200,000 and had become a man without a business and without a family. He still, to anyone who would listen, inveighed against Janet. "Women," he would say, "are all the victors in my generation." He had expected that his daughters would at least telephone him now and then, at least write weekly letters. But Lee was living in London and, what with the Kennedys' frantic lives— Jack moving, moving, with Jackie always in tow, pushing her forward with him at conventions, caucuses, political dinners and meetings (seizing her arm, "I want you to meet my wife, Jackie")—there was very little time in her schedule to devote to her father. When Jackie became pregnant with Caroline, Jack Bouvier learned about it in a newspaper. Of course he was furious. It was just another example of how she "neglected" him.

As for Jackie, one of her pastimes as a little girl— in addition to drawing pictures, painting watercolors, writing bits of verse and short stories—had been making her "predictions." Her predictions were occasioned by births of new babies in the family, anniversaries, graduations, and so on. Everyone gathered around while Jackie read her prediction for the future that the occasion indicated. Her predictions have not necessarily come true. When her half-sister Janet was born, for example, Jackie predicted that Janet would become "the first woman President of the United States." Janet is now a housewife, stationed with her husband in Hong Kong. For herself, on the other hand, Jackie predicted that she would become "Queen of the Circus," and, though admired and sought after by many of the world's bigwigs, would end up marrying "the man on the flying trapeze."

She was very nearly right about that.

11

Having
Babies

FROM A DISTANCE, looking back from the late 1970s
this preoccupation with having babies seems quaint, a
bit old-fashioned. Why should a woman with a slim
good figure, who liked clothes and liked to look good
in them, be willing (much less appear to want) to
spend her first four years of marriage being pregnant
more than half the time?

To begin with, these were the fifties, the bland and
relatively crisis-free Eisenhower years. Our national
memory is so short that, today, those years seem part
of another century. There was no talk, then, of over-
population, of polluting America with too many people. There was no Pill, and abortions were illegal.
There was no talk of an energy crisis, no dire predictions of a future without heat, air-conditioning, or gas-
oline, and the Eisenhower Administration was busily
designing the Interstate Highway System. The future
seemed secure for children. Youth did not riot on
school and college campuses, the blacks (not even
known as blacks in those far-off days) "knew their
place," there were no hippies (remember them? They
came, and went, much later). Boys wore their hair
short, and cut it when their parents told them to. There
was no drug sub-culture, no kiddie porn. It was safe to
walk in Central Park, or in Times Square, at night. Sex
was around, but it, too, knew its place and novelists
closed the door, and the chapter, when the lovers

stepped into the bedroom. Maiden-lady teachers (and maiden gentlemen too) set up housekeeping together (even at Farmington), and probably slept together, but there was no crusade about how "gay" (a term that had a nice, non-controversial meaning) educators might lure the young into experiments with the sin that dare not speak its name. The Catholic Church fretted about what the then-popular practice of "going steady" might lead to.

It was a passive era. In those days, children believed what their parents and their teachers told them. They behaved. They did not rebel, or run away to Greenwich Village or Haight-Ashbury. Children were considered rather nice to have around. In this older, more naïve, all-but-forgotten time, it was what young, educated married people were expected to do —to have children. It was what Farmington girls were told they could expect of life—to marry, to start a family. That was a woman's role, to be a good wife to her husband and a good mother to his children— incredible though that seems at this point in history. Jackie Kennedy had been given this nice-girl's upbringing and education by her parents and her teachers, but in her case there was an even greater reason for wanting to have babies.

To begin with, she loved children. On her beat as Inquiring Camera Girl she liked to interview children because, she said, children always had the brightest, funniest, most interesting and quotable things to say. She loved playing mother to her baby half-sister, Janet, and, later, to her baby half-brother, Jamie. "The children" had always been a unit at Merrywood and Hammersmith Farm, all seven of them: Janet's two, Hughdie's three, and Hughdie and Janet's two. They had always been close. At Hammersmith Farm, the children occupied the entire third floor, which was known as "the children's floor." Then there was Jackie's Roman Catholicism (the Pill or abortion would have been unthinkable to her in those days); to go forth and propagate was one of the teachings of the Church. Who knew that the children of this era would be the troublemakers?

But most important was her feeling that she should be a dutiful wife to her husband. It was what nice girls were supposed to be. That notion had been drilled into her at school, at college, and on her mother's knee. And Jack Kennedy wanted children, and he wanted them right away. He had waited until late to marry, and he wanted to enjoy his children while he was still young. He, too, had grown up in a household full of children, children who had remained remarkably close and loyal to one another. His younger brother Bobby, meanwhile, had been siring children at an astonishing rate and the Kennedys, though close, were also a competitive family. Children were living proof of a man's masculinity, his randiness and prowess, and Bobby certainly seemed to have no problems in that direction. If anything, Jack Kennedy would have liked to go his kid brother one or two better. In those days, the Women's Movement did not exist. Today, Jack Kennedy would have been called a Male Chauvinist Pig. But, in those days, that term did not exist.

In many ways, it was a great disappointment to Jack Kennedy—and a cause of shame and distress to Jackie—that his wife seemed to have a difficult time with childbirth. It was something he had trouble understanding—the miscarriage, the stillbirth, the need for Caesarean sections, the blood transfusions, the long hospital stays that were required in recovery. His mother's children had just popped out, one after another. Still, he wanted children, and Jackie would do her best to give them to him. Most obstetricians recommend no more than three Caesarean sections for a mother. Caroline had been born by her second section. In 1960, Jackie became pregnant again and John F. Kennedy, Jr., was successfully delivered by Caesarean in November of that year. In 1963, she had her fourth Caesarean, and gave birth to a baby named Patrick Bouvier Kennedy, who died thirty-nine hours later.

One trouble, of course, with being a Kennedy was that the family always considered itself in superlatives. Each Kennedy and Kennedy in-law was the "best" or the "most" of something. Jack, for example, was "the most brilliant politician in the country." Bobby was "the best legal mind in the country." Bobby's wife Ethel was "the most energetic" and "the best organized." Patricia Lawford was "the smartest," and her husband "the greatest actor" (even though Peter Lawford's talents tended to belie this). Jean Kennedy Smith was "the most domestic," her husband Steve "the best businessman," Teddy "the most natural," his wife Joan "the most beautiful," and Rose Kennedy was "the most devout." What was Jackie the most of? Well, they had begun boasting that she was "the best read." As a child-bearer, however, she was a disappointment. Though her in-laws never mentioned it, there was always a feeling in the air when she was with them that, as far as having children was concerned she had rather embarrassed them and let the family down. Among themselves they said "poor Jackie." They pitied her. Perhaps, they said, she was too "highly bred." After all, in those days, no one questioned the veracity of Grandpa Bouvier's *Our Forebears* and the connection with all those titled Frenchmen in the past.

In 1957, meanwhile, the prospect that Jackie might finally make him a grandfather did little to elate Jack Bouvier. The fact was that she almost never came to see him, and letters and phone calls were infrequent. She was simply too busy for him now. He had made his will. Except for a few small individual bequests, the bulk of his estate was to be divided equally between his daughters (from it, each girl would receive about $80,000.) He was only sixty-six, but iller than he knew. The drinking years had taken their toll on his liver; in fact, it was cancerous, though his doctors had not apprised him of this. On July 27 he was taken to Lenox Hill Hospital "for tests," he explained. Jackie assumed that her father's condition was not serious enough to require her presence. Six days later, he was dead.

Her father's death, which seemed so sudden, came as a shock. Jackie and Jack flew down from Hyannis Port and, with Lee in London, it fell to Jackie to make all the funeral arrangements, something she had never been required to do before. From her father-in-law's New York apartment, she went to work. Jack Bouvier's life had not been an important one, but she was determined that his death would be treated in an important way. Jackie selected a favorite photograph of her father, and dispatched her husband to deliver the picture personally, by hand, to the managing editor of *The New York Times*. Under ordinary circumstances, a man of Jack Bouvier's slight stature in the community would have warranted no more than a short obituary paragraph in the *Times*. But Jackie reasoned, correctly, that a photograph hand-delivered to the paper by Senator John F. Kennedy would have more than ordinary impact. She wanted her father's funeral to be out-of-the-ordinary, too. Jack Bouvier had been, at his best, a fun-loving man, and she wanted the services at St. Patrick's to convey a sense of his gaiety and love of beauty. Instead of such standard funerary flowers as calla lilies and crosses of white carnations, she ordered garlands of summer flowers in white wicker baskets, and baskets of wild flowers by the altar. For most of her life she had known him as a care-free bachelor, and so she had his casket festooned with white daisies and blue bachelor's-buttons. Later, at the gravesite in East Hampton, she ordered that the burial plot be strewn with thousands more bachelor's buttons.

In addition to the immediate family and his house-keeper, Esther, there were only a few people at the funeral of John Vernou Bouvier III to see Jackie's handiwork—barely two dozen. Most of these did not take the two-hour drive to East Hampton to see Jackie drop the last blue flower on her father's grave.

Of most concern, in the family, was the effect her father's death might have on Jackie's pregnancy. She was in her sixth month, often a crucial one. Naturally, there was great relief in November when Caroline was born—Jack Bouvier's first grandchild and one that he would never see. But, everyone agreed, he would probably have had trouble adjusting to the idea of being a grandparent, just as he had never adjusted to the idea of growing old.

To Jackie, having the baby seemed an almost incredible piece of good luck. The first four years of her marriage to Jack Kennedy had not been without tribulations: the child-bearing problems and Jack's defeat at the convention. He was not a man who took defeats and disappointments easily. Now, however, things looked much better. They were a family at last, with a new house of their own. Presents for the baby poured in from the dozens of aunts, uncles, cousins, in-laws, and step and half-sisters and half-brothers. For months, Caroline was probably the most fussed-over baby in Washington. She was christened Caroline Bouvier Kennedy, after Jackie's sister. It was a nice gesture. Things had not been going all that well for Caroline Lee Bouvier Canfield.

Already a certain amount of competition could be sensed between the Bouvier sisters—a competition in which Jackie always seemed to emerge a step or two ahead. It had begun in their teens. Jackie had been named Debutante of the Year, Lee had not. Jackie had graduated from college with honors, won the *Vogue* prize, turned it down, and had become a newspaper columnist with her own byline within months after graduation. Lee had never graduated from college, had won no prizes, and had had only a brief, unpromising career in journalism. Lee had married a handsome young man of good family who had joined the staff of the United States Embassy in London. Then, within months, Jackie did her one better, and married a much handsomer, much richer, much more glamorous man. Now Lee's marriage had been dissolved by annulment and Lee was living on quietly in London in a rather drab flat. Jack Kennedy, meanwhile, had elevated himself from Congressman to Senator, and was being discussed—though some were saying "America will never elect a Catholic"—as the Democratic candidate for the Presidency in the upcoming election year of 1960. In London, Lee had met a very rich man named Aristotle Onassis, who had taken her out. But, emotionally, he seemed committed to a much more famous lady, an opera soprano named Maria Callas for whom he kept a house in Paris. Now Jackie and her celebrated husband had a baby. Lee did not even have a husband.

With the arrival of the baby, things began looking up for Jack's political career as well, a fact that put him in a better mood and made him easier to live with. In 1958 he was running for his second Senate term in his home state and, for the first time, Jackie campaigned with him around the clock, driving and flying from one end of Massachusetts to the other, smiling, shaking hands, trying to be as charming as she possibly could. While Jack conferred with local politicos, Jackie entertained their wives. She had never done this sort of thing before but one had to admit that she did it very well, always carefully dressed, but simply, understatedly. It was important, when one met small-town voters, not to look too rich, or "too New York." Jackie accomplished this with white gloves, little hats, a simple and short blown-out hair style, very little jewelry and very little makeup. The Kennedys spent election night in Boston, watching the returns come in on television from all the little towns they had visited. Considering that this was during a Republican administration under Eisenhower, Kennedy's re-election victory was overwhelming—a majority of over 870,000 votes.

Yes, things were looking up. But, of course, the Massachusetts Senate race in the fall of 1958 was only a prelude to the big push that was coming up— the push, throughout 1959, for the Presidential nomination at the Democratic convention in 1960 and, following that, the campaign for the Presidency. In the spring of 1960, the crucial year, Jackie was pregnant again. Once again, Jack wanted Jackie to do whatever she could for him. She had become a valuable campaign asset and, though Jack Kennedy was not a particularly demonstrative man, he let her know that he was proud of her. Throughout 1959, Jack had crisscrossed the country again and again—that year he had received roughly 10,000 invitations to speak— and on much of this travel, Jackie accompanied him to breakfasts, dinners, lunches, speeches, press conferences, television appearances. By the summer of 1960, she was in a state of high nervousness—nervous about the outcome of the convention, and nervous about the new baby. Surgery had been scheduled for Christmas Day.

On the night when her husband received the Presidential nomination, Jackie was in Hyannis Port with Janet and Hughdie, and Jack was in Los Angeles. While her mother and stepfather watched the convention on television, Jackie painted, sitting at an easel in a straight-backed chair. It was 5:00 A.M., Eastern Time, before Kennedy's nomination in California was confirmed and the television set in Hyannis Port was turned off, and Jackie put down her brushes. The picture was a whimsical depiction of Jack Kennedy's triumphant return to Hyannis Port. The next morning at ten, she conducted her first press conference as a potential First Lady.

Throughout the next hectic months of campaigning, she wrote thousands of letters in longhand to Kennedy workers all over the country, and turned out a weekly newspaper column called "Campaign Wife." She met with women leaders on questions of feminine importance, conducted press conferences in Hyannis Port and Washington. Though her baby was expected in weeks, she appeared on television shows and at fund-raising teas. Then, following Kennedy's November victory, there was a terrifying ticker-tape parade through New York's financial district where, perched with her husband on the back of an open car, a crowd of an estimated two million people jostled and shoved and flung themselves onto and about the Kennedy car, eager to shake the future President's hand and kiss his wife. The crowds rushed and broke through the police lines, out of control, and at one point nearly turned the car over while its occupants clung to the sides. It was Jack Kennedy's moment of glory and a moment of horror for his frightened and now very pregnant wife.

The moment took its toll. On November 25, Jackie was rushed to the hospital where an emergency Caesarean was performed to deliver her of John Fitzgerald Kennedy, Jr., one month prematurely. For long hours the baby's life hung in the balance but, in the end, he survived. No, being Mrs. John F. Kennedy was not at all an easy job.

12
Jobs

THERE WAS NO course called Assuming Responsibilities at Miss Porter's School for Girls. Nonetheless, the lesson was there: to be taught, to be learned. Some Farmington girls learned it, others didn't. Lee Bouvier, who followed her sister to Miss Porter's, was one of those who appeared to have grasped the principle less well than Jackie. Lee dabbled. She took up things, then let them drop. After the annulment of her marriage to Michael Canfield, she worked at various fashion jobs in and around London. She directed the fashion show at the American Pavilion of the Brussels World's Fair in 1958. None of these enterprises was completely satisfying, long-lasting, or successful. Jackie, on the other hand, had absorbed the upperclass values that Miss Porter's represented.

Upper-class values, of course, are never mentioned as such by the upper class. Nonetheless they exist, they are there, to be grasped and understood and respected. One of the rules that accompanies these values is that one does what is expected of one. Life is a chore, and one carries it off to the best of one's ability. When one is presented with a job to do, one does it. "Go at your fences straight," her horsewoman mother used to tell her. "If you go in crooked, your pony won't make the jump." And, as her grandfather Jack Bouvier had advised her during her first term at Farmington, the key concepts were: *Capacity. Respon-*

sibility. Work. Leadership. Usefulness. Correctness.
Certainly it was hard work being Mrs. John F. Kennedy. She had known it would be before she married him, and had confided to friends that she did not expect an easy time of it. There was the difference in their ages, for one thing, and the fact of his presidential ambitions for another—ambitions that would always come before wife, children, family. Still, she had married him, she had taken on the job. Now that he was going to be President of the United States, the job was simply going to be harder. There was just no other way of looking at it.

In March, 1959, meanwhile, Lee had married a Londoner named Prince Stanislas Radziwill. There were some who thought Lee's remarriage was rather hasty. Five months later she gave birth to their daughter, Anna Christina. The baby was announced to be "three months premature" but, to those who counted on their fingers, even that didn't make the arithmetic come out quite right. The Radziwills had been members of the Polish nobility since the sixteenth century when a title had been conferred upon the family by the Holy Roman Emperor. Stas (pronounced "Stash") Radziwill's father, Prince Janusz Radziwill, had been Poland's Secretary of State and leader of the conservative party before the German occupation of 1939. When Russia invaded Poland, Prince Janusz was captured and sent to a Russian concentration camp. His castle, lands, and town house in Warsaw had been confiscated by the Communists and, when he was finally released from prison, he returned to Warsaw where he had died almost penniless.

His youngest son, however, had been luckier. He had escaped from Poland at the outbreak of World War II and, after spending the war years in Switzerland, had settled in London in 1946, and had gone into real estate. He had founded a company called Metropolitan & Provincial and, in the postwar building boom, he prospered. By the time he married Lee he owned and managed a number of large London business and office buildings, had a Georgian town house in London, a Queen Anne country home called Turville Grange on forty-nine acres of park near Henley-on-Thames, and kept a twelve-room Fifth Avenue apartment in New York as an American *pied-a-terre*. Though the Polish title had no standing in Great Britain—in fact, he had had officially to renounce it when he became a British subject—nor in the United States, he continued to call himself "Prince." And now his wife, whose claim to a title was even flimsier, chose to call herself "Princess." Even more important, Lee, like her older sister, was now the wife of a rich man and was able to move out of her modest digs into a life of luxury.

In 1960, while the American press was eagerly digging up facts about the handsome President-elect and his handsome lady, one of the more glamorous facts about the latter was that she had a beautiful younger sister who was a Princess. How Americans love royalty, even Polish royalty, even though the title technically does not exist! Suddenly Lee Radziwill's photograph was on the covers of the women's magazines almost as often as her sister's. True, Lee had to realize that she was basking only in the reflected glory of Jackie Kennedy. To find an identity of her own would remain a problem for Lee. Still, it is pleasant when all at once the world recognizes your name and face, and pays attention, and Princess Lee enjoyed her new celebrity.

To the family, meanwhile, the most striking thing about Stas Radziwill was how much he resembled Lee's and Jackie's father. Though shorter and stockier than Jack Bouvier, and with a thinner head of hair, he had Jack Bouvier's dark coloring and moustache. Also, since he was more than twenty years older than Lee, he was nearly old enough to be Jack Bouvier.

Jackie's new eminence was shedding glory on other

members of the Bouvier family—to say nothing of the Lees and the Auchinclosses—all of whom were beginning to think of themselves as celebrities of sorts and were enjoying the sensation. The women's magazines interviewed cousins, aunts, step-brothers and half-sisters, all of whom struggled manfully and girlfully to come up with descriptions of what Jacqueline Bouvier Kennedy was "really like." Relatives whom she had not seen for years explained how they "adored" her. Sharing Jackie's spotlight was particularly reassuring for the Bouviers. After all, Grandpa Jack had told them all about the family's glorious, though fictitious, past, and now, after a couple of uncertain generations, it appeared that, through Jackie, the family was to have a glorious present and future. What the cousins failed to notice, however, was that now that her husband had been elected President of the United States Jackie had begun to construct a small cocoon, a chrysalis of privacy around her. Helping to get her husband elected had been one job. Being a First Lady would be another. Feeding the egos of her many relatives was not high on her list of duties.

Naturally, all the relatives received special invitations to the January 20 Inauguration in 1961, and to the various festivities surrounding it. There would be detachments of Marines to escort the family, special buses and limousines for transport. From all over the country, Bouviers and Auchinclosses, rich and poor, planned for the triumphal appearance of two Great American Families in Washington, and worked on their wardrobes. It was to be their greatest day. In *The Bouviers,* Jackie's cousin, John H. Davis, vividly recalls it.

Following the swearing-in ceremony, there was an official luncheon at the Capitol for the President, his wife, and the new members of his government. The relatives, meanwhile, had been invited to a luncheon hosted by Joe and Rose Kennedy at the Mayflower Hotel. It was to turn out to be a rather strange luncheon. After listening to the music, the invocation by Cardinal Cushing, the prayers, the solo by Marian Anderson, the poem by Robert Frost, the oath of office administered by the Chief Justice and, finally, the Inaugural Address, the family headed for the buses that were to take them to the Mayflower. At first, no buses could be found. Finally several buses were located which had large signs reading KENNEDY FAMILY on their windshields. Where were the buses for the Bouviers, Auchinclosses, and Lees, the family inquired. "Oh, you mean Mrs. Kennedy's folks?" they were told by a guard. "They're to go in the Kennedy buses."

At the Mayflower, Rose Kennedy and Janet Auchincloss handled introductions among the assembled members of four families who, for the most part, had never met one another. The Kennedys seemed strangely subdued, almost uncommunicative. Where were the famous Kennedy verve and *élan,* someone wondered. Even Joe Kennedy, who ought to have been ebullient, seemed glum and moody, standing alone, nibbling hors d'oeuvres, responding to congratulations with mere nods of his head. Rose seemed equally nervous and preoccupied. Then, when it was time to eat, all the Kennedys seated themselves on one side of the room, and the Bouviers, Auchinclosses, and Lees sat down on the other with a huge white Rubicon of a buffet table separating the two camps. "The Montagues and the Capulets," someone muttered. The air, far from joyous and celebratory, was edgy with tension. Of course, divergent political leanings could have accounted for this. Most of the Bouviers, Auchinclosses, and Lees were rock-ribbed Republicans, and many had obviously not voted for Jack Kennedy. But, more than that, there was a feeling in the room that the separation was the result of an insurmountable barrier of *class.* The two worlds of wealth represented in the room—one newer, one older—simply could not feel comfortable with one another.

Then it was time to board the KENNEDY FAM-
ILY buses again and go to the White House, to join
the new President in the reviewing stand and watch
the parade. The parade was already forming, and it
was scheduled to continue until six. The day was bitterly cold, with the temperature near zero, and yet
there stood the President, hatless and scarfless in the
icy wind, grinning and waving and cheering each new
unit of the long parade as it came into view. The shiv-
ering relatives joined him on the stand.

As the afternoon progressed, the visiting dignitaries,
one by one, defeated by the cold, began to leave. But
of course the President could not leave. At around
3:30, Jackie whispered something to her husband,
tapped his shoulder, shook hands with Lyndon and
Lady Bird Johnson, and departed. Finally the relatives
decided that they had spent a sufficiently respectful
length of time viewing the parade, and that they
could retreat to the warmth of the White House where
a "Reception for Members of President and Mrs.
Kennedy's Families" had been scheduled following
the parade.

Though the families arrived at the reception more
than an hour early, everything was ready in the State
Dining Room—the trays of cocktails, sandwiches,
cakes, cookies, the tea and coffee services, and a huge
punch bowl filled with Russian caviar. The party
started and, once again, Rose Kennedy and Janet Auchincloss acted as hostesses. Once more, too, the
atmosphere was strained and unnatural. Peter Lawford, for example, was circulating, shaking hands and
accepting congratulations as though he had been
elected President. Rose still seemed nervous. Then
there were the two problem members of the Bouvier
family—the "two Edies," as they were called—"Big
Edith" Bouvier Beale, Jack Bouvier's younger sister,
and her spinster daughter, "Little Edith," then in her
early forties. Big Edie wore strange, eccentric clothes
—shawls, oversize hats, dresses that trailed the floor

behind her. Little Edie, who had been a beautiful debutante in her youth, had become even odder than her mother. Of course, both women had come down from New York to share their cousin's and niece's great moment.

Coyly, Little Edie approached Joseph P. Kennedy to tell him that she had "almost been engaged" to his son, Joe, Jr., and that if the "almost" had become a reality, and if Joe, Jr., had not lost his life in a crash, and if Joe, Jr., had gone on to become President of the United States, then she, Little Edie Beale, would now be First Lady, and not Cousin Jackie. Mr. Kennedy smiled wanly and looked the other way.

By six o'clock, everyone had begun to wonder what was holding up the President. Obviously the parade had gone beyond schedule, and he was still out there, in the cold night, grinning and waving. But even more important, as far as the Bouviers and Auchinclosses were concerned, was the question: where was Jackie? Drinks in hand, the family started an informal tour of the State rooms of the White House. At the foot of the stairs leading up to the private quarters, they were stopped by a Secret Service man. Mrs. Kennedy, they were informed, had left explicit instructions. She was resting in her room, and no one was to be admitted to the upper floor. "But we're her *family,*" the family protested. The guard was not impressed. He had his orders. Did she plan to come down *at all?* The guard had no idea. To the family, this was crushing news. Was it possible that, for them, her own family, many of whom had traveled thousands of miles just to see her, to kiss her, to hug her and congratulate her, she would not come downstairs? Was it possible that, for her very first White House party, the hostess would not appear?

The guests milled about restlessly, wondering: Could she be that rude? Janet Auchincloss, meanwhile, was doing her animated best to fill in for her missing daughter, making light of the situation and assuring everyone that, of course, Jackie would be down momentarily. At around 6:30, Janet managed to penetrate the Secret Service guard and went briefly upstairs. When she came down, her face was drawn. "She's in the Queen's bedroom," Janet said. "She's resting. She's taken a pill. She has five balls to go to tonight." Would she be coming down at all, just for a second, just to say hello? One relative had come all the way from South America just to squeeze her hand. "I don't know," said Janet. Cocktails were passed again.

At a little after seven, the muted sounds from the parade outside on Pennsylvania Avenue were heard to stop. It was over, an hour later than schedule. This meant that the President would be arriving soon, and the relatives joined in a general movement toward the entrance of the State Dining Room. And suddenly there he was, all smiles and handshakes after nearly five hours in the cold, greeting everybody, being hugged, kissed, patted on the back. He accepted a drink, started to circulate about the room, and then asked, "Where's Jackie?" "Upstairs, resting," one of the relatives told him. The President looked momentarily nonplussed. Then he announced that it was probably time for him to go upstairs and dress for the series of balls. Could Jack persuade Jackie to come down, someone asked—at least come to the top of the stairs and *wave* to her family? The President didn't answer. All at once a Secret Service man tapped Michel Bouvier on the shoulder: Mrs. Kennedy wished to see him upstairs. If there was one relative Jackie would have wanted to see, it would have been Michel. Since Bud Bouvier's death, his son had been almost like an adopted older brother to Jackie. Michel spent the next half hour upstairs with the Kennedys as they dressed for the evening.

At around eight, when Michel reappeared, he had no new explanation for the non-appearance of the hostess. She had wanted to rest, he said. And there were five balls that demanded her appearance later on; the first one started at ten. The party in the State

Dining Room began to break up. The relatives, too, had to dress for the ball. They did their best not to show their hurt and disappointment.

What *was* the true reason for this unladylike behavior, which some of the family·thought smacked of insult? Some suspected that Jackie was upstairs sulking, a jealous snit because on this, her husband's day, he was receiving the lion's share of the attention, and she had been forced into the background. Or perhaps some unknown domestic altercation had taken place between the Kennedys prior to the inauguration, and she was venting her anger at him in this way, showing him who was boss. Or of course she could have truly been tired; she had given difficult, premature birth to her baby son just six weeks earlier. Or perhaps, like a movie star who knows she must be rested before close-ups, she was resting in order to make the best possible appearance before the national television cameras later in the evening. Perhaps she was simply heeding her father's coaching: hold yourself back a little, don't give of yourself too freely, don't be too available, keep them guessing and drive them wild. Certainly by not appearing she had made herself the central topic of conversation. Perhaps, John H. Davis says, one of her famous attacks of shyness and uncertainty had overcome her, perhaps she felt she needed all her energy to endure the public appearance later on, perhaps she found it emotionally too difficult to shift gears from the intimacy of a family gathering to the public glare of the television lights. It was also possible that she was fed to the teeth with all four of the battling families: the Bouviers who disdained the Lees and Kennedys, the Auchinclosses who disliked the Kennedys and Bouviers who, in turn, resented the Auchinclosses, and the Kennedys who seemed only to like each other. Or any combination of these explanations might have accounted for her behavior.

But it is also possible that, to her, the evening of January 20, 1961 contained certain priorities. Her appearance at the Inaugural Ball was important, it was mandatory. Her appearance among her family was less important, it could be skipped. She could not have helped but notice how, in recent months, her family had used their kinship with her to add glitter to their own wings. For the moment, she had given them enough. The Inaugural Ball, on the other hand, was part of her job as the new President's wife. She would do it, and do it well. Miss Porter's taught one to rise to great occasions, not to small ones.

Her appearance at the Inaugural Ball that evening was radiant. "She is too beautiful!" Kenneth had moaned, applying the final touches to her hair. She moved, smiling, on her husband's arm through the crowds, in her long white chiffon gown, like a queen, and the television cameras followed. Of course, an Inaugural Ball—or the series of balls that compose it —is really not a ball at all. No one dances. There is music, but it is usually inaudible against the din of conversation, the clatter of plates, the clink of ice cubes. It is really a mass political thank-you bash tossed for all the ward heelers, aldermen, mayors, fund-raisers, staff, secretaries, and bumper-sticker wearers—all who have had a hand, large or small, in the President's victory.

When the relatives of the President and First Lady arrived at the ball, they found themselves pressed in a crush of shouting, shoving people, all straining for a glimpse of the evening's hero and heroine, and ducking the trays of perspiring waiters. There was no chance of getting even close to Jackie or the President. When the ball was over, and the relatives were ready to leave, the Marines who were supposed to escort them had disappeared. The promised limousines and buses were nowhere to be found. Outside the National Guard Armory there was an ugly, shouting scramble for taxis. The relatives straggled back to their hotels as best they could, some on foot. Their Great Moment was over.

13

Camelot

DESPITE HER GLOWING appearance on television during the various stages of the Inauguration, Jacqueline Kennedy, the new First Lady, was by no means the international heroine she was to become. The initial public reaction to her, in fact, was rather cool. She was beautiful, yes, but in a rather exotic way. Her looks fit no accepted American standard: the high cheekbones, the tiny nose, the eyes spaced a bit too far apart. Her figure was slim-hipped, flat-chested, boyish. Also, try as she might, she could not help but look expensive. Even when the public was told that she often bought dresses off the sale racks at Ohrbach's, we somehow knew better. She had a rich girl's look and a rich girl's distance, and a rich girl's aura of awareness of her richness. Americans have never particularly sympathized with rich girls. It is hard to feel cozy with the girl who has everything, including a husband who is President of the United States. In the beginning, the President's wife's influence was felt mainly on Seventh Avenue, where the fashion industry had pronounced her "incredibly chic." The little pillbox hats that she liked to wear in those days provided an unexpected shot in the arm to the millinery business. To the public, she seemed a lovely mannequin more than a flesh-and-blood woman. People didn't call other people "plastic" in the early 1960s, but if the term had been around it might have been applied to her.

John Kennedy, on the other hand, was altogether a different story. He was the All-American Boy made good. One was aware that he was rich, but one forgot about it the instant one heard him talk or saw him flash that grin. With more bushy reddish-brown hair than any man in his forties deserved to have, and with that handsome Irish mug, it was no wonder that he became a youth cult figure. Youth was looking for a hero in those days, bored with a country run by old men, and here the hero was.

What would eventually make Jacqueline Kennedy Onassis the most famous woman in the world, perhaps the most famous woman in history since Cleopatra, was a pattern in her life that was already beginning to develop. She was a woman who had the power to attract glamorous men but also the misfortune to lose them. This is a theme that has propelled any number of enormously popular romantic novels. One thinks of *Gone With the Wind.* Jackie had already lost her doting, glamorous father. By 1961, she had come close to losing her glamorous husband. In New York and Palm Beach society, there was a great deal of gossip about Jack Kennedy's extra-marital dalliances. There is even a Texas gentleman who claims that Jack Kennedy made a sexual advance to *him.* Society gossip can often be discounted but, at the same time, it is often true that the truth behind the gossip is much more scandalous than the gossip itself. Jack Kennedy liked beautiful women, and considered himself a proficient sexual athlete. Some of the rumors were no doubt true.

It is known that some of her husband's wanderings had, in the early days of the marriage, caused Jackie to consider divorcing him, and that she had discussed the matter with both the Kennedy and Auchincloss families. It has also been said, and never denied, that at the time Joseph P. Kennedy offered his daughter-in-law a million dollars in cash to remain with his son, and that Jackie accepted it. She and her sister had always had something of an obsession about security—

financial security—just as their mother had. That million dollars, if the tale is true, would have provided her with the first real money—of her very own—that she had ever had. In any case, she had decided not to let the glamorous husband go, though she would lose him soon in a manner she could not have dreamed.

Meanwhile, it was not long before Jackie Kennedy began to emerge as a personage in her own right—as a star of a magnitude larger than her husband—and it occurred, interestingly enough, during the Kennedys' state visit to France in May of 1961. That was the beginning of Camelot. No one, furthermore, had any idea that it was going to happen and, in fact, State Department officials planning the visit were somewhat nervous about what the French reaction to Jackie might be. The French do not always take warmly to Americans—particularly to Americans of French descent. Every stress and circumflex of her French accent would be scrutinized, criticized, commented upon. She had, furthermore, become an American fashion figure, and no one knows more about fashion than the French. Her clothes, her hair style, her makeup—all would be examined and analyzed by the finicky French, and reported in the frequently over-fastidious French press.

But when Jackie stepped off the plane at Orly, wearing one of her little trademark pillbox hats and a simple wool coat, the enormous crowd that had gathered to greet the Presidential couple began to chant, *"Vive Jackie! Vive Jackie!"* The crowd virtually ignored the head of state who was traveling with her. Along the route of the motorcade to Paris, another crowd, estimated at over 200,000, continued the chant—clapping enthusiastically when the first limousine, bearing President Kennedy and Charles de Gaulle, came into view, and bursting into a deafening roar at the appearance of the second car which contained Mme. de Gaulle and Jackie. With the French, it appeared that she was an instant and overwhelming success. There was a 101-gun salute in the Place de la Concorde, and then more cheering throngs at the Quai d'Orsay where the Kennedys had been given the state suite. Outside the Elysée Palace, where the de Gaulles had scheduled a luncheon for the Kennedys, there were still more crowds, more noisy cheers, and, following the luncheon, there was an even wilder demonstration in front of the Red Cross Child Welfare Clinic where thousands of people crushed through police barricades screaming for Jackie. That evening, back at the Elysée Palace again for the state dinner, the rue St. Honoré was jammed with people standing in the rain for a glimpse of their new idol as she stepped from her car in a Greek-style gown by Oleg Cassini.

The next morning, the press was ecstatic. *"Comme elle est jolie!"* the captions proclaimed under her front-page picture, and the fashion editors were unanimous in their approval of her clothes, her coiffure, and her perfect French accent. Even the stony-faced Charles de Gaulle had been turned to jelly by her looks, her manners, her poise, her smile, and that faultless French. There were, in the meantime, a few problems. For one thing, everyone in France with the name of Bouvier—a name almost as common as Smith or Jones in America—was claiming to be Jackie Bouvier's cousin, and the United States Embassy and the United States Information Service were deluged with calls and letters from alleged relatives who wanted to meet her. At the Embassy, extra switchboard operators had to be hired to deal with the insistent, the angry, the disappointed callers. Also, it had been decided in Washington that, since Mrs. Kennedy was an American fashion figure, she should appear only in dresses by American designers. The Paris couturiers had invited her to a private showing of their collections, but this invitation had been declined on the theory that American housewives, back home, would not look kindly on a First Lady who spent an afternoon admiring gowns by Dior, Givenchy and Chanel. At a press conference for French and American newspaper women, she was asked why she had turned down the invitation to the fashion show, and had replied, "I have more important things to do." This had nettled the French couturiers somewhat. As a result, at the last minute Jackie executed a change of plan. For the dinner that was to be given for the Kennedys at the palace of Versailles on the second night of their visit, Jackie had planned to wear another Cassini gown. Instead she chose a gown of white satin, studded with rhinestones, with a red, white and blue bodice by Givenchy. She topped her hair with a diamond tiara and, when she made her entrance into the glittering Hall of Mirrors, there was cheering again, and more cheers for Hubert de Givenchy when he appeared. The couturiers were mollified.

The dinner at Versailles was considered one of the most important social events in the history of the Republic, and to be invited to it conveyed such status that a number of highly placed Parisians and members of the American colony, who felt that they should have been invited but were not, hastily scheduled urgent trips that would take them out of town on the night of June 1, so that their omission from the list of guests would not be noticed by their friends. The climax of the gala evening came after dinner when guests repaired to Versailles's Louis XV Theatre for a ballet performance, and when Jacqueline Kennedy, in her tiara, entered the royal box and rose to attention as the French and American national anthems were played, she looked like a reigning princess from some foreign, far-off realm. So complete was Jackie's success in France that, on the last day of his visit, President Kennedy was moved to make his famous laconic comment to the Paris Press Club, "I am the man who accompanied Jacqueline Kennedy to Paris, and I have enjoyed it."

The triumph in Paris was followed by a state visit to London, and dinner with Queen Elizabeth and Prince Philip at Buckingham Palace. The British reaction to Jacqueline Kennedy was as warm and enthusiastic as the French, though somewhat more Britishly muted and polite. The news, meanwhile, of the tremendous reception which the First Lady had had in Paris had made its way quickly back to the United States. All at once she was a giant American heroine. She had devastated the undevastatable Charles de Gaulle, she had improved United States relations with France enormously. The slumbering giant awoke, and all at once Jackie Kennedy's face blossomed on the covers of all the magazines. The *Ladies' Home Journal* came promptly forth with a gushy series of articles on her, later turned into an even gushier "official" biography, by Mary Van Rensselaer Thayer. Mrs. Thayer's account oozed with fawning praise. In Mrs. Thayer's account, Jackie's childhood had been idyllic. The Bouviers' rancorous divorce was dismissed in a sentence, along with her father's and uncle's drinking problems, the terrible moment at the wedding, and all the years of bitterness and recrimination between Jack Bouvier and the Auchinclosses. Mrs. Thayer faithfully repeated the falsehood that the Bouviers descended from an "ancient house of Fontaine near Grenoble," and that Louise Vernou was a "daughter of a Frenchman of noble family." *McCall's,* meanwhile, pointed out that the Lees were "an aristocratic offshoot of the Lees of Virginia." Magazine editors discovered that even a mention of Jackie Kennedy's name on their covers meant an instant sell-out on the newsstands. She was box office. A Broadway producer, Stuart Ostrow, launched plans to mount a musical comedy based on her life. Of course this was only the beginning. And, as it turned out, it would never end.

What America had suddenly discovered was that, for years, it had been thirsting for elegance, for aristocracy, on an important national level. This was surprising, because Americans had always assumed that America was the land of the common man, of Lincoln and his log cabin. But now, it seemed, even the humblest housewife in the Kansas plains longed to dream of princesses, of titles and tiaras, of jeweled gowns, of heiresses and coronets. We had become tired, it seemed, and bored, with all those dowdy ladies in the White House. What an unromantic stream of plumpness and plainness they had been, those First Ladies of our memory—chubby little Lou Hoover; tall, gawky Eleanor Roosevelt; dumpy Bess Truman; Mamie Eisenhower in her silly little-girl bangs. Lou, Eleanor, Bess, and Mamie—even their names dripped with dullness and ordinariness. But now, with Jacqueline Bouvier Kennedy, we finally had a lady who had style, who had glamour, who had money, who had class. She represented concepts we had been ashamed to admit we cared about, such as "good breeding," "elegance," and "fine things." Her particular enthusiasms—art and European history—no longer seemed effete and sissified, the bailiwick of limp-wristed librarians and nice old men who sold antiques. Suddenly they seemed *important* interests. Because she represented porcelain polish and perfection, we began to expect that there was nothing she could not do, and do *right*. This was not a woman, we expected, who would ever stamp her foot or scream at her husband, who would sob, or curse, or sometimes have one too many cocktails or sometimes have trouble sleeping. What we expected, of course, was a dream, a princess from a fairy tale, a person who had never existed and who never would.

14

First
Lady

DURING HER FIRST months in the White House, it seemed to her friends, and particularly to her close relatives, that Jackie had "changed." Now that she was becoming so famous, they said, she was also becoming a bit self-centered. The fame, it seemed, was going to her head. She had, they said, begun to high-hat them and they, who remembered her as a chubby little girl in pigtails and jodhpurs, considered this a most unfortunate development. What they—the Bouvier relatives, specifically—resented was the fact that they had expected, when Jackie became First Lady, to be invited to the White House for dinner on a regular basis. Now it seemed that these invitations were not to be forthcoming. Her non-appearance at the family party on the day of the Inauguration still rankled, and now it seemed as though Jackie, as a giant public luminary, no longer wanted to share her position in the spotlight with anyone. In their New York apartments and in the East Hampton summer houses, the Bouvier relatives sulked. When they saw her face on the covers of their magazines, they sneered. They were, after all, more than a little jealous of her. And they wouldn't have minded it so much if they hadn't also felt neglected.

There was no question that Jackie's life had entered a new phase; the wife of a President has many "duties," more than a few of which are boring. There are, for example, those required teas and luncheons for Senate wives, a number of whom might be women the President's wife would never normally care to meet. There are state functions, where the hostess of the White House is expected to be present. All these chores consume time and, though having servants and secretaries helps, each First Lady's day contains a few items that one would rather die than do, and yet, because of who one is, must do. And, through it all, are constant, annoying reminders that, in the end, one is only who one is by virtue of what one's husband is. One is only the First *Lady*. He is the Great Being.

After Jackie's wildy enthusiastic reception by the French, Jack Kennedy realized, more clearly than ever before, what an enormous political asset his wife had become. She provided something that the Kennedy family had never had before—elegance and style. None of the other Kennedy women had it, but Jackie did, and the public loved it. As they say in the theater, it "played." Politically, Jackie was a highly exploitable property. Jackie, meanwhile, in the glowing aftermath of the French visit, had also realized how valuable she had become to her husband, how much he needed her to fill what was essentially a decorative role. The marriage had become, by now, little more than a matter of mutual convenience—a union of two mercurial, strong-willed, stubborn people who, like so many children of the rich, were rather used to getting their own way, and were not happy when they didn't. Any romantic love that might have once existed between them had long since evaporated and, though close friends were aware of the hard little looks that sometimes passed between them, all that was left was a need to put the best public face on things. And so a perfectly sensible business deal was struck during those first White House months. She would supply the elegance, the charm, the class that he wanted. And he, in turn, would let her do pretty much whatever else she chose.

She had decided to expend her efforts as First Lady

in three general directions, each of which reflected one of her personal interests. She bore the genes of designers and decorators and so, not surprisingly, she wanted to renovate and redecorate the White House, to turn it into "the prettiest house in America." She had also decided that the level of White House entertaining could be raised and, since she was no mean shakes as a hostess, she decided that it should be the First Lady—not professional hostesses such as Mmes. Mesta and Cafritz—who should provide Washington's most notable entertainments. Finally, she wanted the White House, and the President, to support an area largely neglected by previous administrations—the arts. In addition to all this, she intended to find time for one or two things that were purely and simply for personal pleasure.

She had found the decor of the executive mansion dismally institutional and museum-like, and the furniture a hodgepodge of unrelated styles and periods. The house, she felt, should be refurnished and decorated in the period in which it was built, the early 1800s. She asked Henry F. du Pont, who had created the Winterthur Museum in Wilmington, to provide overall supervision of the project, and she next set up the White House Fine Arts Committee, with David Finley, former director of the National Gallery of Art, as chairman. A bill was passed through Congress establishing the White House as a National Monument, and the position of White House Curator was created. By the fall of 1961, the White House Historical Association had been added to the list of committees that were toiling to face-lift the mansion. A campaign was launched for private funding of the project, and it was immediately successful. Gifts of money, antiques, and paintings poured in from museum officials, gallery owners, and private individuals. Out of basement storage rooms in the White House itself came antique treasures that no one knew were there. It seemed to Jackie unfortunate that no official guidebook for visitors to the White House had ever existed, and so she asked John Walker of the National Gallery to supervise the preparation of one. The National Geographic Society was asked to provide photographs for it. A few months before the completion of the renovation, Jackie Kennedy conducted her famous guided tour of the almost-finished mansion. All three networks aired the tour, and an estimated 56,000,000 people turned on their sets that night—at the time, a record television audience—and more contributions poured in. In all, more than $2,000,000 was raised and spent on Jackie's project.

When it was completed, there was no question that it looked it. A Cézanne hung in the Green Room. The Red Room had been completely done in the American and Empire style. The Blue Room had been redone in the manner that it had been during the presidency of James Monroe, complete with reproductions of the open-armed chairs Monroe had originally specified for the room. In the Diplomatic Reception Room, Jackie had placed antique scenic wallpaper by an early nineteenth-century French designer named Zuber. When the redecorating was done, only one room in the mansion was left untouched: Lincoln's bedroom.

Though no taxpayers' money had been involved, there was a certain amount of grumbling in some quarters about Mrs. Kennedy's extravagance. It was certainly true that she didn't believe in cutting costs. She had originally admired the Zuber wallpaper in a house in Maryland and, when it was donated to the White House, it cost $12,500 to take it down and re-hang it. The American Institute of Interior Designers in New York was publicly critical of this, since the paper could have been reproduced at a fraction of that cost and M. Zuber's original printing blocks were still available. The president of the Institute sneered, "I don't know how faded the paper is, but some people like old, broken-down things because they are old and broken-down. Maybe Mrs. Kennedy is one of those."

With her new French chef, René Verdon, Jackie was also determined to return White House entertaining to the *grand service,* and for this she was also criticized. Inspired, for example, by President de Gaulle's dinner for the Kennedys at Versailles, she decided to stage the dinner for the President of Pakistan, Mohammed Ayub Khan, on July 11, 1961, at George Washington's former home, Mount Vernon. A huge tent was set up on the lawn overlooking the Potomac, and guests were ferried down the river in the Kennedy yacht, *Honey Fitz,* and two other boats which had been borrowed from the Navy. An orchestra played for cocktails on each boat. When guests arrived at Mount Vernon, they were served mint juleps in silver cups. The food, which had been prepared at the White House and included such dishes as *poulet chasseur, couronne de riz clamart* and *framboises à la crème Chantilly,* was also transported down river by boat in Army field kitchens. Tiffany and Bonwit Teller created the table decor. After dinner, in line with Jackie's credo that every entertainment should include something "cultural," the National Symphony performed a concert in the open air. It all sounded expensive, as indeed it was, and this time it *was* taxpayers' money.

She had decided to eliminate stiff, formal dinners, with guests seated in rows along either side of a long dining table. Instead, she substituted small round tables for six or eight. Often, to avoid problems of protocol —and guests who might feel they had not been seated in a place of sufficient importance—she had guests draw their seating from slips of paper in a silver bowl. It had to be admitted that Mrs. Kennedy's parties were imaginative and fun—different from anything Washington had seen in years. For her October party for Premier Abboud of Sudan, an after-dinner Shakespeare recital was offered by members of the American Shakespeare Festival Theatre. For a dinner for Governor and Mrs. Muñoz Marin of Puerto Rico, a cello concert by Pablo Casals was offered, and the dinner guests included prominent American musicians and composers. In April, 1962, a dinner party honored all the Nobel Prize winners in the Western Hemisphere, and Fredric March read from works of American Nobelists in the past. It was at this gathering that President Kennedy made his famous comment, "I think this is the most extraordinary collection of talent, of human knowledge, that has ever been gathered together at the White House, with the possible exception of when Thomas Jefferson dined alone." Jackie made sure that talent—musical, literary, artistic—was always included at her White House parties. For example, at her May, 1962 party for the French Cultural Minister, André Malraux, Isaac Stern, Leonard Rose, and Eugene Istomin played as a violin, cello, and piano trio, and the guest list included Robert Lowell, Arthur Miller, Andrew Wyeth, Saul Bellow, Elia Kazan, and others from the fields of arts and letters.

At the same time, Jackie Kennedy had made it clear to her husband that, in addition to being his official hostess, she intended to enjoy the luxury of some private time for herself. In the autumn of 1961, for instance, she announced that she intended to depart, alone, on an extended trip to Asia and the Far East. Her purpose? She simply wanted to tour that part of the world. The President's advisors were horrified. Mrs. Kennedy was proposing a pleasure trip, unaccompanied by her husband or children, during a period which would not only include the Thanksgiving holiday but also both children's birthdays. The American public, they insisted, would never stomach that. Finally she agreed to postpone her trip to the following spring.

Her Asian journey, which consumed most of March and April of 1962, was enthusiastically followed by the press. Americans read of their glamorous First Lady being entertained by maharajahs and potentates in India and Pakistan. Lavish parties and receptions were put on for her at every stop in her tour. She was treated like a queen by regents of remote principalities, and was floated through the Shalimar Gardens and other exotic places that most Americans had either never heard of or only dreamed of seeing. Of course there were some angry reactions to all this. She was being treated like an official visitor, even though hers was a private trip. Where was her husband? Who was caring for her small children? How much of the taxpayers' money was paying for these travels and the entourage of secretaries, Secret Service men, the maids, the hairdresser? Still, most Americans, at heart, found the details of the Royal Voyage fascinating. They seemed, somehow, to understand her need for the trip. They forgave her, and she got away with it. She returned to the United States to find her popularity greater than ever. Barely three months later she was off again, again *sans* husband, for another extended trip—this time to Italy where, among other things, she had a private audience with the Pope in which she petitioned for an annulment by the Vatican of her sister's first marriage. Again, eyebrows were raised. But somehow she had reached the point where, as far as the public was concerned, she could do no wrong and, again, she was forgiven.

Throughout this period, however, a much more important thing was happening. Its scale might be limited but, for her, it was to be one of her life's most significant achievements. She was learning how to play on her public. At first, it had been almost instinctive, tentative, but now, with growing aplomb, which would become magnificent mastery, she was learning to *manage* her celebrity. Celebrity must be managed, of course, because it is such a fragile commodity that it can easily be destroyed. Most movie stars, particularly women, never learn the trick. Movie stars protest that they cannot go out on the street without being recognized, followed, intruded upon, begged for autographs and snapshots. It's dreadful, the stars complain, to live in a fishbowl of fame. Even more dreadful, on the other hand, are the moments when they are not recognized, not pestered. It is a dilemma that stars face throughout their careers—thirsting for fame, publicity and recognition, and then resenting what the fame, publicity and recognition bring with them—the public's feeling that stars are public property.

But most movie stars have not had Jackie Bouvier Kennedy's background and training: her father's lessons in how a woman should keep herself inaccessible, fascinating, intriguing, exasperating; her mother's knowledge of society's rule which states that you speak and behave in a manner that suits the occasion, regardless of what you may actually think and feel. And so Jackie was realizing that she could treat her public, which already numbered in the millions and was growing, exactly as she could treat an admiring escort at a Princeton prom: politely, pleasantly, aloofly. You laughed at the escort's little jokes, you tried to make him feel important, but when the escort's hand squeezed your waist too tightly, you gently pushed the hand away.

The squeezing paw of the public could be treated in precisely this fashion. She would give of herself just so much, no more. The result of the technique was that the public—from so many newspaper stories, magazine covers and articles—thought they knew a great deal about Jacqueline Kennedy. At the same time, they were uneasily aware that they knew very little—that there was more, somewhere, to know. There would always be more to know about her, and so the public would remain frustrated and, of course, intrigued.

One of the things Jackie had asked her husband to buy for her was a country house, a weekend retreat, where she could ride. It was called Glen Ora, and was in Middleburg, Virginia, in the heart of horse country, and not far from the Auchinclosses' Merrywood. Sometimes the President weekended there with her, and sometimes he did not and, particularly during the winter hunting season, she would go to Glen Ora by herself, with the children. It was a lovely, peaceful place.

The President and his wife went there together when *both* chose to. One afternoon, the French economist, Jean Monnet, drove down to Glen Ora for a meeting with the President. As his French Embassy limousine turned into the gates of the estate, Monnet was surprised to see that there were no guards or police at the entrance. He continued up the long drive and, again, there was no sign of anyone. His car was parked in the circle in front of the house and there was the front door, unattended. The first sign of life Monnet spotted was a lone figure walking toward him across the grass —a man in slacks, sweater, and tennis shoes. It was the President.

Monnet was shocked by the lack of security at Glen Ora. Later he said, "Anyone could have come up that drive and shot him on his own lawn. Along the driveway of Charles De Gaulle's country place, there's a sentry posted every twenty meters."

But for her retreat in the country Jackie had not wanted an armed camp with guards and sentries.

In the winter of 1963 she was pregnant again, and the public eagerly watched her pregnancy. And when, on August 9, Patrick Bouvier Kennedy was born, and died two and a half days later of a respiratory infection, the public's heart went out to her. As a result, there were nothing but sympathetic feelings for her when, barely ten days later, she flew to Athens and boarded the yacht *Christina* belonging to Aristotle Onassis, her sister's friend, for a cruise of the Aegean islands. The Radziwills had been in Athens when the news of the baby's death arrived and, at dinner with Onassis, who loved to surround himself with celebrities, Onassis had suggested that a cruise might ease Jackie's grief. Lee had telephoned her sister, relaying the invitation, and Jackie had accepted. Also invited on the cruise were the Radziwills and Franklin Roosevelt, Jr., and his wife, Suzanne.

Among the public no eyebrows were raised this time

by the fact that, again, the First Lady was traveling without her husband, nor by the fact that Mrs. Kennedy was the only unescorted woman on the yacht and Mr. Onassis was the only unescorted man. Nor was anything made of the fact that, at the time, the legendary Greek shipowner was heavily in debt to the United States Maritime Administration, and that the cruise for the President's wife might smack, to some, of bribery. At that point Jackie had become, to her public, just what her father had said she had been to him—"all things holy."

15

At Sea with Ari

THIS WAS NOT the first time Jackie had been aboard the *Christina*. She and her husband had been invited on for cocktails one afternoon in Monte Carlo, when Jack Kennedy was still a junior Senator from Massachusetts, and when the purpose had been to meet Sir Winston Churchill, who was then Mr. Onassis's pet guest. At the time, Jackie had confided to friends that she found the *Christina* a bit vulgar, a rich man's garish toy. The yacht sported, among other things, its own yellow twin-prop, five-seat amphibian airplane, and a deck-top swimming pool whose bottom could be elevated to deck level to create a dance floor. The other details of the boat were, to say the least, exuberant.

He had owned the *Christina* since 1954 when a North German shipyard had completed the conversion of a 1,600-ton Canadian frigate, *Stormont,* according to his specifications. These included a circular staircase lined with vitrines to the bridge deck and the owner's private quarters, a three-room apartment. In the book-lined study hung El Greco's *Ascension,* a collection of Russian icons, a number of swords in golden scabbards—a gift from Arabia's King Saud—and a number of whaling trophies. The master bedroom, dominated by an eighteenth-century Venetian mirror and a dressing table set out with gold-plated combs, brushes, and cosmetics jars and bottles, led to a mirror-lined dressing room and the owner's bathroom. Onassis considered his bathroom his *pièce de resistance.* It was an exact replica, in Sienna marble, of the bath in King Minos's lost Palace of Knossos in Crete, with inlaid mosaic flying fish across the walls.

Downstairs was the grand salon, which could be converted into a motion-picture theater, and the all-white dining room with a round table and wall paintings by Marcel Vertes. Then, on the poop deck, was the enormous smoking room with a grand piano and a big open fireplace made out of carved lapis lazuli which, Onassis liked to say, cost four dollars a square inch. Then there was the bar with its walls covered with antique parchment maps, with tiny models of famous ships in glass cases, with barstools covered with white whale-skin—"Made from the testicles of a whale," he liked to joke—and supported by giant whales' teeth. Then there was the children's room, made for his children when they were small, with wall murals by Ludwig Bemelmans, an electric organ, and a music box disguised as a Monte Carlo fruit-vending machine. Outside was the pool, its floor decorated with another mosaic of the Minos Palace—a large reproduction of the fresco of the Minotaur and the Dancing Acrobats covering an area of sixteen square yards.

Below, along a corridor, were the nine double guest cabins, each with baths, showers, wash basins with fish-mouth faucets, lavatories and bidets of different-colored marble, each done in a different style, and each named after a different Greek island—*Chios, Crete, Ithaca, Lesbos,* and so on. Jackie Kennedy was given *Ithaca,* which Lady Churchill had preferred, and which had also been inhabited by Greta Garbo and Maria Callas. In each guest cabin were instructions on how to telephone the Maids' Cabin (two trained ladies' maids and a number of valets on permanent call), the Pantry Galley for food, the Bar for a drink, or the Laundry. There was also a ship's hospital, complete with surgical and X-ray equipment. There were forty-two telephones aboard the *Christina,* and she required a crew of fifty—"More than I need to run a forty-thousand-ton tanker," Onassis used to say in mock dismay.

When Ari Onassis planned a cruise, he usually acted on the supposition that a yachtful of dazzling international celebrities automatically guaranteed a gay, stimulating and congenial group. It didn't always work out that way, however. Every Hollywood hostess knows that she cannot surround her dinner table with nothing but first-magnitude stars. There must always be a few unknowns, to support the giants and to give the giants confidence, to remind them pleasantly that all are not as blessed as they. Otherwise, the giants will spend the evening trying to outrank and upstage each other, and everyone will have a ghastly time.

This often happened among the enlarged egos Ari liked to gather aboard the *Christina.* The ructions that took place were legion, and a number of his guests had had to set up their own little rules about when they would, and when they would not, accept an invitation to a cruise. Greta Garbo, for instance, declined to go aboard when Maria Callas was to be present; nothing personal, but why should Garbo be willing to share her luster with another, somewhat younger, woman? Callas herself would never come aboard when Sir Winston was a guest. The aging Churchill used simply to ignore her, and for a woman such as Mme. Callas it was most difficult to be ignored.

Jacqueline

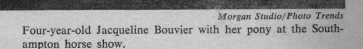

Four-year-old Jacqueline Bouvier with her pony at the Southampton horse show.

August 1949. Sailing for France for a year of study.

(Opposite above) Jacqueline with younger sister, Lee. East Hampton, 1935.

(Opposite below) With her parents in 1933.

1952. Inquiring photographer for the *Washington Times-Herald*.

Magnum

September 12, 1953. Hammersmith Farm, Newport.

(Inset above) With fiancé, Senator John F. Kennedy. Hyannis Port, June 1953.

(Inset below) Leaving the hospital after Senator Kennedy's near death following spinal surgery in 1954.

Mrs. John F. Kennedy, politician's wife, at 1958 conference (inset) and during the 1960 presidential campaign.

Massachusetts headquarters,
election eve, 1960.

Hyannis Port the morning
after the election.

United Press International Photo

Escorted by Frank Sinatra to the pre-inaugural gala.

Inauguration Day, January 20, 1961.

Cornell Capa/Magnum

Cornell Capa/Magnum

Cornell Capa/Magnum

(Inset) An almost private moment.

A relaxed President and First Lady at the end of a formal White House dinner in 1962.

At Versailles with French President Charles de Gaulle in 1961 during the trip that brought her worldwide attention.

United Press International Photo

Vienna in 1961 with Soviet Premier Nikita Khrushchev.

United Press International Photo

Camera Press/Photo Trends

On a private trip to India
in 1962. With Indira
Gandhi (above) and with
Indira Gandhi and Prime
Minister Jawaharlal Nehru
(below).

Marilyn Silverstone/Magnum

With President Ayub Khan of Pakistan.

Emperor Haile Selassie of Ethiopia being welcomed by President and Mrs. Kennedy in 1963.

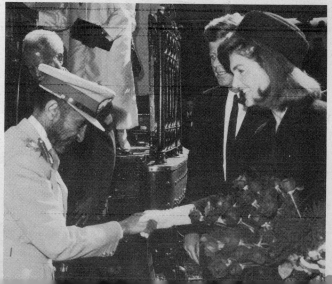

Leaving the hospital after the death of their newborn son in August 1963.

A quiet summer with Caroline in Ravello, Italy.

Never away from the cameras' scrutiny.

November 25, 1963.

(Above and lower left) Inauguration of Kennedy Memorial at Runnymede, England, in 1968.

Private audience with Pope Paul VI in 1966.

After she emerged from mourning the rumors began about Jacqueline Kennedy's romantic interests. Among the candidates were Mike Nichols (above) and Lord Harlech.

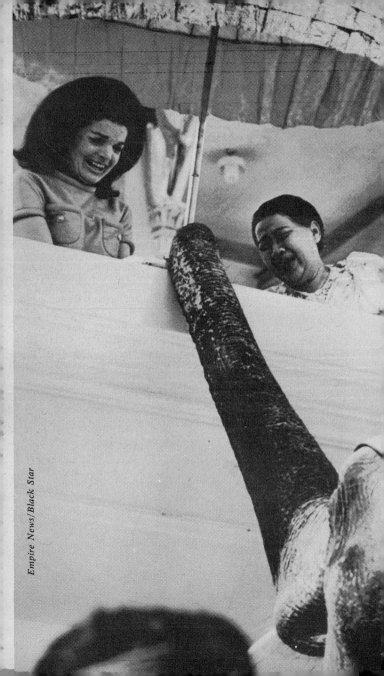

In Cambodia in 1967 for the dedication of a boulevard to her late husband. (Above) With Prince Norodom Sihanouk.

June 1968. Leaving for Los Angeles (accompanied by Roswell
L. Gilpatric) to be with Robert Kennedy after he was shot.

October 20, 1968. Jacqueline Bouvier Kennedy marries Aristotle Onassis.

Syndication International/Photo Trends

Mrs. Aristotle Onassis in London.

Schoor/Paterson/Liaison

With her husband and former mother-in-law, Rose Kennedy.

With stepdaughter Christina Onassis.

Leridon/Liaison

Nightclubbing in Paris.

January 1973. Arriving at the hospital to visit her dying step-son, Alexander Onassis.

With Christina Onassis after Aristotle Onassis's death in March 1975.

Rose Hartman/Black Star

"The Smile."

Nights on the town with . . . Frank Sinatra.

Oliver Smith.

Skip Stein.

Pete Hamill and Roosevelt Grier.

Consulting editor at The Viking Press (with Bryan Holme), the first of her publishing jobs.

Kevin McCarthy.

The most important thing about a yacht cruise, meanwhile, is that it is not the cruising that counts; it is the stops. For this reason, a proper cruise must be planned in exacting detail, with as few successive days spent at sea as possible. Otherwise, boredom quickly sets in, even on a vessel as lavishly equipped for diversion as the *Christina*. By the middle of the second day out of port, the familiar, heavy signs of weariness and lassitude will have begun to creep into the proceedings. The guests will sleep until noon, and will arrive on deck looking haggard and feeling, more than likely, hung over. Drinks are tried in an effort to recapture the spirit of the night before. The talk is of what took place in the wee hours of it—and, as a rule, with who had too much to drink and what happened as a result thereof. When the weather is bad, the air of *ennui* becomes even more pronounced.

On days at sea, Ari would usually appear at a little past noon to greet his guests and to tell them a new joke he had heard over his ship-to-shore phone. Then, for a moment or two, there would be a bit of that noisy, off-color talk that only the very rich and very secure can carry off successfully—barracks language in peerage accents from famous heads wrapped in Hermès scarves. But then, on days at sea, this too might pall. The talk could become small, very small. Poker might be tried, or craps, or bezique, or backgammon, or "Towie"—the rich-man's- three-handed bridge game—and, over yawns and glassy looks, more drinks. To lighten spirits, Ari might offer to show a movie—he kept a steadily changing library of first-run American or foreign films—and meanwhile everyone would wait for the *Christina*'s next port of call.

Some of the other forms of entertainment devised by the *Christina*'s host smacked of desperation. Once, to relieve the torpor of the third day out, Ari announced that lunch would be served on the sunken floor of the drained swimming pool. Soon after the meal was served, however, he ordered the water turned on. To their surprise, if not to their delight, his guests soon found themselves—along with chairs, tables, and their lunch—floating squealing to the top. When Onassis's inventiveness wore thin, more extreme measures were taken to entertain his guests—as happened once when the yacht was passing through the Strait of Messina, between Italy and Sicily. Ari, like most Greeks, was fond of food—though his favorite dish was a plate of sliced raw onions drenched in olive oil—and the small talk had been reduced to its tiniest. The subject of the conversation was groceries. Ari mentioned a shop in Athens that sold a pastry he particularly favored and, this news drawing a spark of interest among his guests, he suddenly announced that they must all have a sample of this delicacy right now. Immediately, the *Christina*'s yellow seaplane, the *Piaggio*, was dispatched with its pilot. A radio-telephone call was placed to the shop in Athens. The plane sped eastward across the Mediterranean to Athens, where the oven-hot pastry was being rushed to the airport. Loaded aboard, the tarts headed westward again to join the *Christina* at Palermo. The feat infused a lagging cruise with new excitement, and everybody said, "Isn't Ari wonderful?" and, "Who else but Ari. . . ."

Still, such frolicsome episodes were relatively rare. Onassis spent more time aboard the *Christina* than in any of his mainland houses—in Paris, Buenos Aires, Monte Carlo, Athens and on the island of Skorpios—and it was really a floating office. He was invisible most of the time, in his study, on the phone, doing business, leaving his guests to fend for themselves. In fact, most of his friends admitted that he had no particular talent as a host. The *Christina* usually sailed from port at midday, to allow guests as much time as possible to recover, in bed, from the previous evening. After brunch and drinks, they would wander back to their staterooms to nap or change clothes for the cocktail hour. During the day Ari would make one or two appearances, acting cordial, then quickly returning to his telephone. Unless the boat were due at another port for dinner, the cocktail hour was lengthy, and dinner was served late.

Alcohol was usually the evening's only pastime. Guests lingered around the bar, sitting on the whale's-testicle stools, or on the open patio beside the dance floor-swimming pool, getting drunker. Many evenings Ari would fail to show up at all. At the same time, Onassis was considered a rather moralistic (some said downright prudish) host, and this had a dispiriting effect on certain guests who expected a more laissez-faire attitude on board the world's most famous pleasure ship. He made it quite clear that all affairs of passion, should they occur, must transpire entirely behind closed stateroom doors, and were not to be discussed with others. A few of his friends found this rule cramping. Also, unlike other owners of yachts in the Mediterranean, Ari did not offer young members of his crew as escorts to unescorted ladies. A strict line of status between guests and crew was drawn. In fact, Ari once fired a sailor whom he had seen squiring a lady guest. On the first stops of the August cruise for Jackie, Ari had closeted himself in his quarters. Jackie was not pleased. Through the Roosevelts, she let it be known that she expected him to escort her when she went ashore. Almost reluctantly, he did.

Onassis had learned about the importance of mid-cruise stops the hard way. Once, the *Christina* had pulled into Venice the day after one of the most important balls of the Venetian social season—and the disappointment of Ari's passengers was quite evident. Another time the *Christina* was bound for Marbella on the southern coast of Spain where, Onassis assured his friends, Ava Gardner waited to join them. But when the yacht arrived in Marbella, Miss Gardner had departed for London, having left Spain two days earlier —a bitter blow to Ari. He quickly learned to plan his schedule of stops with extraordinary care, his secretary was ordered to keep a calendar of European social events and to keep track of who was where, and he stopped counting on people as famously unreliable as Ava Gardner.

When the *Christina* docked, her passengers would head for shore with remarkable alacrity. And on shore, life was determinedly gay—so gay, indeed, that often a note of desperation seemed to enter the activities, just as occasionally it did at sea. Mrs. Bob Considine recalls one evening in Majorca when Ari's guests took over the orchestra in a local club. The late Elsa Maxwell played the piano, and Prince Rainier and Maria Callas tried their hands at a variety of other instruments. At the height of things, photographer Jerome Zerbe snatched off Millie Considine's wig, put it on his own head, and asked Princess Grace for a dance. At another party, this one in Monaco, twenty-two members of a Hawaiian and Mexican orchestra were flown in from somewhere, and when the music was still not boisterous enough to suit Ari, he and Callas set out to prowl nightspots for more musicians. They led the new musicians back to the *Christina*—Ari at the head of the procession, like the Pied Piper, and Maria just behind him, tootling on a saxophone.

"The *Christina* was most fun when she was at anchor," Ari's friend Melina Mercouri once recalled. But even in the lightest seas—and even with costly new stabilizers that Ari had installed—her most ardent admirers admitted that the palatial showpiece didn't ride as well as other yachts, such as Lady Docker's legendarily ugly *Shemara,* or the *Giviota,* which used to be owned by the Chilean millionaire Arturo Lopez-Wilshaw. The *Christina,* stabilizers notwithstanding, tended to pitch, yaw, twist, and wobble from side to side. Maria Callas was one of Onassis's very few friends who had made the full twenty-four-day Atlantic crossing aboard the boat. The trip was so rough that many crewmen were too seasick to work, yet Maria did not seem to mind. It was early in her romance with Ari, and even in the worst weather, she would appear with him on deck. They would sit side by side in deck chairs, like young lovers, or, according to one crewman, "walk like sleepwalkers" holding hands.

Though the *Christina* had two French chefs, most guests admitted that the food aboard the yacht was undistinguished—another reason why the stops at ports were looked forward to so eagerly. Onassis had no palate for the subtleties of French cuisine and, caring little, exercised scant supervision over what his kitchen staff prepared. There were other, less obvious, shortcomings to life aboard the *Christina*. Its crew had been called "the worst paid in the Mediterranean," and by the time of Jackie's August cruise, the original German and Greek sailors had all left Onassis, and he was settling for young, inexperienced part-time seamen, picked up here and there for short periods, and they were always complaining about the quality of the food served them.

For all his wealth, Ari Onassis was something of a tightwad. It had been a fellow yachtsman, Embericos, who first persuaded Onassis of the importance of making petty economies, particularly where they involved the crew. "Look into the garbage cans in the crew's kitchen," Mr. Embericos had advised. And, grotesque as it seems, Onassis had done just that. He had made a surprise visit to the crew's kitchen and, yanking the lids from the garbage pails, plunged his hands deep into their unlovely contents. Coming up with handfuls of uneaten spaghetti, he cried angrily, "Why has this food been thrown away?" From then on, the strictest buying economies were undertaken and, when Jackie Kennedy boarded the yacht the crew was being served no vegetables except beans, no meat but frozen chicken. In the crew's quarters, Ari had become known as *skilapsaro*—the shark.

Of course none of this fazed Ari Onassis. But the whole style of the *Christina,* its jukebox opulence, his humdrum menus, and the boisterous, roughneck style of its burly host, the raucous quality of his entertainments, did seem remarkably at variance with the dainty style in which Jackie Kennedy had redecorated the White House, her lovely candlelit parties, her concerts, recitals, and quartets—compared with Onassis, their styles seemed to blend like olive oil and Chanel Number Five. And yet Jackie enjoyed her cruise on the *Christina,* the leisured visits to the ancient Greek islands where she shopped for gifts for friends and her children. Dining one night in a mountaintop restaurant overlooking the sea, she said that she had never had a pleasanter, more relaxed time.

When at last the cruise was over, she seemed almost sad to leave. But there were things to do, official duties to peform, back home in Washington, and she had to face them. There was, among other things, a trip to Texas coming up. For it, her husband had told her to assemble a wardrobe "that will show those rich Texas broads what it's like to be well-dressed." She was going home to do just that.

16

Widow

WHEN IT WAS all over, she seemed to fall apart. When she spoke of the assassination in Dallas, and the events that followed it, her account was so disjointed as to be incoherent. Her speech slurred, her eyes darted, she seemed frightened of everyone and anything that moved. The realization of what she had undergone had seemed to strike her all at once when she moved out of the White House and into the Georgetown house that Averell Harriman had made available to her—a delayed reaction, an aftershock. She suddenly looked, her relatives and friends thought, terrible—disheveled, haggard, with dark circles under her eyes, and she seemed to have lost all interest in her clothes or her appearance. In the weeks following Kennedy's murder, those close to her began to be afraid that Jackie was losing her mind.

One thought of crazy Aunt Edith Beale in her ramshackle mansion in East Hampton, spending most of her days in an unmade bed, boiling potatoes for her meals from a hot plate on a bedside table—the house full of cats and their droppings, raccoons in the attic that were encouraged with loaves of bread left out for them. Edith had always been peculiar, but it was after her husband had left her that she had begun to disintegrate into what she was now. Would Jackie follow that pattern? One thought, too, of her father and uncle Bud, both killed by drink. Would that become Jackie's fate as well? Of course it wouldn't, but in those winter weeks following the funeral and the burial at Arlington, her family was deeply worried. One of her Bouvier uncles by marriage died, and when Jackie paid a condolence call on her aunt all she could talk about was death. Death consumed her, it followed her wherever she went, it would not leave her alone; was she herself perhaps an angel, or agent, of death? Her father had died, three of her five pregnancies had ended in death, and now her husband was dead. Everywhere she went were reminders of death as more and more memorials to John F. Kennedy were dedicated all over the world—streets, plazas, airports.

Of course, as the world knows, from the moment she stepped off the Presidential plane at Andrews Air Force Base on the night of November 22, 1963 in the glare of the television cameras, to the afternoon of November 25, when she lighted the eternal flame at Arlington, she was magnificent. Later she would say that, at the time she felt as though she had suddenly been given superhuman powers, powers she had never remotely suspected she possessed. It was as though an invisible pair of white wings had been provided that would carry her, buoy her like a great bird, through those next few days. On the plane she had been urged to change her dress, which was spattered with blood. She refused. No, the television cameras and the world must see the blood, must react with shock at what had happened. The public must shudder and clutch at its throat and avert its eyes in shame and horror. What had happened must be brought home to the public with as much violence as the deed itself had entailed, and the bloody skirt would do it. It was a theatrical gesture, to be sure, but it was a moment for drama, and she knew it.

When she arrived at the White House that night, her mother and Hughdie were waiting. She was urged to take a sleeping pill. She refused. She would have to be up at 4:00 A.M. to begin planning for the murdered President's funeral and she wanted to be possessed of all her senses, not groggy from a pill. She talked and talked, going over what had happened again and again, never crying, refusing to change the dress, the bloodied stockings. The children, when the news had come from Dallas, had been whisked to the Auchinclosses' house in O Street. She ordered them returned to their own beds in the White House. They—particularly Caroline—had to be told. She could not quite bear to do this, and this task fell to their nurse, Maude Shaw, who (as she recalled later to William Manchester) went to Caroline's room and said, "Your father has been shot. They took him to a hospital, but the doctors couldn't make him better. So, your father has gone to look after Patrick. Patrick was so lonely in heaven. He didn't know anybody there. Now he has the best friend anyone could have . . . God is making your father a guardian angel over you and your mother, and his light will shine down on you always.

His light is shining now, and he's watching you, and he's loving you, and he always will."

For some reason, Jackie wanted her mother to sleep in Jack Kennedy's bed. Then, as she moved toward her own bedroom she suddenly turned to her stepfather and said, "Uncle Hugh, I don't want to sleep alone." And so Hughdie Auchincloss—dear old Hughdie, whom many people found old-fashioned and not a little dull, who never had much in the way of conversation and no humor whatsoever, but whom no one could say was not invariably kind—went into her bedroom and lay down beside her on her bed, and held her while she tried to sleep.

Part
Three

17

Celebrity

THERE WERE TOUCHES provided to the President's funeral, made at her insistence, which were pure theater. Yet for some reason, they worked. There was her decision, for instance, to walk the eight blocks from the White House to the services at St. Matthew's. It was both a dramatic decision and an unusual one. Funeral processions on foot are rare in the United States and other English-speaking countries; they are a Latin custom. And yet she had known instinctively how moving it would be, to the public in front of their television sets, to see the President's widow walking, her veiled head slightly lowered, her shoulders straight, in the strong, good stride of an accomplished horsewoman. The walk added a note of grace and also of humility. Originally, she had wanted to walk all the way from the Capitol to the church, but she was dissuaded from this with the argument that many of the elder statesmen in the procession might not have the stamina for such a journey.

St. Matthew's had been her decision also. The Church hierarchy had wanted the funeral held in Washington's huge new Shrine of the Immaculate Conception, the largest Roman Catholic church in America. But Mrs. Kennedy was adamant. The smaller, older St. Matthew's had been where the President had worshiped, and by demanding a setting that was less pretentious she achieved an effect that was emotionally much more powerful. Then there was her choice of the Black Watch pipes to accompany the President's bier on its journey to the cathedral. Normally, one of the Armed Forces bands would have been chosen to provide the music, but the Black Watch had performed a tattoo on the White House lawn just nine days earlier, the President had admired the haunting sound of the bagpipes, and so the Black Watch was given the assignment.

Practically every detail of the funeral was planned and orchestrated by Mrs. Kennedy for maximum effect. On the Saturday before the Monday services, a memorial mass had been scheduled at the White House. It was to have been celebrated in the Family Dining Room, where an impromptu altar had been set up in front of rows of folding chairs. The minute she entered the room, however, she had decided that the setting was not sufficiently dignified, and the mass was moved to the East Room, where the President was lying in state under chandeliers draped with black bunting. Then there was her choice of Arlington National Cemetery for the burial. The rest of the Kennedy family was very much opposed to this. They felt strongly that he should be buried in the family plot in Brookline, Massachusetts, with his older brother and all the other Kennedys. But once again Jackie was determined to prevail. He belonged, she said, not to her or to the Kennedys but to the nation. Arlington it would be. Then there was her controversial decision to have an eternal flame burn at the gravesite. Once again, this seemed very European, modeled as it was on the flame that burns at the Tomb of the Unknown Soldier beneath the Arc de Triomphe in Paris. There were some who felt that an eternal flame was going a bit too far in the direction of theatricality. But, once again, Jacqueline Kennedy prevailed and, today, when one visits the gravesite at Arlington, and watches the dancing light for a moment or two, one cannot help but agree that her decision was the right one.

The two most stirring moments of the funeral were provided by the President's widow alone. At the end of the services at St. Matthew's, she reached out her hand and briefly touched the casket, and, at a whispered reminder from his mother, little John Kennedy saluted it.

Following the burial, there was a reception at the White House and if, at that point, Jackie had seemed drawn and haggard and exhausted, no one would have blamed her. For the last three days she had had almost no sleep. But, instead, she was almost radiant, standing in the Red Room receiving a long procession of dignitaries—Charles de Gaulle, Prince Philip, Haile Selassie, Eamon de Valera—smiling, shaking hands, offering a personal word of thanks to each in the huge line. On and on the procession went, and she showed no signs of flagging, murmuring, again and again, "Thank you so much for coming . . . Thank you so much . . ." And even when the procession ended, and the reception was over, her day was not ended. What most people, in the turmoil of the past few days, had forgotten but what she had not, was that the day of the funeral, November 25, was also John F. Kennedy, Jr.'s, third birthday. Upstairs, in the Family Sitting Room, the birthday party was under way. Places were being set at table—with John at the head—and presents were being arranged. Soon she would join the rest of her family for the party, the lighting and blowing out of candles, the opening of the presents—trucks, a fire engine—the noisemakers and paper hats, the singing and the games, the birthday cake and the ice cream. It had been suggested to her that, in light of the circumstances, the festive birthday party might have been postponed. She would not hear of it. John might be too young to understand his father's death and the funeral, but he could not have understood putting off the party he had been looking forward to for weeks. And it seemed to his mother perfectly appropriate that three days of sorrow and mourning should close with a gay celebration of life.

In a sense, Jacqueline Kennedy may have planned her husband's funeral too perfectly. Its emotional impact had been so powerful, her role at the center of it had been so pivotal, her dignity and composure so complete, that to the public—to the entire world—she emerged as a kind of paragon. By the evening of November 25, 1963, Jacqueline Kennedy had become the most famous woman in the world and the most admired. The world now expected nothing short of perfection from her in everything she undertook, or said, or did. What the world expected of her now was, of course, the impossible, and whenever she would fail to deliver the impossible the world would question her, and wonder why.

At the same time, there was a large part of the public that was more cynical, more jealous. They were convinced that their great idols all had feet of basest clay, and they were now voraciously waiting for a good look at those feet. To some, she seemed *too* perfect. They longed to see Jackie Kennedy make that first false step that would reveal her ordinariness.

Every move she made was examined and dissected, analyzed and laid open for interpretation. Why, for example, after emerging from her period of mourning, would she allow herself to be photographed outside a fashionable restaurant wearing a mini-skirt? It made her look bowlegged. Why would she allow herself to be escorted to a Manhattan discotheque by a somewhat younger man (director Mike Nichols)? Was it proper that she had appeared at the Seville Fair in a Spanish costume, complete with combs and mantilla? Why was she cruising the Adriatic on the Charles Wrightsmans' yacht, and not staying home and caring for her children? Was a man like Frank Sinatra sufficiently reputable to be her friend, as he appeared to be? A part of her public, at least, seemed to want to turn her into a kind of chic, national nun. She was criticized as much for things she did not do as for things she did. She had failed to vote in the 1964 Presidential election. At the dedication of the Jacqueline Bouvier Kennedy Garden at the White House she had failed to attend. Why? Whom was she high-hatting now? Did she consider having lunch with Marlon Brando more important than these weighty national events? Others complained that she was spoiled and pampered. She was the first widow of an American President to have Secret Service protection for herself and her children, for example, and to be provided with an office and a secretarial staff at taxpayers' expense —she, a rich woman, who had benefited handsomely from her husband's will.

One trouble was that newspaper and magazine editors had discovered that her face, on their covers, was box office, that not even the news of another marriage for Elizabeth Taylor sold more newspapers and magazines. Manfully the editors labored to satisfy their readers' cravings for Jackie stories. And the editors' problem was that a great deal of what she did did not make particularly exciting story material. It was not hot copy that she was devoting a lot of time to creating the John F. Kennedy Memorial Library at Harvard, and to the monument that was to mark his grave at Arlington Cemetery. Readers would merely yawn over details like these. Readers wanted to know about the men in her life, whether they stayed over for breakfast, and what they ate. These were details, needless to say, which she was unwilling to reveal.

She did not, meanwhile, go out that much, nor did she entertain that often. She herself had embarked upon a policy of granting no interviews to the press, and her press secretary, Pamela Turnure, had become extraordinarily agile and adroit at fielding questions from the press with bland, uninteresting answers. Faced with this frustrating situation, the editors and Jackie-writers had two choices. They could resort to a keyhole approach, which involved bribing doormen, delivery boys, servants, neighbors, waiters, bartenders, taxi drivers, anyone who might have glimpsed one of her comings or goings. Or they could simply make things up. As the months wore on following President Kennedy's murder, this approach was taken with increasing frequency. As a giant public figure, furthermore, there was no way she could fight back with denials of these stories without calling more attention to them and selling more newspapers and magazines.

Her initial reaction to the fictitious reports about her doings, as well as to stories which contained a germ of truth and which had obviously been extracted from servants and tradespeople, was anger. It began to seem to her that the same "they" who had shot her husband in Dallas were now bent on commercializing and degrading her. She became suspicious of everyone. Her friends were instructed not to talk to reporters under threat of banishment from her threshold forever. Pamela Turnure was told not to reveal even such simple matters as what current books she was reading or what breed of dog she liked, lest that information be exploited for commercial purposes. A young woman who was giving piano lessons to Caroline Kennedy and who revealed that fact accidentally to a journalist begged that it not be included in a story (of course it was), because she might lose her pupil. A cook who let it be known that Mrs. Kennedy was dieting was fired. Still another cook, Annemarie Huste, was dismissed because Mrs. Kennedy suspected that Annemarie planned to write a book about her boss. (Actually, Annemarie was writing a cookbook, and has since published two cookbooks, neither of which contains references to Mrs. Kennedy.) A private limousine service which Jackie occasionally used was advised that no individual driver could be dispatched for her more than twice, so that no man would have knowledge of her frequent destinations. All these precautions were taken in the name of a single goal: privacy for herself and her children.

It was for privacy that, in the autumn of 1964, she moved from Washington to New York and into a fifteen-room cooperative apartment at 1040 Fifth Avenue, overlooking Central Park, the Metropolitan Museum, and the reservoir. New York has a reputation of being a blasé city, used to seeing celebrities on the streets, a city where a celebrity, though noticed, is usually not pestered, a place where a certain amount of anonymity can be achieved. In Jackie's case, however, this would turn out to be only partly true. She had no sooner moved into 1040 Fifth than scores of the curious lined the park benches opposite the building, waiting for a glimpse of their heroine emerging. Though the building already had exceptional security, with its new tenant the security measures escalated. Soon neighbors in the building were complaining that they could not get deliveries from local shops and services, because of the gamut of inspections deliverymen had to go through before they could leave or enter. Laundresses complained of being frisked by Secret Service men in the basement laundry room. Still, the address had some personal advantages for Jackie herself. Her friends, the McGeorge Bundys, lived in the building. Her sister Lee lived just down the street at 969. Her stepbrother, Yusha Auchincloss, was just a few blocks away at 1105 Park Avenue. Farther downtown, Jackie established a four-room office where she could headquarter her Kennedy Library work at 400 Park Avenue, assisted by secretaries Pamela Turnure and Nancy Tuckerman.

In the offices of the newspaper and magazine editors, meanwhile, there was no visible abatement in the thirst for more Jackie stories. If anything, the thirst seemed to increase, to have become unquenchable. The more she tried to keep her private life a secret, the more curious about it the public seemed to be. The more she barricaded herself behind elaborate screens

145

of privacy, the greater seemed to be her allure, her mystery, and the more heated and sophisticated became the attempts to invade that privacy. If she lunched at a certain restaurant, the proprietor or his public-relations man would quickly telephone the news to *Women's Wear Daily,* whose photographers would be waiting for her when she came out the door. That newspaper had christened her "Her Elegance." One New York photographer, Ron Galella—whose peeping Tom techniques included hiding behind loaded coat-racks with his camera and aiming it through windows —was particularly merciless in his pursuit of her. He was, he explained, just another working stiff, trying to earn a living; he could sell photographs of Jackie for quite a bit of money. East Side dress shops developed various tricks to persuade customers that Jackie shopped at their establishments, and to move merchandise—such as accepting fake telephone calls and saying, within customers' earshot, "Yes, Mrs. Kennedy, we have that little top in your size. Shall I have it sent over?" Immediately all the little tops on the rack would be snatched up.

It began to seem, in fact, that if she really wanted privacy she was using the wrong tactic. If, for example, she had agreed to hold monthly press conferences—at which she was very skillful—and to answer reporters' questions on some sort of regular basis, the saga of her daily life might have begun to seem considerably less dramatic and provocative—even dull—and the public's interest in Mrs. Kennedy's doings and opinions might have diminished to no interest whatsoever. But there were some who suspected that this was not really what she wanted, either.

She was trying, of course, to reconcile two irreconcilable forces—fame and privacy. She enjoyed both. Having had, and liked, a taste of life at the center of the stage, she was unwilling to give it up. Publicity, particularly when it is flattering, is gratifying, and she courted that kind. When, for example, she visited

Spain as the guest of the Duke and Duchess of Alba, when she visited the Spanish Ambassador to the Holy See in Rome and had another audience with the Pontiff, and when she voyaged to Cambodia to be entertained by Prince Sihanouk and visit the jungle ruins of Angkor Wat, she graciously posed for the photographers from *Life* and *Look,* and was not at all displeased when these cultivated, high-toned activities made the covers of the glossy magazines. But at the same time she could not seem to accept the fact that sniffing at the heels of the responsible journalists ran, inevitably, the gossips. She could not have the splendors of Angkor Wat without the bitchy babblings of Suzy Knickerbocker. What she wanted was to have her cake and eat it too—always a difficult request.

What she also needed, it began to seem in the months following the President's death, was someone to lean on, to take care of her, to guide and comfort her. Once, when she was small, Janet Bouvier had received a telephone call from a New York policeman who said, "I have a little girl here. I can't make out her name, but she knows her telephone number. Is she yours?" It was Jackie. She and her nurse, it seemed, had become separated in Central Park, and while the nurse searched frantically for her, fearing that she had been kidnapped, Jackie had calmly walked up to a policeman and said, "My nurse is lost."

Now, in a sense, her nurse was lost again. Though she had no lack of social poise and charm, there was also a side of her that was soft, dependent, uncertain and insecure. She needed a stronger person whose elbow she could take. At first, that elbow had been provided by her father. When he had failed her, she had turned to Uncle Hugh. Uncle Hugh had been replaced by an even more dominant figure, Jack Kennedy, and she needed to be dominated. Though she hadn't always relished the things he had told her to do, she had usually done them obediently enough. She had grown up in a man's world—of money, business, power, and

147

politics—where a woman's role was much more passive. Women were cared for by men who provided a woman with her "security," as Janet Auchincloss often put it. Now that Jack was dead, where was Jackie's security to come from?

More and more she had begun to rely on an even more forceful personality than her late husband, his younger brother, Bobby. During the days following the assassination, he had been a tower of strength for her. Those details of the funeral that she had not planned herself she had planned with Bobby Kennedy. All through that next year, while she was living in Georgetown, Bobby had been her most frequent visitor. He had wholeheartedly assumed the position of head of the Kennedy clan, and had become the surrogate father of Jackie's children—taking them on outings with his own brood of nine. Now that he was a Senator from New York, he was frequently in Manhattan, and was always popping in on Jackie at the apartment to keep her company and see how she was doing. He had become her chief collaborator on the Kennedy Library project and, when he was not in town, they talked on the telephone almost daily. There was nothing romantic in the relationship—Bobby was one of the most solidly married men in Washington, and Jackie got along well with bubbly, giggly Ethel—but he had become her mentor, her guardian and protector. Soon there was no decision, small or large—her children's schooling, for example—that she made without discussing it first with Bobby, and hearing what he had to say. He was so reliable, so dependable, she often said. And she still needed to depend.

18

The

Book

ONE OF JOHN F. Kennedy's favorite writers had been William Manchester. Kennedy particularly admired Manchester's books and articles that had dealt with foreign affairs and, in 1962, the tall, diffident Massachusetts-born author and Wesleyan University professor had interviewed Kennedy extensively for a book published that year, *Portrait of a President,* which Kennedy had also liked. Therefore, shortly after the assassination, when publishing circles learned that Manchester was planning a book on the events in Dallas, it seemed an appropriate marriage of author and subject matter.

Meanwhile, another tall, diffident man, Evan Thomas, had become a senior editor at the prestigious New York publishing house of Harper & Row, and had more or less established himself as Harper & Row's special expert on dealing with the writings of Very Important People. In late 1954, when Senator Kennedy was recovering from the second of his two back operations at New York's Hospital for Special Surgery, Kennedy sent two chapters of a book he was writing to Thomas, and asked Thomas whether he thought the project showed promise as a book-length work, or should be developed as a series of magazine articles. The book was to be called *Profiles in Courage,* and Kennedy was writing it flat on his back, on a board propped up in front of him, from extensive research that was being fed to him by his friend Theodore Sorensen. (Later, it would be rumored that Kennedy had written very little of the book himself, and that Sorensen had done most of the actual writing, though Kennedy took full credit for authorship.) Evan Thomas liked what he read, and immediately went to visit Kennedy at the hospital. He persuaded Kennedy to consider his material as a book, which Harper would be eager to publish. *Profiles in Courage* was published in January, 1956, and in his preface Jack Kennedy had written, "The editorial suggestions, understanding cooperation and initial encouragement which I received from Evan Thomas of Harper & Brothers made this book possible."

Profiles in Courage was an immediate success, and seemed to mark the beginning of a long, sunny relationship between Harper—and Evan Thomas in particular—and the Kennedy family. In 1957, Jack Kennedy's book won the Pulitzer Prize for biography, and the book went into a number of later editions— Inaugural, Memorial, Young Readers, and Perennial paperback. In all editions, including foreign, book clubs, and paperback, the book sold millions of copies. (When the Memorial edition was published in 1964, Harper turned over all its publisher's profits to establish a John F. Kennedy Memorial Award in biography and history.) Evan Thomas had gone on to be Kennedy's editor for *The Strategy of Peace,* and had consulted with Sorensen in the White House while *To Turn the Tide* was being put together—a collection of President Kennedy's statements and speeches from his election through the 1961 adjournment of Congress. Another volume of Kennedy speeches, *The Burden and the Glory* was in preparation at the time of the assassination.

In the meantime, Evan Thomas had also become Bobby Kennedy's editor, and Harper his publisher. Harper had published Bobby's *The Enemy Within,* an account of the Senate's investigation of labor and management, and this had been followed by *Just Friends and Brave Enemies,* and *The Pursuit of Justice*—all Kennedy titles had developed something of a drum-roll sonority. When Thomas first heard of the William Manchester project, however—from Pierre Salinger who had stayed on in the White House under Johnson —he had little interest in it. It seemed to Thomas an attempt to commercialize a national tragedy. Also, William Manchester at the time was under contract to Little, Brown & Company. But it was not long before Thomas received an invitation to come to Bobby Kennedy's office. Bobby Kennedy explained that Mr. Manchester had been "authorized" by the Kennedy family to do the book, that Manchester's would be the definitive volume on the assassination, that the Kennedys had agreed to cooperate with Manchester and no one else on the subject, and that the family wanted Harper & Row to publish the book. To relieve the aura of commercialism from the project, Bobby asked that Harper—though not the author—turn over the bulk of any publishing profits from the book to the Kennedy Library. The enitre family was solidly behind Mr. Manchester, Bobby explained, and so was Jackie, who would make a single exception to her rule of silence with journalists, and would submit to a series of taped interviews with Mr. Manchester. On this basis, Evan Thomas agreed, and requested Little, Brown to release Manchester from his contract. In the gentlemanly way of publishing houses, Little, Brown agreed to the release.

What was to ensue was to turn out to be not gentlemanly at all. In March, 1966, William Manchester submitted his manuscript to Harper & Row. It was titled *The Death of a President,* and it was a bulky package of typescript. Thomas and two associate editors read the script with mounting enthusiasm; it was going to be, they felt sure, a huge success. In the process of this initial reading, Thomas routinely queried a number of facts and passages, suggested certain deletions and additions, and proposed a few structural changes and revisions—all of which an author normally expects from a conscientious editor. Bobby Kennedy, meanwhile, had asked that two of his friends, John Seigenthaler and Edwin Guthman, be permitted to look over the manuscript. This seemed reasonable enough. Seigenthaler was publisher of the *Nashville Tennessean,* and Guthman was news editor of the *Los Angeles Times,* and had won a Pulitzer Prize for news reporting. A book, Bobby Kennedy seemed to feel, could not have too many editors.

Copies of Thomas's edited manuscript were prepared for Seigenthaler and Guthman and, with that, editing the book became the project of a committee. Following the rule that anyone who is asked for advice will give it, both Seigenthaler and Guthman had suggestions for revisions, deletions, and additions, and naturally the two men did not necessarily agree with one another. It was then necessary for Evan Thomas to begin shuttling between New York, Washington, Los Angeles, and Nashville in an attempt to collate all the various editorial comments and to bring them together into some sort of cohesive whole. Next, Bobby Kennedy asked that a copy of the manuscript be given to Arthur Schlesinger, Jr., the author of *A Thousand Days,* which the family considered the definitive work on the Kennedy presidency. Schlesinger read the manuscript, and had comments of his own.

Though it might have begun to seem as though too many cooks were already at work ruining the stew, William Manchester had, in the meantime, given a reading copy of *The Death of a President* to his friend and fellow Wesleyan professor, Richard N. Goodwin. Goodwin was also a friend of the Kennedys and, it seemed to Manchester, might serve as a useful mediator between the author and the House of Kennedy and their many advisors. Richard Goodwin added his thoughts on the book, and it was now Evan Thomas's thankless job to sort out comments from six different critics—criticism that now ran nearly as long as the original manuscript. The two people who might have been expected to have the strongest reactions to the book—Bobby Kennedy and Jackie—had not read it. They did not want to.

A note of urgency had also entered the proceedings. Through the publishing grapevine it had been heard that another, unauthorized book on the assassination was in the works at a rival publishing house, and Thomas and Bobby Kennedy agreed that it was essential that *The Death of a President* get to the bookstalls as rapidly as possible. Because of the hurry, Manchester was persuaded to accept nearly all the proposed alterations and emendations of Mssrs. Seigenthaler, Guthman, Goodwin, Schlesinger, along with what the three Harper & Row editors had to say, and the result—a considerably emasculated version of the original—was rushed to the printer. Manchester's literary agent, Don Congdon, had meanwhile sold serialization rights of the book to *Look* magazine, which planned to begin publishing installments in the late summer of 1966.

Bobby Kennedy had approved of the *Look* serialization, and on July 29 he sent a telegram to Manchester, saying:

Should any inquiries arise re the manuscript of your book I would like to state the following:

While I have not read William Manchester's account of the death of President Kennedy I know of the President's respect for Mr. Manchester as an historian and a reporter. I understand others have plans to publish books regarding the events of November 22, 1963. As this is going to be the subject of a book and since Mr. Manchester in his research had access to more information and sources than any other writer, members of the Kennedy family will place no obstacle in the way of publication of his work.

However if Mr. Manchester's account is published in segments or excerpts I would expect that incidents would not be taken out of context or summarized in any way which might distort the facts of, or the events relating to, President Kennedy's death.

This seemed a fair enough green light, and certainly neither Harper nor *Look* had any intention of summarizing or distorting facts.

The news of the *Look* serialization, however, and the price that Manchester was reportedly being paid by the magazine—$665,000—brought Jackie strongly into the picture for the first time, and she was furious. She immediately asked Manchester and *Look* to cancel the serialization agreement. The reason, she said, was that serialization would be harmful because sections "might be printed out of context." Of course she had no idea whether the magazine planned to print portions "out of context" or not, and the whole concept of "out of context" is a particularly fuzzy one. In a sense, any magazine serialization is printed out of context since the reader must wait to see what happens from one issue to the next. On the other hand, the aim of any serialization is to give the reader, at the end of the series, a completed context. Since Jacqueline Kennedy had steadfastly refused to read the book she was on particularly shaky ground.

The reasons she did *not* give for objecting to the *Look* serialization were more interesting. For one thing, the *Look* deal, one of the biggest in magazine history, certainly smacked to her of commercialization, of exploitation of her husband's murder, the exact things that Evan Thomas had found distasteful about the project to begin with. *Look* was a big, glossy, popular magazine—one of the most commercially successful in the country at the time. It had lots of mass, not much class. If, say, the book were to be serialized in a smaller, more genteel magazine like *American*

154

Heritage or the *Kenyon Review,* that would not have struck her as so outrageous. At one point she had said —somewhat naively, to be sure—that she had expected that the Manchester book would be "a little black reference volume," buried away in library shelves for scholars of history. The fact that the book was obviously being treated as a huge commercial property came as a shock.

And doubtless there was another unconscious reason. Many rich people do not at all like the idea of writers or artists becoming rich. The rich like to think of themselves as "patrons" of the arts, and certainly Jackie was a patron of the arts in good standing. She had often said that the people she most enjoyed being around were writers, painters, photographers, but perhaps what she really meant were writers, painters, and photographers who needed her help, her support, her patronage. Writers were supposed to be lonely souls who slaved away in dark little Greenwich Village garrets and had trouble meeting their fuel bills. Until *Look* came along, William Manchester had fitted that category nicely—a professor at a small New England college, struggling to support a wife and three children, whose previous books, though well received critically, had had small sales. The *Kenyon Review* would not have handed him $665,000 for his work. It was the thought of him making all that money from her husband's death that must have outraged her most of all.

The fact that John F. Kennedy had made quite a bit of money from *Profiles in Courage* seemed quite irrelevant. Her husband had been a statesman, not a writer, and his books had been mere adjuncts to his statesmanship. Sections of *Profiles in Courage,* in or out of context, had been serialized in *Harper's Magazine.* Well, *Harper's* had more cachet than *Look.* If it had been $600 from *Harper's* and not $665,000 from *Look,* she could probably have accepted it.

Now there was a series of meetings between Thomas, several other Harper editors, Mr. Seigenthaler, and

Jackie's press secretary Pamela Turnure. Passages in the book were carefully marked for Mrs. Kennedy's consideration, and further deletions and changes were offered in hopes of mollifying her. Evan Thomas suggested diplomatically that Mrs. Kennedy and Manchester get together and communicate directly, rather than through intermediaries, in hopes of working out some amicable solution. On the one hand, everyone wanted Mrs. Kennedy to be happy with the book because of who she was. On the other hand, no one saw any reason—legal or otherwise—for obeying her instructions absolutely.

In the meantime, as she had expected, Bobby Kennedy had sprung to Jackie's defense. Now he, too, opposed the *Look* serialization, though he had previously approved it. There was a bizarre meeting at Bobby Kennedy's Hickory Hill in Virginia between Manchester, Bobby, and Richard Goodwin, during which Bobby, splashing in the swimming pool, would fire questions at Manchester and then duck his head underwater when Manchester would try to answer. At the same time, Jackie's objections had prompted all the other advisors on the book—Seigenthal, Schlesinger, Miss Turnure, *et al.*—to come up with all sorts of new lists of suggestions and proposals for changes. The Kennedy-Manchester controversy raged in the press and, with so many copies of the manuscript floating around, it was possible for the press to obtain and quote long sections of supposedly "offensive" material from the book, which only added fuel to the fire.

Meanwhile, while a great many other people were making suggestions for changes, deletions, additions, and other emendations to his manuscript, William Manchester was making some changes of his own. He decided, among other things, to revise the dedication page. The book had originally been dedicated: "For the two who loved him most. And for all in whose hearts he still lives—A watchman of honor who never sleeps." Perhaps it sounded too windy, too mawkish. He decided to delete "For the two who loved him most." He has never said who "the two who loved him most" were intended to be. "It was a very personal thing," he says. But he does say that neither of the "two" he had in mind was Jackie.

A "final" reading on behalf of the Kennedy family by Richard Goodwin was scheduled for November. Nineteen sixty-six, to have been the book's publication year, was slipping away, but Goodwin, it seemed, could not read the proofs because he had departed for a holiday in Italy. William Manchester left for a rest in London. Kennedy representatives continued to barrage both *Look* and Harper with more requests for changes, and both book and magazine publication were postponed until some indefinite date in 1967.

On November 21, 1966, Jacqueline Kennedy summoned both Evan Thomas and Cass Canfield, Harper's editor-in-chief, to her apartment. She asked them to carry a letter which she planned to write to Manchester in London, along with a report which Richard Goodwin had promised to write concerning changes in certain passages. Canfield and Thomas enplaned for London where they delivered the letter and report to a weary Manchester who, on reading both documents, agreed to make all the suggested changes. Leaving the London meeting, an also-weary Cass Canfield—who, for a while, had been Jackie's sister's father-in-law—merely shook his head and commented, "Both those girls like to get their own way."

Then both Cass Canfield and Gardner Cowles, chairman of *Look,* wrote to Jackie to say that the changes she wanted had been made, and suggested that Richard Goodwin and Evan Thomas meet on December 12 to discuss ways in which these supposedly final changes could be incorporated into what it was hoped would be a final book. But on that date Jackie changed her mind again. The changes were not enough. That morning, her lawyers served summonses on both Harper and *Look,* and editors at both companies were informed that there was no basis for further discussion since the matter was in the hands of her attorneys. Four days later, the summonses were followed by Mrs. Kennedy's weeping appearance at the Supreme Court of the State of New York where she asked for an injunction that would forbid the publication of the book by either Harper, *Look,* or William Manchester.

Now the case was on front pages of newspapers across the country, and newspapers, television, and radio stations issued editorials on the controversy. Some sympathized with the President's widow and argued that she was being misused by an avaricious publisher and a greedy, insensitive author. Others took the stance that she was attempting to rewrite American history according to a version which she preferred, that an author's privileges to report the truth were being wilfully curtailed, and that the public's right to know the facts was being abridged by a stubborn, power-mad woman. The publishers issued statements saying that the manuscript had been released by the Kennedy family. The family issued a statement saying that their agreement with the publisher had been breached, and for the next few weeks more long excerpts of the still-unpublished book were printed, digested, discussed.

Finally, on January 16, 1967, the case was settled out of court when William Manchester capitulated and offered to turn an even larger share of his earnings from the book to the Kennedy Library than he had originally offered to do. Mrs. Kennedy, Harper, and Manchester issued a joint statement saying that all differences had been resolved, and that the historical record had in no way been censored. When, in 1968, Harper & Row sent the Kennedy Library a check for $750,000, representing the first year's earnings of *The Death of a President,* Jackie issued a statement to the *New York Times* in which she said, "I think it is so beautiful what Mr. Manchester did . . . all the pain of the book and now this noble gesture, of such generosity, makes the circle come around and close with healing."

As for the public reaction to the case, it was similar to that of the press—mixed. Some people felt sorry for Jackie, felt that she had placed too much trust in William Manchester, and that he had tried to betray that trust. Others, more cynical, noted that it had not been until Manchester had agreed to turn over much of the earnings from his book to her pet project that she had agreed to stop harassing him. Still others, who had admired her stoic composure at the funeral, were disappointed with Jackie, embarrassed by her tearful appearance at the court house, and thought it too bad that she seemed to have become unbuttoned, to have let down the side, to have lost her famous cool. Still others viewed her behavior as a display of autocracy and bad temper; she had actually thought she could rule the country by dictating what the country could and could not read. Up to then, her strong point had been her *politesse*. She had been America's Queen of Manners, but in the Manchester affair she had tried to be Queen of Power.

Later on, William Manchester would ruefully recall hints that he had received from her—from the days when they had first sat down together, over icy pitchers of daiquiris, to tape her recollections of the assassination—that she had begun to take an imperial view of herself and her position. In a letter to another author who wanted to write a book on the same subject (a carbon of which she sent to Manchester), she wrote that she had "hired" Manchester exclusively for the job. "If I decide the book should never be published," she added, Manchester would be "reimbursed" for his time and trouble. Though no hiring had taken place, and no reimbursement had even been discussed, this was the way she chose to think of the arrangement. Then there was the point, at the height of the controversy, when she had said to Manchester, rather flippantly, "If it's money you want, I'll give a million." Finally there was the point, having decided definitely to fight the book and said that she knew she was going to win, when she had tossed in the comment, "Anyone who is against me will look like a rat—unless I run off with Eddie Fisher!" In the beginning of their relationship, Jackie had impressed William Manchester as "a very great tragic actress." Later, he would comment that the woman in history she most reminded him of was Marie Antoinette.

Most saddened by the episode, perhaps, was Cass Canfield, the courtly, aristocratic gentleman publisher of the old school. Jackie had been an old friend. Now they no longer spoke. At the time, one of Canfield's favorite restaurants for business lunches had been the Lafayette, in East 50th Street. The fashionable watering place was also one of Jackie's favorite lunching spots. Now, when he would telephone for a reservation, he would be gently told that Mrs. Kennedy had also booked a table for the same date, and so he would go somewhere else for lunch.

In the end, the Kennedy-Manchester affair had become a situation in which no one could possibly win, in which there could be no victors. In fact, in the battle over Manchester's book, everyone lost. The public lost because, despite the joint statement, it was obvious that the book *had* been censored, and by a number of heavy hands. Harper & Row lost. When *The Death of a President* was finally published in April, 1967, it was assumed that what had once been touted as "the book of the century" would remain at the top of the Best Seller list for at least a solid year. But —perhaps because the public had read so many published excerpts from it already, and felt they didn't need to buy the expensive book—the book was a best seller for only a few weeks, and sales were disappointing. Bill Manchester lost, because the book did not either make him rich or earn him nearly as much money as he might have expected. Jackie Kennedy and her Kennedy Library lost because the publishing profits from the book were also smaller than they might have been. And Jackie herself lost a certain share of her former public esteem.

If anyone gained from the affair it was Bobby Kennedy. No one could help but admire the manly way he sprang to the defense of his embattled, widowed sister-in-law—taking her side in the matter even though it had meant reversing his former position, the bold young knight to the rescue of the fair, if perhaps misguided, maiden. Less than a year after the publication of *The Death of a President*, Bobby Kennedy announced his candidacy for the presidency of the United States, and entered the primaries. The consideration with which he buoyed and cared for Jackie, the way he availed himself as a substitute father to her children—all these things were by now well known and would stand him in good stead politically. He had seen what an important political asset Jackie had been to his brother. Now he could see how, in a different way, she could become a political asset to him, and could envision her, perhaps, looking beautiful on the Inaugural dais with him—not standing beside him, of course (that would be "Old Moms" Ethel), but just a few places down.

19

Filling
a Gap

You REMEMBER EXACTLY where you were and what
you were doing when momentous events occur. You
might have been bringing in the garden furniture to
store for winter when the news of John F. Kennedy's
assassination came blaring from an open window of a
passing car. The impact, in November, 1968, when
the world learned that the President's widow was
about to marry an aging Greek shipping tycoon named
Aristotle Onassis was not quite in the same category.
But it was stunning nonetheless. The public reeled
and gasped at the news. Instantly Jackie dropped
again, and sharply, in the public's esteem. The most
coolheaded reaction to this news was simply: *Why?*
And yet it is likely that the event might never have
taken place had it not been for Bobby Kennedy's murder, barely five months earlier, in Los Angeles.

Once more she had lost a strong, assertive older
man whose emotional leadership she needed. The second Kennedy assassination had been shattering
enough, and the ensuing days were even more harrowing. Robert Kennedy's funeral had none of the dignity
that his brother's had had—nor was there any likely
way it could have. It had the wild, distraught quality
of the final act of a Greek tragedy—the curse of the
House of Atreus was being drawn to its conclusion.
The funeral train bearing Senator Kennedy's body
struck and killed a bystander. Storm and fury, the

gnashing of teeth and the beating of breasts seemed to fill the air. And outside 1040 Fifth Avenue throngs of people milled in the streets for a morbid chance to glimpse Jacqueline Kennedy in grief again, while sidewalk vendors set up pushcarts selling hot dogs and frozen custard. The scene outside her building alone might have been enough to cause Jackie to lose faith in her public forever.

One of the first to call at the White House and to offer his condolences after the death of the President had been Aristotle Onassis. He and Jackie had remained friends. There had been frequent dinners in New York in the months following Jackie's move to the city, and there had been more cruises aboard the *Christina*. After Bobby Kennedy's death, Onassis offered her what he inevitably offered his friends—another cruise—and she accepted. When he first proposed marriage, she had demurred. She had consulted her mother and her sister. She asked the advice of Cardinal Cushing, and of others in the Kennedy family. Their reactions to the idea had been mixed. Most opposed to it had been Janet Auchincloss. She thought that the difference in their ages (more than twenty years) was too great, and she had also heard that, though Onassis could be charming, he had a ferocious temper. There were also those who said that Lee had once hoped to marry Onassis and her marriage to Radziwill had already begun to fall apart. But actually Lee urged her sister to accept the marriage proposal. Still, Jackie vacillated.

Then Bobby died, and another great emotional prop was knocked from under her life's support. Who would be her salvation now? There was Ari Onassis, another powerful father-figure reaching out to help. Happiness, it sometimes seems, is the bird in the hand. He offered her a pleasant life. He would make few demands. She could live where she wished. And, though she was now comfortably rich—she would surely never face the poorhouse—she still felt that

163

curious need for "security," financial security. Perhaps it was the growing-up years in the Depression, her mother's complaints about the size of her alimony payments, her parents' constant bickering over dentists' bills, the graveside quarreling among the Bouviers over wills, estates, and trusts—whatever it was, she had learned to draw an equation between money and peace of mind. Onassis offered money to an almost unlimited degree. Consulting almost no one this time, she decided to say yes to him.

To the public, the reaction to the news was one of shock. It seemed as though Ari, the shark, had managed to swallow a particularly juicy fish, and as though Jackie, the poor fish, had swum greedily into the shark's jaws where, though a captive, she was confident of finding treasure. The announcement came with such startling suddenness, for one thing. There was absolutely no public preparation for it. Though Jackie and Onassis had been seen together here and there, the columnists had not made an "item" of them, there had been no hint of a romance. Even Jackie's close relatives were completely taken by surprise. On the day the news broke Jackie had been supposed to have lunch with one of her Bouvier relatives, her cousin Michelle Crouse. Two hours before they were to meet at the restaurant, Nancy Tuckerman had telephoned Mrs. Crouse to break the date because Jackie was flying to Europe. No explanation for the trip was given. Like everyone else, Mrs. Crouse first read about what had happened in the newspapers. Even Nancy Tuckerman was jolted by the news and, when she expressed astonishment, Jackie merely said, "Tucky, you don't know how lonely I've been." Loneliness, then—it was reason enough, and the only reason she would give.

Of course the public would quickly supply her with reasons of its own. At first the reaction was anger at both parties in the marriage—at the aging, swarthy foreigner who, with his ill-gotten billions had managed to purchase America's fairy princess, and at the princess herself who was obviously money-mad, a woman no better than she should be, who had sold herself for an old man's gold. Quickly the reaction turned from anger to mockery. Within days, dozens of off-color Onassis jokes proliferated, most of which centered on alleged activities on their wedding night. *Women's Wear Daily,* which had dubbed her "Her Elegance," now began derisively referring to the pair as "Jackie O" and "Daddy O." The public refused to accept "loneliness" as a motive, nor would it buy the notion that romantic love or any tender feeling was behind Jackie's move. It had to be greed, pure and simple. When the news came out that he had settled something in the neighborhood of five million dollars on her in a pre-marital contract and, in addition, had showered her with a number of precious stones as a wedding gift, the public's worst thoughts were confirmed. She had done it. She had "run off with Eddie Fisher."

Onassis's motives in marrying her were equally suspect. Everyone knew how he liked to surround himself with celebrities from whom he seemed to feel he acquired a certain borrowed luster—Garbo, Callas, the Richard Burtons, Sir Winston Churchill in his dotage, so senile that he seldom knew where he was and yet a perpetual guest on the Onassis yacht. He used these people as window-dressing, as decoration, and they in turn used him for free rides, drinks, and meals. Now he had bagged the biggest celebrity of all, the former American First Lady who, with her connections, would send the former telephone operator and tobacco importer, the crudely educated boy from Smyrna, sailing into the pages of the *Social Register*. As far as the public was concerned, the motives of both Jackie and Ari were base and venal.

Meanwhile, even people who knew and admired them both were forced to admit that they found the union a little odd. In addition to the difference in their

165

ages, there was the difference in their personalities and the styles of life they favored. Ari was rough-hewn, outgoing and gregarious. He drank and swore like a trooper, and loved to stay out all night in the bars of night clubs and noisy discotheques. Jackie was quiet and introspective, disliked large parties, hated bars, and if she stayed up late it was with a book or sketching at her easel. Jackie preferred menus that included desserts such as *framboises à la crème Chantilly*. Ari liked his plates of raw onion slices. Jackie cared about fashion. Ari had no interest in clothes, his shirts were usually rumpled and his suits usually looked as though they had been cut for someone else. Still, there was not a little of Jack Kennedy about him. He, too, was a tough fighter who had fought his way to the top. He was a gambler who liked to win. He was also very much like Jack Bouvier—swashbuckling, party-loving, a lady-killer, a big spender and a *bon vivant*. Or, rather, like the man Jack Bouvier had liked to think of himself as being.

For weeks following the wedding on the island of Skorpios, newspapers, magazines and television were filled with speculation about it. The Presidential election and the Vietnam peace talks were all but forgotten as writers and commentators wrestled with the general question: *why?* What, besides his money, could she see in him? What besides her celebrity, could be her usefulness to him? If the American reaction to the wedding ranged from disappointment to disapproval, the reaction in Europe was one of outrage. A great American lady, it seemed, had turned out to be little more than a tramp who would sell herself for wealth and membership in the freewheeling international set. The attitude expressed in *France Soir* was typical. It called the marriage "sad and shameful."

A year later, in *The Bouviers,* his book on the family, her first cousin John H. Davis felt called upon to offer some sort of explanation, or excuse, for his relative's behavior. "Jacqueline," he wrote courteously, "like many Bouviers, especially her father and grand-father, is highly susceptible to beauty, luxury, and great wealth. Who could put more beauty, luxury, and wealth into her life than Aristotle Onassis? A Greek island all her own. Apartments in all the capitals of Europe. One of the most luxurious yachts in the world. A fortune that made the money President Kennedy had left her seem modest in comparison. A privately owned airline. If in November 1963 'the cloud-capp'd towers, the gorgeous palaces . . . the great globe itself' had been taken away from her, now she would have them back again." Well, yes, perhaps that was part of it, but Mr. Davis's interpretation still made her sound awfully self-indulgent and material-istic.

Her old friend Letitia Baldridge, who had been her social secretary at the White House, had another ex-planation. "She had become a woman without a job," Tish Baldridge says. "Being married to Jack Kennedy was a full-time job. After he died, there was the Ken-nedy Library and then Bob Kennedy's campaign to keep her busy. She's always needed something to do. Onassis offered her a job, as the wife of another very busy man."

What no one may have stopped to consider was that Jackie, at that point, may have been as disgusted with her public as they now appeared to be with her. She had seen the public's worst side—its pettiness, its intrusiveness, its massive bad taste, its collective clod-dishness. In the milling, noisy crowds outside her home during the day while Bobby Kennedy fought for his life—women with their hair in rollers, munching chili dogs and brandishing Instamatics—crowds that made her neighbors devoutly wish that she lived some-where else, she saw, in that scene alone, her public behaving in far worse a fashion than anything she had ever done. If this is my public, she may have thought, then the hell with it. She may have thought—escape! Damn their hides, she may have thought, I will show them I can do exactly as I want, thumb my nose at the slobs, go off to Greece where there's a man who wants me, who can protect me from this sort of thing, where I can slip out of my girdle and lie in the sun. The public, she had learned, would always be around. When she came back, as she would, she would have her public back again but, when she did, she would have it most definitely *on her terms*.

20

Mother

ONE JOB THAT Jacqueline Kennedy had always taken with great seriousness was motherhood. It had been her determination, from the time of the President's death, that her children be allowed to lead completely private lives and, as a result, John and Caroline Kennedy became two of the most protected children in the world, more inaccessible than any royal prince or princess. Outside the tight circle of family, friends, schoolmates and teachers, the walls surrounding the Kennedy children became impregnable. For years their fortress was patrolled by the United States government in the persons of two Secret Service agents assigned to each child, as well as by the family itself and by nurses, governesses, and servants—and the screen of secrecy descended from Jackie herself. "I want them to grow up like normal kids," she would often say. In the process of achieving that goal, of course, she managed to accomplish just the opposite: her children became public curiosities. Both John and

Caroline Kennedy grew up quite aware that they were rather special people, though each reacted to the knowledge in a somewhat different way.

When Jackie first moved to New York, she chose her children's schools, primarily on the basis of their proximity to 1040 Fifth Avenue, and she chose Catholic schools—the Convent of the Sacred Heart, just up the street, for Caroline, and St. David's, around the corner, for John. Later, deciding that both children should also have a secular education, she moved Caroline to the Brearley School on the East Side of Manhattan, and John to the Collegiate School, on the West Side. Her choice of schools was interesting. She did not send Caroline to Miss Chapin's School, which she herself had attended as a girl. Miss Chapin's and Miss Spence's have always been considered New York's two "snob" elementary private day schools for girls. Brearley, though less fashionable, has a reputation for seriousness and academic superiority. Chapin and Spence are known as "rich girls' schools." Brearley is a smart girl's school. Similarly, if Jackie had been choosing John Kennedy's school for fashionability, she would have chosen Buckley or St. Bernard's. Instead she chose stalwart old Collegiate—an excellent school, though on the wrong side of town.

There would be other differences between Jackie's own education and the kind of education she wanted her children to have. Though Jackie had loved Miss Porter's, she chose the less exclusive, more academic Concord Academy in Massachusetts for Caroline when it came time for boarding school. Jackie and Lee had both attended the fashionable sessions of Miss Hubbell's dancing classes, held weekly during the winter months at the Colony Club, where little girls wore their best party dresses and little boys wore Eton jackets and white gloves. There would be none of this for Jackie's children. Instead, Jackie would hire ballerina Maria Tallchief to give Caroline private ballet lessons. (Alas, Miss Tallchief was forced to conclude that

Caroline Kennedy had no talent for ballet.) Jackie had been presented to society at an elaborate debutante party in Newport. There would be no debut for Caroline, who would mark her coming-out year studying art and art history in London. In fact, though many people assumed that in marrying Onassis Jackie was settling for a society kind of life, society and its rituals were what Jackie and her children were deliberately eschewing. Caroline, for example, became eligible for her own listing in the *Social Register* in 1969, and John in 1974. It was not for several years after these dates that Jackie would permit either of her children to be listed in society's little black-and-red book. Until they were old enough to know what society was all about, she seemed to be saying, she did not want them to be considered a part of it.

After their mother's marriage to Onassis, the children's lives continued in the strict but gently guided pattern that Jackie dictated. The great dread, of course, was kidnapping and, after the marriage to Onassis, the dread was much more acute. To the Secret Service protection which the children had already, Onassis added bodyguards of his own. The Secret Service men drove Caroline to Brearley each morning in an unobtrusive car, and stationed themselves outside her classroom door throughout the day. In the afternoon, they escorted her back to the waiting car for the drive home. She could not stroll home with her friends the way the other Brearley girls did. In John's case, he was escorted down from the Onassis apartment and was picked up at the door by the Collegiate bus. The Secret Service men then followed the bus in an unmarked sedan. He was then taken to his first class, and the men repaired to the school basement, where they generally played gin rummy all day long. At the end of the school day, the process reversed itself.

John at least could enjoy the camaraderie and horseplay of the school bus, but there were other restrictions. One of his best friends at Collegiate, for example, was a boy named Barry Cramer. Barry Cramer loved tennis. John himself was an indifferent tennis player—indeed he did not seem brilliant at any sport. Nonetheless, one summer in the early 1970s Barry Cramer had been planning to go to Androscoggin Camp in southwestern Maine, where tennis was the specialty, and when the subject of summer camps was brought up at 1040 Fifth Avenue, John announced that the only camp he would be willing to go to was Barry Cramer's. Jackie then telephoned Barry's mother to ask her about Androscoggin. After the initial shock of realizing that she had Jacqueline Onassis on the other end of the line, Mrs. Cramer described the camp and then added, "But I do think you should know that it's primarily a camp for Jewish boys." Jackie replied that that didn't matter, as long as there was a way for John to attend Sunday mass. Mrs. Cramer said that she was sure this would present no problem. For a while, John was scheduled to go to Androscoggin. Then, all at once, there was another of the periodic kidnap threats. Plans for a summer camp for John had to be cancelled.

To make up for his disappointment, Jackie suggested to John that he invite Barry to come with the family to Skorpios for a summer visit. Barry accepted, and flew over as a guest of the Onassises. The summer, however, was not an unqualified success for either boy. On his return, Barry announced that the trip had been "mostly a big bore." There had been no tennis. Not even a cruise on the *Christina* had amused him. That was "pretty boring, too," he said. He added, "The *Christina* has a pool on it, but it doesn't have a tennis court."

At their respective schools, meanwhile, it was necessary to give the Kennedy children a certain amount of special treatment and attention. At both Brearley and Collegiate, all teachers and staff were required to sign documents swearing that they would never talk to

171

outsiders about Caroline or John. Similar agreements had also to be signed by all those employed in the various Onassis households, and by tutors who came in and out to give the children lessons. Servants were not even permitted to give their own names to reporters.

All applicants for household or tutoring jobs were screened and interrogated by Nancy Tuckerman. Officially, with the remarriage of her boss, Nancy had become an employee of Olympic Airways, though her job remained that of Jackie's private secretary. While Jackie's private, unlisted telephone number was regularly changed, it was always possible to be switched to the apartment by calling the main number of Olympic, to which the apartment was now connected by a tie-line. Nancy was both efficient and tough—with the kind of toughness in dealing with unwanted calls and business that her employer may not have lacked, but disliked having to exercise. All calls to Jackie were screened by Nancy, and so were the children's calls, both outgoing and incoming.

Once an outsider had been screened and accepted by Nancy, however, communication became somewhat easier, almost simple. A young woman who was engaged to give Caroline piano lessons was surprised, on her first visit, to find the Onassis household a relaxed and easy one. Gone were the tensions and suspicions that had surrounded the initial interviews and screening process. She found Caroline a quick, cooperative, and cheerful pupil, with a young teenager's natural reluctance to practice. The piano tutor liked the informal atmosphere of the job and the informal atmosphere of the apartment, where the lady of the house often strolled about in jeans and a T-shirt, and was surprised by the fact that the Onassis butler served tea in his shirtsleeves. The children showed her John Kennedy's collection of model ships in his bedroom, and Caroline Kennedy's wall of framed mementos of her father in hers. She also admired Jackie's breezy relationship with her daughter. "When a lesson was over, she'd come into the room and say, 'Okay, kid, time to hit the books'—even though Caroline, who was a brilliant, straight-A student, didn't really need to hit the books all that much." The piano tutor, however, did find it a bit disconcerting to arrive at the apartment at the appointed hour for the lesson, only to be told that her pupil had been whisked off to Skorpios, or to Capri, or to the coast of Spain, and no one had remembered to notify her. But she was always paid in full for these missed lessons, with checks printed "Jacqueline Bouvier Onassis," and signed by Nancy Tuckerman.

Other Brearley and Collegiate parents also found the Kennedy children a somewhat intimidating presence at their own children's schools, and quickly learned to be apprehensive and uncommunicative when the subject of the Kennedy youngsters came up. It began to seem as though they, too, were expected to keep an oath of silence on the matter and, in fact, they were. They, it was made clear, were on their honor not to discuss Caroline or John. Jackie, of course, was aware of this, and worried that the frightened attitude of other parents was affecting her children's social life —which it naturally was. Parents of John's and Caroline's classmates were often too intimidated to invite the Kennedy children to their own children's parties, and, when Jackie heard of a party to which her children had not been asked, she frequently found herself in the position of telephoning parents and requesting that her children be included. When her children did go to parties, she had begun to make it a general rule that she herself would not attend them, on the theory that her presence would merely draw unnecessary extra attention to their presence. On the rare occasions when the children were permitted to make a public appearance—such as at the Robert F. Kennedy Pro-Celebrity Tennis Tournament in Forest Hills, for instance—she did not appear with them. (At one of these, John Kennedy, grumbling about having to be an usher, kept repeating, "I don't really know how to *do* this.")

And yet, whenever it appeared that either child was in the remotest way being used as a tourist attraction, Jackie was there immediately. Once, in Marbella, Spain, the proprietor of the Marbella Club announced that Caroline Kennedy would appear as a guest star in a bullfight he was staging. Quickly an Onassis jet descended on Marbella, and Caroline was whisked away.

One technique which Jackie used to shield her own small brood from "outsiders" was to surround them, when they were out-of-doors, with hordes of other children who were roughly her children's size. In this she had only to tap the resources of the child-laden clan. When all the Kennedy children were at play, it was hard to differentiate one from another because, as Art Buchwald once said, "All Kennedy children look alike. Do not ask your host or hostess which child belongs to which family. Nobody knows and it will only embarrass them." At Jackie's weekend house in Bernardsville, New Jersey, meanwhile, her next-door neighbor was Murray McDonnell, a member of the wealthy Irish Catholic McDonnell and Murray families. Murray McDonnell's mother had sixty-five grandchildren and six great-grandchildren, and when the Kennedy children joined the McDonnell children, the Kennedys were lost in a scramble of arms and legs.

In personality and temperament, Jackie's two children turned out to be quite unlike each other. It is as though each were a reflection of one side of their mother's two-sided nature—John headstrong, a little arrogant, and mercurial, and Caroline shy, studious, sometimes even solemn. As a child, John Kennedy was full of sauce and energy, with more than a little of the hell-raiser in him—a handful. At the 1966 wedding of his half-aunt, Janet Jennings Auchincloss, to Lewis Rutherfurd in Newport, John Kennedy was a page. During the ceremony, he kept taking sly pokes in the ribs of young contemporaries and, during the reception, he ran about in his velvet jacket and silver-buckled shoes, chasing the Auchincloss ponies with a stick, trying to drive them into the reception tent, while a brace of Secret Service men chased after him. Several of his relatives began to feel that his knowledge of his own celebrity was making him a trifle bratty—cocky, arrogant, too full of his own importance for his own good. For as long as they could remember, both children had been trailed by photographers wherever they went and John, when recognized or when a stranger called out his name, might either respond with a grin and a friendly wave, or make a face, stick out his tongue, waggle his fingers in his ears, or utter one of several familiar four-letter words. On the other hand, he was well-liked at Collegiate, where his grades were fair to average, though his shenanigans were occasionally disruptive in the classroom.

Caroline was quite another matter. She was always a serious student and, through her growing-up years, much of her mother's efforts were spent trying to broaden Caroline's interests in other, non-scholastic areas. Though Jackie, as a two-year-old, had been taken to the dog show for her birthday, where she had been photographed for the society pages, Jackie's fourth birthday treat for Caroline had been to take her to a rehearsal of the Bolshoi Ballet, where there were no photographers. In addition to the lessons from Miss Tallchief, Caroline was also enrolled in the American Ballet Theatre School in New York where, to her mother's disappointment, she dropped out about half-way through the course. "I love ballet and she doesn't," her mother said sadly. Caroline did, however, inherit her mother's love of horses. Long before she was a teenager, Jackie began educating her daughter's palate —instructing her in *haute cuisine,* along with *haute* everything else. At first, these efforts met with only limited success. At a luncheon with Brearley classmates at New York's La Caravelle restaurant, Caroline ordered a first course of *artichauts vinaigrette,* and then followed this dainty dish with an order of steak and French fried potatoes. John, meanwhile, became fascinated by exotic dishes and, discovered in the kitchen of 1040 Fifth at the age of six, working with pots and pans, he explained, "I'm making my own wiener schnitzel."

In her firm but gentle way, it was clear that Jackie wanted her daughter to be perfect in every way—in appearance, in manner, in walk and gesture, and in taste. For clothes, Jackie sent Caroline to one of her favorite designers, Halston, though Halston commented at the time, "She has no innate sense of style yet. She's not very adventuresome. She'll say, 'No, I don't want to try that on.' She tends to dress up in little-girl dresses, or else it's a shirt and blue jeans. She's not the teeny-bopper type at all. She'd look better in a shirt and sweater and boots." Caroline, of course, was old enough to be deeply affected, even traumatized, by the murder of her father, whom she worshipped, and by the later murder of her uncle Bob. ("No little girl can go through two horrors like that without its leaving a deep, permanent scar," says one relative.) For years, she shuddered at even a photograph of a firearm. She was old enough, too, to respond to the death of her infant brother, and to be aware of her parents' grief over that loss. Perhaps it was to offset these dark memories that Jackie tried to infuse Caroline's life with beauty, art, style, elegance.

Perhaps it was Caroline's extensive training in elegance and sophistication that made her, even as a young girl, appear more at ease in the company of adults than with boys and girls her own age. For her eighth birthday, Caroline was asked what she wanted, and her answer was that she wanted writer George Plimpton, then thirty-eight years old, to come to her party. Plimpton came and posed for his picture in the middle of a group of little girls. Plimpton and other friends of her mother's, such as Josh Billings and Leonard Bernstein, served as substitute fathers for

Caroline—taking her on hikes, boat trips, skiing trips —before Jackie's remarriage, and Caroline often listed these men as her "best friends."

Still, she has always been very much her mother's child. "She has her mother's histrionic streak," says a friend. "Jackie and Caroline are both stubborn creatures. Neither one likes to be told what to do. Caroline also has, when she wants to use it, her mother's distance and reserve." Caroline's reserve displayed itself, early on, in her relationship with her new stepfather. It was not that Caroline appeared to resent or dislike Onassis, but just that their characters didn't quite seem to match. Onassis, meanwhile, got along splendidly with young John and, when the boy was saucy or rambunctious, was able to bring him sternly into line— just as, friends noticed, Ari was able to bring Jackie into line. When a Brearley friend asked Caroline how she liked her stepfather, Caroline hesitated, thought a moment, and then said, "Well, he's away a lot." She displayed toward Onassis the same cool skepticism which she did toward Lyndon Johnson when the latter cozily suggested that she call him "Uncle Lyndon." Caroline whispered to her mother, "Is he really my uncle?"

When Caroline began her first year of boarding school at Concord, Jackie took a house nearby. Several of her friends questioned the wisdom of this move. "Caroline has so little freedom and independence already, she should be allowed to enjoy as much as she can get," said one. "Jackie mother-hens her too much." But another cousin, John Davis, said, "What a lot of people don't realize is how much Jackie *needs* Caroline. Caroline's the main emotional support in her life. They're terribly close. Watching the two of them together, talking, gossiping, with their heads together discussing some problem, it's more like watching two sisters, or two very dear friends, than mother and daughter. It's not at all the same way with John. John can be irritating, and Jackie gets irked with him. But

177

not with Caroline. They're like one soul. What I wonder is what would happen to Jackie if and when they ever have to be parted."

Once, in a pensive moment, Jacqueline Onassis said, "The trouble with me is I'm an outsider. And that's a very hard thing to be in American life." The same might be said for her children—her daughter in particular—who were so sheltered from outsiders that they became outsiders themselves. Being outsiders, and being the children of the world's most famous mother, was difficult and, as the children grew up, the difficulty was brought home to them more and more.

But then Jackie, who had once dreamed of becoming the "Queen of the Circus," had never really wanted to be an ordinary woman, or to lead an ordinary life, in ordinary circumstances among ordinary people. She had wanted to be extraordinary, to be something special. Under her photograph in her Farmington class yearbook there had appeared the following data:

Jacqueline Lee Bouvier
"Merrywood"
McLean, Virginia
"Jackie"

Favorite Song: Lime House Blues
Always Saying: "Play a Rhumba next"
Most Known For: Wit
Aversion: People who ask if her horse is still alive
Where Found: Laughing with Tucky
Ambition: Not to be a housewife

She had certainly managed to achieve that ambition. It was an ambition she harbored for her daughter also.

21

The
Team

IT WAS NOT always the most serene of marriages. It was not that Jackie and Ari did not get along with one another. They did, for the most part, particularly when they were alone together on the private island of Skorpios. But the trouble was they were so seldom alone. Onassis was a multi-national businessman who kept the complexities of his far-flung deals and enterprises for the most part in his head. His office was where the nearest telephone was and, to help him keep track of what he was doing—buying a hotel here, selling an oil tanker there, trying to settle a long-shoreman's strike in some distant port—there was the Onassis entourage, his retinue. He was always surrounded by at least a dozen swarthy, tense, fast-thinking men—many of whom chattered back and forth with him in languages Jackie couldn't understand. This was not a retinue of sycophants or toadies. Each man in the retinue had his area of expertise, his duty, and Onassis saw to it that he did it. There was no dead wood on the Onassis team. Onassis liked to boast, for example, that though he had a large battery of lawyers on his payroll, he had never sued anyone. The lawyers' job was to keep him out of trouble, not to cause it.

It was the omnipresent retinue that Jackie found most distracting and irksome. Jack Kennedy had had a retinue, too, but at least Jackie had been able to grasp what the endless conferences, hastily-called meetings, late-night phone calls and abrupt changes of plans were all about. But, in the case of Onassis, only he really understood what he was doing. Each man on his staff might know a part of it, but only Onassis was able to encompass the full picture. Occasionally, she would ask him what such-and-such hasty session or emergency telephone call had been about, but he would be unable to answer her in a way that made any sense. The full scale of his business life was such a mystery to her—as it was to almost everyone associated with him—that it finally seemed better not to ask. Onassis was not the kind of husband to whom you could say, over an evening cocktail, "Well, how was your day, dear?" His days were too complicated for anyone but him to comprehend.

Some members of the Onassis team she grew to like, and they grew to like her. Others, it was clear, rather resented her, and thought of her as a woman who was coming between them and their boss. Some treated her in a somewhat cavalier fashion—entering a room, acknowledging her presence with a mere nod, and then going into a heated, whispered conference— in Greek—with Ari. Jackie found this rude. Also, it was quite obvious that her husband valued the advice and opinions of his advisors more than he valued hers.

There was one member of the Onassis retinue that Jackie grew particularly to dislike. That was Johnny Meyer, the baby-faced, balding, fun-loving publicity man who, before joining the Onassis group, had served in a similar capacity for another very rich man, Howard Hughes. Johnny Meyer was well known in moneyed society all over the world, wherever the wealthy gathered—in Palm Beach, Paris, New York, Monte Carlo, and St. Moritz. And one reason everybody liked Johnny, in addition to the fact that he was always full of juicy gossip, was that, despite his expensively tailored suits, there was always something a little raffish about him, something faintly disreputable. Someone once commented, "Johnny Meyer would sell his own grandmother down the river for a buck." To which the reply was, "He would, except he already sold her down the river ten years ago." That was the kind of aura that followed Johnny Meyer wherever he went.

Once, at a Connecticut house party, Johnny Meyer was telling one of his stories and, as he told it, the details became more and more preposterous. Finally one guest spoke up and said, "Johnny, that just *can't* be true." With a look of indignation on his plump face, Johnny Meyer leapt on top of a coffee table, struck a pose, raised his hand heavenward and cried, "May God strike me dead if that isn't exactly what happened!" With that, the coffee table collapsed underneath him. That was the kind of story people liked to tell about Johnny Meyer all over the world. It was part of his roguish charm.

Johnny's job with Onassis was to *manage* Onassis's publicity. Onassis, unlike other Greek shipping tycoons, who generally liked to keep their names out of the newspapers, loved publicity. That was one reason why he liked to have famous people on board the *Christina*—Princess Margaret and Tony, Princess Grace and Rainier, Margot Fontaine, Cary Grant, the Kennedys, and so on—for the publicity. He loved to be photographed, and to have his doings chronicled in the press. Johnny Meyer's job was to see that Onassis got only the right kind of publicity, the glamorous kind, and to see to it that if there were any slightly sordid or questionable details in his boss's social and business life these facts were concealed from the media. Of course there were some matters that Johnny could not control. After Ari Onassis's marriage to Jackie, for example, Ari continued to see Maria Callas occasionally. Their houses in Paris adjoined, they had remained friends, and he had settled a substantial sum of money on his former mistress when he left her to

marry Jackie. Sometimes, word of these clandestine
visits leaked to the newspapers. When this happened,
part of Johnny Meyer's job was to see to it that the
new Mrs. Onassis did not see the papers that day.

Not long after the marriage some resourceful photo-
journalists had moored a boat some distance off
Skorpios and, using a telephoto lens, had succeeded
in photographing Jackie on the beach where she had
been sunbathing in the nude. These photographs they
had succeeded in selling to an Italian newspaper,
which published them, and eventually they made their
way throughout the globe—much to Jackie's understandable distress, embarrassment, and anger. Even
though the episode had been completely out of Johnny
Meyer's control, she tended to blame him for it. Surely
there was something he could have done to suppress
the nude photographs; surely the pictures and nega-
tives could have been purchased for a price, and
destroyed. Jackie had never really succumbed to
Johnny's charm, and had not cared for the offhand
way he treated her. Now she complained to her husband bitterly about Johnny. But Onassis was nothing
if not loyal to the men who served him, and he listened to Jackie's complaints politely, and did nothing.
Relations between Jackie and Johnny Meyer became
considerably chillier, if not hostile.

Then, not long after the nude-photographs-of-Jackie
fuss, there was a similar to-do involving Ari. Someone
had come up with some nude photographs of *him,* and
these, too, were about to be published. Johnny Meyer
was the first to hear the news, and he quickly obtained
copies of the prints and hurried to inform his boss of
what was about to happen. When he arrived at 1040
Fifth Avenue, Jackie met him at the door and led him
into the living room. Rather coolly, Jackie asked him
what he wanted. Meyer replied that he wanted to see
Mr. Onassis. "What for?" Jackie wanted to know.
Meyer opened the envelope of photographs and
showed them to her. After looking quickly through

them, she tossed them on the coffee table with disgust. "You *must not* show these to him," she said. "He'll be terribly upset. I won't let you upset him so."

Meyer replied that Onassis would learn about the photographs soon enough. Meyer's job was to alert and forewarn Onassis of their existence, and to see what Onassis wanted to do about them, how he wanted to handle the situation. But the more Meyer insisted that he had to show the photographs to his boss, the more Jackie insisted that he not do so. The argument became quite heated and, in the middle of it, Onassis walked into the room. What were they arguing about, he wanted to know. "More of Johnny's *drivel!*" said Jackie, indicating the photographs.

Onassis went to the coffee table and picked up the pictures. He sat down on a sofa and slowly and thoughtfully examined each print. He scrutinized each picture, shaking his head. Then he went through the collection again. Finally he looked up at Meyer and, in his soft voice, said, "Johnny, these aren't *recent* pictures. These must have been taken at least ten years ago. Look—I've lost a lot of weight since then." It was Onassis's final comment on the situation, and Jackie turned on her heel and stalked angrily out of the room.

There was not a great deal Jackie could do about the Onassis team except accept it, and put up with it. It came with the man she had married, it was part of the package. She was aware that some of the members of the team resented her, and there was little she could do about that, either. Gradually she stopped complaining about the intrusions, the interruptions, the constantly ringing telephone, the fact that everywhere they went they were surrounded by a large group of people, most of them Onassis-team members. Just as docilely she accepted the nightclub life style he preferred. At the opening of the new El Morocco Club in New York, she appeared with him, and the Onassis party—numbering about ten, including Johnny

Meyer—was given a front and center table, and remained until the wee hours. In Paris, he liked the stylish *le Club Privé,* and she joined him for long evenings there, along with various members of the team. "He tamed her," says a friend, and it was true that with a look or with a gesture—a raised finger—he could turn any signs of recalcitrance on her part into smiling obedience. Cheerfully enough, she usually went along with anything he wanted her to do.

True, she liked to tease him. Her favorite target was Ari Onassis's lack of taste in clothes, and at times she could twit him unmercifully on that subject. "Look at him," she would say in front of others. "He must have four hundred suits. But he wears the same *gray* one in New York, the same *blue* one in Paris, and the same *brown* one in London." Ari generally ignored these verbal sallies. She put up with him, he put up with her.

And it was true, he was away a lot. In addition to the Fifth Avenue apartment, Onassis also maintained a suite of rooms at the Hotel Pierre. Often, working late, he would find it easier to stay at the Pierre rather than go home, even though 1040 Fifth Avenue was little more than twenty blocks up the street. Jackie accepted this arrangement. Then there were his business trips—often extended ones—all over the world. Occasionally she would accompany him on these trips, but usually she would not. On his business trips, she felt rather in the way. Still, wherever he was—out of husbandly solicitousness or because he liked to check on her—he telephoned her faithfully every night.

It may not have been a marriage that involved much physical passion, but it was a convenient one. And there were times when having the Onassis team at her disposal could be definitely helpful. Not long after her marriage to Onassis, for example, an antique dealer in Sag Harbor, Long Island named Otto Fenn spotted a man's portrait in a sale. Handsomely framed, there was something about the face in the painting that struck Mr. Fenn, and he bought it for a small sum. Even if no one wanted the portrait, he decided, the frame would bring something. But when he had brought the painting back to his shop, the man's face began to haunt him. It looked familiar, the face of someone he had either known, or seen a photograph of, or read about. There was some resemblance, in the face, to Clark Gable, and yet Fenn was certain the man was not Gable. Finally, Fenn realized who it was. The portrait was of Jackie Onassis's father, Jack Bouvier.

Otto Fenn had read that Jackie and her father had been close and so he photographed the portrait and sent a picture of it to Mrs. Onassis, suggesting that she might like to purchase it. Within a few days, there was a reply from Nancy Tuckerman. Mrs. Onassis would indeed like the portrait, and an agreement on the price was reached (Mr. Fenn chose not to disclose the price Mrs. Onassis paid for her father's portrait, but it is safe to assume that the antique dealer made a tidy profit). He then removed the portrait from its frame, and shipped the painting to 1040 Fifth Avenue.

A few days later, there was another polite letter from Nancy Tuckerman. It had been assumed, she said, that the price of the painting included the frame. Mrs. Onassis had expected to receive the painting in the same frame she had seen it in in the photograph. Mr. Fenn just as politely replied that Miss Tuckerman was in error. What he had offered for sale was the painting only. If Mrs. Onassis wanted the frame as well, that would be extra. There now followed a series of telephone calls, back and forth between Mr. Fenn and Mrs. Tuckerman. The dickering for the frame remained polite, but grew more persistent. Mrs. Onassis wanted the frame. She had expected to get it with the portrait, and was unwilling to pay extra for it. She felt she was entitled to the frame. Mr. Fenn continued to maintain that the frame was a valuable one; he could not part with it without charging an additional fee. Finally, he suggested that, instead of a fee, he might let Mrs. Onassis have the frame in return for some other sort of consideration.

There was silence, then, on the subject of the frame for about a week. One day, however, a messenger arrived at Mr. Fenn's shop with a long, slim envelope. In it were two first-class round-trip tickets to Athens on Olympic Airways.

It was a solution in which everyone profited happily. Mr. Fenn and a friend got a free trip to Greece. And Jackie got the frame she wanted for her father's portrait—also, as it were, for free.

22

Poor Relations

ONE OF THE problems with being rich is that one is always being asked for money. One quickly learns to be very hardheaded and ruthless about these requests because, the more one gives, the more relentless become the demands. From the moment her marriage to Onassis was announced, Jackie began to be deluged with requests for donations. Some came from legitimate charities and philanthropies, but many more came from individuals. Daily, in the mail, came piteous tales of widowhood, bereavement, and loss. The letter-writers told of crippled children, terminal cancer cases, houses lost by fire, insurmountable medical bills, husbands who had been unjustly thrown in jail. How many of the stories were true it was impossible to tell.

Some doubtless were, and a number of the tales were genuinely pathetic. Still, all these letters, unanswered, went directly into the waste basket.

But there were some requests she could not ignore. There was the problem, for example, of her father's younger sister, Aunt Edith Bouvier Beale. Jackie's grandfather had always urged Jackie's father to "Take care of Edith." Within the limits of his resources, Jack Bouvier had done his best. Jack, in turn, had passed on the admonishment to take care of Edith to his daughters, and there was no question that Edith needed taking care of. Edith had once dreamed of becoming an opera singer, and in the family she was explained as being "artistic," which was another way of saying "peculiar." After her husband, Phelan Beale, divorced her, Edith's behavior and style of life became more outlandish. She had inherited a twenty-six-room shingled mansion on two acres of shore property in East Hampton, which she never left, and she had allowed the house, Grey Gardens, to deteriorate around her, and the lawns and gardens had been left to grow into a jungle of tall weeds and trees. On the house, shutters dangled from a single hinge, and rents in the rusted screens admitted a flow of wildlife. Downstairs, fleas swarmed from the rotting upholstery of whatever furniture remained.

Hardly anyone in the family visited Edith anymore. Still, everyone was aware that she was there. Also there was her unmarried daughter, Edith. In the family, they were "Big Edie" and "Little Edie." Little Edie had once wanted to be a dancer and had gone to New York to pursue this career, where she had lived respectably enough at the Barbizon Hotel for Women. But after Big Edie's divorce, her mother had persuaded her only daughter to come back to Grey Gardens and care for her and, over the years, Little Edie had become even more eccentric than her mother. Little Edie dressed as no Farmington girl (which she had been) had ever done—wearing black mesh hose, high-heeled shoes, bathing suits over sweaters, head scarves fashioned out of skirts, blouses, and aprons to conceal her bald head—the result of an illness or of Edie having shaved it, no one quite dared ask. The two Edies had taken up a life together that was spent in bickering and recriminations—Little Edie berating her mother for having sent away her one serious suitor, Big Edie complaining of Little Edie's bad temper and neglect—even though it was a life of mutual dependency. By the late 1960s, the two women had run through the small family trusts that had supported them, and now they were virtually paupers—a pitiful embarrassment to the family.

By 1971, their neighbors in the fashionable resort community had turned against the Beales and their slovenly style of living. An inspector from the Board of Health had visited Grey Gardens, and found them living ankle-deep in trash, garbage, and cat and human excrement. He had declared Grey Gardens a health hazard to the community and, because the two recluses were Jackie Onassis's close relatives, the story made front page headlines across the country. Jackie and her sister were as surprised and appalled as everyone else to learn of the condition to which their aunt's and cousin's lives had deteriorated. Jackie and other relatives quickly came forward to assist the Beales, and some $30,000 was spent to put Grey Gardens into a state that would satisfy the Long Island town authorities. Of course, not even $30,000 was sufficient to restore the big house to anything like the elegance that had originally been intended for it, but at least the sanitation problems had been relieved. Jackie volunteered to pay the recluses' water, oil, and electricity bills on a continuing basis, and to place a monthly food allowance for them in their bank account. Other relatives agreed to take over other expenses.

The family felt sorry for the Beales but, after all, that the two women would eventually find themselves in some sort of predicament had not been entirely unexpected. It was, however, with a sense of shock that the family learned of an almost simultaneous development—Hughdie Auchincloss, it seemed, was going broke. It had started with the 1969–70 stock market decline—the so-called Nixon recession. A number of Wall Street brokerage firms had found themselves in deepening trouble, and one of these was Hughdie's Washington-based Auchincloss, Parker & Redpath. In 1970 a number of firms simply went under while others—like Hughdie's—struggled to stay afloat despite a feeling of panic, trying to deal with computers that were spewing out wrong answers, accounting systems that had been taken for granted but that were actually so inefficient that no one knew for sure whether trades were being made for the correct customers, whether stock certificates were being sent to the right people, or who was owed what.

Hughdie Auchincloss had always been of the Old School of stockbrokers. He had experienced panics before, seen the market crash as it had in 1929, and seen it rise again to new heights following World War II. For the past several years, furthermore, he had been in semi-retirement, spent little time in his office, had assumed that his business would take care of itself and, like everyone else, that he would always be splendidly rich. But when, in the early 1970s, the economic situation failed to improve, and he realized that his firm faced bankruptcy, he felt compelled to step in. He did what Janet later described as "a very noble thing," and decided to try to save his foundering company with his own personal money. To some, it might have seemed not a noble but a foolish thing—sending good money after bad. But that was what he did, and into Auchincloss, Parker & Redpath went all the Jennings millions he had inherited from his mother. Eventually, the firm was saved through a merger with Thomson & McKinnon & Co., the names Parker and Redpath were dropped from the letterhead, and Hughdie's name was placed at the end of the reorganized firm of Thomas & McKinnon Auchincloss. But the Jennings millions were gone.

It was hardest, perhaps, on Janet. She had gone through a similar financial reversal with her first husband. But it was also hard on Hughdie because he realized, by late 1970, that he was probably going to have to sell Hammersmith Farm, which had sheltered five generations of Auchinclosses. Merrywood had already been sold, and the only other property he owned was his O Street town house in Georgetown, in Washington. Hammersmith Farm, the last working farm in Newport, with its seventy-five acres, had become something of a white elephant. Property taxes alone ran to over $31,000 a year. In addition to the main house, with its ten master bedrooms, there was a sixteen-horse stable, an hexagonal children's playhouse, plus numerous other garages, barns, and out-buildings. No one, Janet argued, could manage to live on that scale anymore. But Hughdie loved Hammersmith Farm—perhaps even more than he loved Janet.

One could see why. The main entertaining room of the house was not the formal sitting-room but the big, west-facing room that the family had always called "the deck room," perhaps because, in it, one had the feeling of being on the deck of a ship. The decorative style of this room could probably best be described as "eclectic"—an unself-conscious mixture of Victorian and eighteenth-century pieces, comfortably worn leather chairs and sofas, a fireplace tall enough for a man to stand in. The deck room seemed to have happened, rather than been furnished (though Lee Radziwill liked to take credit for having "decorated" it), and the effect was of cozy clutter. In one corner stood a portable television set where Hughdie liked to watch professional football games. In another was a brown bearskin rug, head and all, which a hunter friend of Janet's once sent her as a gift and in which her various dogs always took an alarming interest. Suspended from the ceiling in the center of the room

swung, in endless slow gyrations, a stuffed pelican
that Hughdie himself once brought down with his own
gun. One could see, in the deck room, the central
theme of Hammersmith Farm. It was not so much a
house built for ostentation as for a family—a big family, with many children. John Winthrop Auchincloss
who built the house in 1892 was one of nine; he
himself had six, and Hughdie had five plus his two
stepdaughters.

One of the last had been his youngest daughter Janet. When Janet Jennings Auchincloss had her debut
at Hammersmith Farm in the summer of 1963, there
were over a thousand guests, including seven foreign
ambassadors, two United States senators, a retired associate justice of the Supreme Court, along with
the Angier Biddle Dukes, the David K. E. Bruces, the
Harvey Firestones, the Winthrop Aldriches, the
Sheldon Whitehouses and the Claiborne Pells. It had
been the most lavish debutante ball of that or any
other Newport season in memory. The President and
Mrs. Kennedy had not been able to be there, but they
had sent Janet the bouquet of flowers that she carried,
and announced that they would entertain for her at the
White House during the coming Christmas season—
a season that did not come for President Kennedy.

By the 1970s, however, the house had begun to
wear something of the air of a memorial. Perhaps this
could not be helped. Framed, in the entrance hall, was
the Presidential flag that had flown from the foot of
the lawn when the President visited, and photographs
of him were everywhere—there with his wife, there
with his children, there with Hugh Auchincloss, Jr.'s,
twin sons. Upstairs, in the study off the room he used,
was a desk with a bronze plaque listing the various bills
he signed into law there. On the top floor, the children's floor, the rooms were usually empty now. The
long upper hallway was lined with photographs of departed Auchinclosses and, though the pictures showed
happy scenes, one could not help but be struck with a

sad sense that the greatest days of the great house were over.

Weekday mornings, Hughdie Auchincloss, dressed in the comfortable tweeds of a gentleman farmer, would spend an hour or so in his book-lined office off the entrance hall, surrounded by more family photographs, doing, it seemed, not much of anything. Then he would climb into his blue Bentley and drive down to the water's edge. He might spend the morning there, sitting on the dock where the presidential flag once flew, fishing for mackerel and chatting with groundsmen and farmhands. Lunch was at one. After lunch it was time to move into the deck room for any football games on the television. At five, it was time for a nap before dinner.

A letter from one of the children became an event that would make the day. Suddenly Janet Auchincloss would hurry into the room, crying reproachfully, "Hughdie, *Hughdie!* Why didn't you tell me there was a letter from Janet?" Waving its pages covered with rounded, girlish, boarding-school script, she would reach for her glasses and, even though he had already read the letter, sit down to read it aloud to him—a long letter from the Orient, full of news.

Janet wanted to thank her mother for the records and the check—"She's teaching some French classes, so I sent her the French records. Then I remembered she has no record player with her, so I sent her the check and told her to buy one as my birthday present." Janet, Jr., told her mother how she and her young husband celebrated a wedding anniversary in Hong Kong —she cooked his favorite chicken dish for him: "The chicken simply *wouldn't* thaw, though I kept pouring boiling water over it again and again—finally I threw it at the kitchen wall in a fit of pique . . ." "And look how she spells it," her mother cried. "P-e-a-k." Little Janet then described a scene in a Hong Kong hotel lobby which she and her husband witnessed—young soldiers who had been on furlough there departing for

Vietnam: "I stood on the steps, and as one of them passed by he smiled at me, and I smiled back and said, 'Good luck. . . .' " "Of course she's such a *baby,*" said Janet, and her eyes became suddenly melancholy.

Even before the economic debacle of 1970, Janet had begun to talk of renting the big house at Hammersmith Farm and summering at some smaller place. She had also begun to talk of loneliness. Then, in the spring of 1966, she had embarked upon a project to breathe new life into the old place. The old windmill, which once lifted water for the house, stood idle, and she had an idea: Why not move it down to the water's edge and remodel it. She and Jackie spent weeks hiking about the farm in search of the perfect spot and, when they thought they had discovered one, the two women had themselves raised on a forklift tractor so they could appraise the view from above. Working with walkie-talkies between the main house and a prospective site, Janet and Jackie also tried to place the windmill where it would do the most for the *house's* view. It became a familiar sight in the summer of 1966 to see Jackie and her mother—one woman craning from a window of the main house, gesturing and shouting directions, and the other, skirts blowing, perched high on the platform of the forklift, half a mile away. At last they settled on a site—and tragedy struck. A workman, preparing to move the building, was using an acetylene torch. The windmill caught fire and burned to the ground.

But Janet had had her heart set on the project, and so she decided to build a new windmill. When it was finished, it was quite a bit more than the old windmill was to have been. There were four floors with an elevator between, out of consideration for Hughdie's emphysema, one room to a floor. There was a large room for entertaining on the ground floor, a living-dining room on the next, a bedroom on the next, and on the top, a glass-walled studio that took in a view of the entire bay, and a generous portion of the Atlantic Ocean as well. The new Auchincloss windmill became the talk of Newport, and Janet announced that from then on she and Hughdie would spend their summers in the windmill and the children and grandchildren could use the big house—if they wished.

But the trouble was that they didn't seem to wish. Then came 1970, and Hughdie's troubles. All Hughdie's lawyers, his financial advisors, and his wife told him that he must sell Hammersmith Farm. Maintaining it now was just too much of a financial drain. But stubbornly Hughdie refused. He had promised himself that he was going to die there, and he was going to keep that promise. He would go to the poorhouse first, rather than sell the farm. After he died, Janet could do what she wished with the place, but not before.

Why, people began to wonder, didn't Jackie come forward to help her financially troubled stepfather and mother? She was married to one of the richest men in the world. Wasn't there something she could do to help them save the house—the house she had grown up in, made her debut in, had been married in? She had always claimed that she loved the house, claimed that she loved her Uncle Hugh who had stepped in and given her away when her own father had let her down. Suddenly her financial support of her two eccentric relatives in East Hampton began to seem awfully niggardly. Thirty thousand dollars, after all, was no more than a week's mad money for someone like her. She had airily offered to buy off William Manchester for "a million." Could she be that cold-blooded?

It wasn't that simple. For one thing, Hughdie Auchincloss was certainly too proud, too Scotch and Presbyterian, to have accepted any largesse from Jackie had she offered it, and so, very likely, was Janet. Nor would the Auchinclosses have accepted money from Onassis had he offered it and, it should be noted, he showed little interest in the money problems of his new in-laws. Also, as Jackie knew, the Auchinclosses were still far from the poorhouse. What had happened was that a huge fortune had become a very much smaller fortune. By American standards, the Auchinclosses were still wealthy. They would continue to maintain Hammersmith Farm much the way the Bouviers had continued to maintain Lasata after 1929—by dipping into a dwindling supply of capital, and not altering their expensive way of life all that much. And Jackie's own portfolio of stocks had been unkindly buffeted by the Nixon recession. The premarital funds Onassis had settled on her had become considerably diminished, and though she had suggested that he replace them, he had demurred. For most of the luxuries she obviously enjoyed, she depended on the tolerance and indulgence of her husband.

At the same time, child of the Great Depression that she was, she continued to be uneasy about the security of her financial future, and the financial future of her children. Even after her remarriage to Onassis, she harbored a widow's fear of poverty and old age with no one to care for her. And, she may have wondered, how much could she really count on from Onassis? In terms of marriage and romance, he had no great record of stability. If he tired of her, as he had tired of other women, where would she be?

Once, to a friend, she had complained, "You know, everyone talks about how rich I am. I'm not really that rich. I have a few thousand in my checking account, some savings, a few stocks and bonds." Then she had added with a nervous laugh, "Of course there are a lot of things I can charge to Olympic Airways."

For all this, new tales of Jackie's miserliness coupled with extravagance began to circulate. A former White House aide alleged that after her elegant parties Mrs. Kennedy ordered all unfinished drinks to be poured back into the bottles and decanters they had come from. A former maid announced that Jackie saved S & H Green Stamps. A New York real estate man said that he could not sell an apartment at 1040 Fifth

Avenue because the lady who lived on the floor above
—Mrs. Onassis—hung her panty hose out on the window ledge to dry. It was also reported that she insisted
that her stockings and panty hose be ironed. It was
said that after washing her handkerchiefs she dried
them by pressing them wet against a mirror. It was
also said that her bill for clothes ran close to a million
dollars a year, that she bought compulsively everything
in sight. When one spent that much money on adornment, how could one *help* but be well dressed?

At the same time it was said that she was a piker.
She had made her contribution to the Beales' welfare
only after their degraded circumstances had become a
public scandal and a public embarrassment to herself.
She was a super-spender on consumer goods and services and the latest fads and fashions but she was also,
at heart, a tightwad—that had to be the answer. It
was all surmise, of course, because no one had the
answer to her character but herself, and she would
not reveal it.

23

The

Smile

AT ABOUT THE same time, the publicity about John
F. Kennedy was beginning to disintegrate. Judith
Exner had not yet appeared on the scene with her
memoir of scandalous disclosures, but reports were
starting to appear in the press about lurid Presidential
goings-on—naked romps with easy women in the
White House pool on nights when Mrs. Kennedy was

out of town, and so on. True or not, these were the sort of things the public now seemed to want to read about, and the gossip writers wrote about them willingly. The man who had been a golden hero to youth of the early sixties was dead, and Camelot was over, and now it was hard to believe that he or it had ever really existed. The stories now were petty, mean, and small—as small as the tales of Jackie's panty hose—but the tabloids printed them. Somehow, they had to be endured.

For someone such as Jackie Onassis, so squarely in the public mind, the only way to endure such public pillory was to suppress it from *her* mind. To have dwelt upon it would have led to paranoia. She insulated herself from it, built as impervious a wall as she could between it and herself. It was the only way. Farmington had taught her to rise to occasions and, though her life seemed to contain more occasions to rise to than most people's, she would continue to do her best.

At first, it wasn't easy. It is never easy to know that the public is watching and reporting your every move, and even some non-moves, but, by training herself to ignore the reports, she was learning to deal with them. Inevitably, some of the rumors that circulated about her and her former husband reached her ears and, inevitably, at first, they angered and depressed her. But she was becoming tougher, getting better at putting up the insulation, until she would reach a point where nothing could touch her. And of course she had a lot of help from friends. Nancy Tuckerman, her best friend from Farmington days, was a marvelous insulator. The two women had known each other and worked together for so long now that they almost seemed like the extension of the same personality, and thought and reacted to situations in the same way. All Jackie's mail and telephone calls were screened by Tucky, and Jackie's trust in Tucky was complete. Jackie didn't read the tabloids or the gossip magazines or the scandal sheets that were sold on supermarket check-out counters, and the kind of stories that were appearing about her were not printed in *The New York Times.* Nancy knew what she might or might not like to watch on television, and the children's television programs and reading matter were similarly edited. When Jackie passed a newsstand, which was seldom, she trained herself to look the other way. And of course her friends, and the world in which she moved, never talked to her about any of the matters which the gossip sheets printed. At large social functions, she learned to arrange the friends in flanks around her, and the Onassis team served as additional protection. If a reporter broke through the phalanx of friends and protectors, and managed to blurt out a rude question, she simply smiled and turned away.

Part of the insulation, the only part that showed, was the smile. The smile had changed enormously over the years. Early photographs show Jackie with a shy, tentative, uncertain smile. She seemed afraid to part her lips over her teeth. By her debutante days, however, she had developed a flirty, head-tilted-to-one-side coquettish smile. Later, posing campily with a hugely long cigarette holder, she had found a wicked smile, a smile that seemed to say she was a party to some splendidly naughty and delicious secret. But now the smile—and it had taken work—had perfected itself into something that was both radiant and ingratiating, enthusiastic and brave—a theatrical smile that was at the same time human. It was a smile of such a quality that, when faced with it, there was almost nothing one could say or do. The smile of Jacqueline Kennedy Onassis was more than insulation. It was armor. Her smile had grown from a little-girl nothing to a big-girl something. The Jacqueline Onassis smile would become her trademark and her most effective weapon.

But the smile could not protect her children. This was the basis of her continuing complaints against Ron

Galella. Galella was a photographer who made a fairly handsome living from his specialty of snapping pictures of celebrities in unguarded moments and, in the process, earning the undying enmity of the famous themselves. Galella's sneak tactics had already resulted in scuffles with such people as Frank Sinatra and Paul Newman. Now his favorite target had become Jackie, Caroline, and John. Actually, a number of the pictures he took of Jackie were extremely flattering. Spotting her crossing a city street while his car waited for a light, he called out, "Hi, Jackie!"—and aimed his Nikon. Before she realized who he was, she turned, flashed the smile, and then quickly turned her head the other way. But Galella got his picture—a memorable one of a pretty woman in a hurry, smiling, with her hair blowing across her face.

Relentlessly, wherever she went, he pursued her and her children—materialized, out of nowhere it seemed, on both sides of the Atlantic. Onassis was philosophical about the situation. "Publicity is like rain," he said. "When you're soaking wet, what difference do a few drops more make?" But Jackie grew increasingly annoyed. Why couldn't Johnny Meyer, who was supposed to "control" publicity, do something about it, she demanded. At one point, Jackie ordered one of her Onassis-assigned bodyguards to confiscate Galella's camera. At another, she had him arrested. Finally, on the basis that Galella was harassing and invading the privacy of herself and her children, Jackie consulted the lawyers who had represented her in the Manchester affair—Paul, Weiss, Rifkind, Wharton & Garrison—and asked them to take Galella to court.

Ari Onassis was appalled. It had been part of his business philosophy never to sue anyone. Ignore the man, he advised her. He will eventually tire of the game and go away. Sue him, and the public will interpret you as vindictive and mean—as mean as you seemed when you tried to stop the publication of William Manchester's book. Johnny Meyer agreed. The publicity that would ensue from a court battle with someone of Galella's ilk would only be bad and would convey to Galella a degree of status and importance that this member of the *paparazzi* didn't deserve. But Jackie, whose low opinion of Johnny Meyer's advice was already established, did not agree. She wanted to sue, she said, "on principle." She sued, and Galella countered by suing her for trying to interfere with his right to earn a living.

The public reaction to these developments was as Meyer and Onassis had predicted. The public tended to sympathize with Galella—a humble, hard-working man of immigrant extraction who was being harshly and arbitrarily persecuted by a rich and arrogant woman. Once more, it seemed, she was losing her famous cool and, bent on getting her own way, was forgetting her once-ladylike manners. She was not, it seemed, rising to the occasion as she usually did—and even the occasion seemed petty. Privately, Onassis approached Galella on the street and asked him whether some out-of-court settlement couldn't be made in order to get the unpleasant case out of the papers. Galella explained that his Jackie pictures were an important source of income for him, but that he would promise to leave her alone for $100,000. To Onassis, this figure seemed ridiculously high, and negotiations were broken off at that point. To this day, Galella believes that an agreement could have been reached if Jackie had not been so determined to defend her "principle."

In the end, Jackie won a victory of sorts. Galella and his camera were enjoined by the court to come no closer than within a fifty-yard radius of Mrs. Onassis and her children (though with telephoto lenses, fifty yards is not an unmanageable distance between a photographer and his subject). And when the bill for her legal services in the proceedings arrived, the victory seemed decidedly a Pyrrhic one. It was for over $200,000. When she presented this to her husband, he was outraged.

The Galella affair, and what it had cost in terms of time, money, and bad press, was one of the first warnings of future storms that would toss the marriage of Jackie and her second husband. Money arguments—the most destructive kind that can occur between a husband and a wife—became more frequent. In the beginning, of course, it had all been quite different. He had literally showered her with money and expensive gifts. Among his wedding gifts to her had been a pair of heart-shaped ruby earrings and an enormous ring to match—at a cost, reportedly, of about a million dollars. In 1969, for her fortieth birthday, unable to find enough orchids in Athens to be flown to her in Skorpios, Onassis settled for twelve dozen red roses, along with more stones—including a diamond necklace, a diamond bracelet, diamond earrings, and a forty-carat diamond ring worth another million. For good measure, he added another pair of earrings encrusted with diamonds and rubies. In a book which Fred Sparks wrote on the first year of the Onassis marriage, Sparks claimed that Onassis had spent $20,-000,000 in that year alone—most of it on things for Jackie. Though that figure may be exaggerated, even half that sum would be impressive.

By the early 1970s, however, rumors had begun to circulate that all was not as well as it might be between the Onassises. Perhaps, during that lavish, no-holds-barred first year, he had spoiled her, because it was obvious that the style of living she preferred had become more costly. Sometimes, flying back and forth to Europe on Olympic Airways, she asked for—and got—the entire first class compartment to herself. At the very least she wanted two seats, so she could stretch out. At the same time, she was having personal money problems. As part of their pre-marital contract, Onassis had turned over to Jackie $3,-000,000 in tax-free government bonds. She had decided, against his advice, to invest some $300,000 of this in the stock market and, in the so-called Nixon recession of 1970, she had lost most of it. When she suggested that he replace this, he declined and suggested, somewhat sarcastically, that if she needed money she could sell some of the millions of dollars' worth of jewels he had given her, and which she rarely wore, keeping most of it in safe-deposit vaults. Or she could sell the Van Gogh or the Picasso or the El Greco that he had given her for the Fifth Avenue apartment—or any number of valuable paintings that he had given her from his vast art collection.

He had also contracted, prior to the marriage, to give her $33,000 a month for the maintenance of her apartment and automobile, for clothing, hairdressers, medical expenses, and staff, plus $5,000 a month for each of the children. Suddenly it seemed that that was not enough, and there began to be almost daily calls from Nancy Tuckerman to Creon Brown, Onassis's financial manager, asking for more funds. In his recent biography on Onassis, Frank Brady reports that at one point Jackie said to Ari, "Things simply can't go on this way in the house any longer!" To which Ari replied, "That's too bad. They'll just have to." He then, according to Brady, left strict instructions with his office not to pay his wife a penny more than the sums established in their agreement.

In New York, it was rumored that the Onassises no longer lived together under the same roof, that his permanent address was now the Pierre and that hers was 1040 Fifth Avenue. Brady disputes this, however, and reports that, when he was in town, Onassis frequently slept at the apartment, where he had his own room, but—to avoid being taxed as an American resident—it was important that Ari keep the Pierre as a transient address, and that the apartment remain in her name only. But their life styles had begun to collide. Jackie liked to rise early in the morning to have breakfast with her children and see them off to school.

Careful of her sleep, she preferred on most nights to be in bed with a book by ten. Onassis, on the other hand, was a night person, who liked to drink and party and night-club till dawn, and rise in the afternoon. Jackie liked the theater, films, ballet, opera. Onassis had no interest in any of these entertainments.

More and more the press noted Jackie being squired about New York by most of the same escorts who had taken her out before her marriage—Leonard Bernstein, Mike Nichols, Peter Duchin, Frank Sinatra. The *New York Post* published a photograph, meanwhile, of Onassis dining at Maxim's in Paris with none other than his former mistress, Mme. Callas. To those who questioned the status of what seemed to have become an obvious "open marriage," Ari Onassis issued the following statement:

Jackie is a little bird that needs its freedom as well as its security and she gets them both from me. She can do exactly as she pleases—visit international fashion shows and travel and go out with friends to the theater or anyplace. And I, of course, will do exactly as I please. I never question her and she never questions me.

It all sounded sweet enough, and certainly very civilized and modern. They had agreed, from the beginning, that each would lead an independent life. But under the veneer of goodwill and sophistication, there were occasional cracks. When Jackie's photograph appeared in the papers with another man, there were angry telephone calls from Ari, from wherever he might be, demanding an explanation. And, when the widely circulated photograph in the *Post* appeared, a tearful Jackie immediately flew to Paris to demand—and get—a contrite apology. In 1973, perhaps to dispel all the rumors of a marriage on the rocks, Jackie tossed a surprise party for her husband in the Champagne Room at El Morocco to celebrate their fourth wedding anniversary. At the party, both Onassises did their best to present a picture of wedded bliss and, during the evening, squeezed elbows, kissed, and hugged each other several times.

But even the most open of open marriages can come to grief when the issue at hand disintegrates to that of money. Onassis had begun to chide his wife for extravagant spending and she, needless to say, resented this. After all, she might have wondered, hadn't he seemed to *want* her to be extravagant—after that totally extravagant and spendthrift first year, and after all the paintings, the rubies and the diamonds? Had she read his signals all wrong? She had assumed that lavish spending was in his blood, the thing he liked most to do. Since he had seemed, at first, to get so much pleasure out of spending money on her, had she been doing anything more than what he expected of her? What she may have failed to realize was that, like a wealthy child who quickly tires of the most expensive toy, Onassis had simply become bored with her.

In the autumn of 1973, Jackie announced that she wanted to go to Acapulco—to commemorate the tenth anniversary of Jack Kennedy's death in the place where she and Kennedy had spent their honeymoon. Onassis could understand, more or less, and sympathize with her reasons for wanting to make this sentimental and nostalgic journey, though a few pangs of jealousy and resentment over the purpose of the trip would have also been understandable, and forgivable. Still, he agreed to make the Mexican pilgrimage. But the trip did not go well. In addition to the romantic reason she gave, it seemed, Jackie had another purpose in mind for visiting Acapulco. She wanted to buy a villa there. Onassis was opposed to this. He had, he said, plenty of houses already. Still, while Onassis spent his days by the pool, Jackie shopped for real estate. The more she wheedled for a villa in Acapulco, the more adamantly he opposed it. They argued about it, and the argument continued bitterly on the private plane that brought them home. Finally, in disgust, Aristotle Onassis got up and changed his seat to another part of the plane. There, for the remainder of the trip, he busied himself with paperwork, scribbling on large yellow sheets of cap—"writing letters," he explained.

But he wasn't writing letters. He was re-writing his will.

24

End
of an Epoch

FOLLOWING THE SECOND Kennedy assassination, Jackie had seemed so shattered and disoriented that, once again, those close to her had begun to fear that she might lose her sanity. In her mind she seemed to confuse the events in Los Angeles with the events in Dallas and, at times, even spoke as though her husband were still President of the United States, and as though she were still First Lady. As a result, when, shortly after Bobby's murder, she announced her intention to marry Aristotle Onassis, her family and legal and financial advisors decided that, before such a momentous step was taken, certain things should be settled. Since she was about to marry a much older man, the terms of her financial future should be made clear. This was the basis of the famous pre-marital contract which was worked out in New York between Onassis's lawyers and banker André Meyer, senior partner at Lazard Frères & Company, who represented Jackie. Jackie and Onassis, according to all reports, never personally discussed the matter, though each was kept informed of the negotiations.

The details of the contract have never been made public but, according to Frank Brady, a former Onassis employee, Christian Cafarakis, did see a copy of the agreement as it was being drawn up, and was able to recall a few of the 173 clauses in it. Among other things, Onassis agreed to give Jackie $3,000,000 in tax-free bonds outright. Further, she was not required to give Onassis a child. The pair agreed that they only needed to spend Catholic and summer holidays together and that, for the rest of the time, they could come and go and live as they wished, and where they wished. They agreed that separate bedrooms would be provided for each whenever both were under the same roof. If the couple decided to separate, the following provisions were strictly set up: if Ari left Jackie, he would give her $10,000,000 for each year of the marriage; if Jackie left Ari within five years, she would receive only $20,000,000; if she left him after five years, she would receive $20,000,000 plus a trust fund of $180,000 for the next ten years. If Ari died while still married to Jackie, she would get $100,000-000. If Jackie died before her husband, all her property and money would go to her children, but they would be supported by Onassis until each was twenty-one years old.

There was more. Jackie was to receive an allowance for maintaining her apartment and automobile up to $10,000 a month. Medical expenses, hairdressers, cosmetics, and so on were budgeted at $7,000 a month. She was given a clothing allowance of $10,000 a month, an allowance for servants and bodyguards of $6,000 a month, and each of her children was given an allowance of $5,000 a month to cover their education, clothing, medical expenses, and spending money. It was, to say the least, a generous agreement. If it all sounded a little cold-blooded and mercenary, and if it made it appear that Jackie placed an exceptionally high price on her duties (not spelled out in the agreement) as a spouse—well, it must be remembered that in marriages between wealthy persons such pre-marital agreements are not really uncommon, though most are not of such Olympian proportions. And, Jackie's counselors pointed out, having everything spelled out in black and white would insure that there would never be any disputes between the couple over money, which was important in a marriage where money would loom as so large a factor. About this, of course, the counselors would turn out to be wrong.

But beware, someone might have reminded her, of Greeks bearing gifts. Onassis was a wily man, far wiser in the ways and uses of money than she. He had not made his fortune by being sweet to people. He could be charming, but he could also be irascible, and he had a famous temper. He was a man who never forgot a friend, and who never forgave an enemy. He could be generous, and spend money regally, but he could also fly into a rage at being overcharged a dollar on a restaurant tab. As far as is known, he never gave a cent to a charity, though he helped support several dozen relatives. To a man who had learned how to buy governments, buying a mere woman was child's play. Following that scene on the plane back from Acapulco, he set about systematically to subvert the terms of the pre-marital agreement.

Under Greek law—at least as of early 1974—a widow automatically received at least one quarter of her husband's estate. Upon Onassis's death, in other words, Jackie confidently expected to receive an inheritance of at least $125,000,000—perhaps even as much as $250,000,000. In May, 1974, however, three months after the Acapulco trip, Onassis's personal lawyer, Stelios Papadimitrou, visited the Greek Minister of Justice, and a meeting was arranged with Minister Stelios Triantailou, the purpose of which was to change that law. Triantailou was one of the most powerful figures in the Greek junta and, whether or not any money changed hands at that point, the mission was almost immediately successful. Barely a month later, the Greek parliament passed a law titled "For the Settlement of Hereditary Questions of Greek Citizens Living Abroad." The law stipulated that, in the event of the death of a Greek citizen, a marriage contract drawn between the Greek citizen and a foreigner was legally invalid, and that the foreigner had no claim to the estate of the Greek citizen. (It is hard to imagine to which "Greek citizen" the new law might have applied, other than Onassis.) There was no mention of the passage of this law in the Greek press which, of course, the junta controlled, and so Jackie and her New York lawyers were unaware of the fact that she had, in effect, been disinherited.

It is curious that he felt he had to be so devious with her—that he had been unable to deal with her honestly and directly—as curious as the fact that he had felt unable, in the end, to control her spending. Perhaps it was just the Byzantine way his mind worked: he could not confront a problem head-on, that would be too simple, but only through convoluted machinations involving governments, agents, go-betweens and emissaries. Perhaps he had never intended to honor the pre-marital agreement, and it was just an elaborate charade to entice her into marrying him. Now he seemed to be preparing to shed himself of her, but in a roundabout way. He had always had trouble letting his women go. A strong-willed grandmother had dominated his childhood and early youth, his sisters had remained forces in his life, he still spoke nostalgically of his first wife, and he had never completely broken off his relationship with Callas. In a way, he was awed by women, a little frightened of them, and he was particularly awed by Jackie. It was as though she possessed a power over him that he didn't quite understand—possibly the aura of "class" that she managed to convey. She was not the earthy, tempestuous Maria Callas, who, when the occasion arose, could talk gutter language as efficiently as he or any of his dock-workers. He had married, instead, someone whom he considered to be a lady and he, in his heart of hearts, knew he was no gentleman. He had heard the name that his deckhands called him behind his back: *skilapsaro.*

He did not, however, intend to die and leave her completely penniless. He had presented her with what he described as an "amendment" to the original premarital agreement in which she was asked to agree to accept, following his death, an income of $200,000 a year for life, plus $25,000 a year for each of her children until they reached the age of twenty-one. She signed this readily, supposing that the new document meant that she would have an income of $250,000 a year *in addition* to the millions she assumed she would one day inherit. What she was actually accepting was a tiny share—less than two per cent—of what might have been her inheritance from him.

His complaints about Jackie's spending, meanwhile, continued—never to her directly, but to associates, secretaries, friends. Jackie, whom he had certainly spoiled at first, resented—could not understand—what she considered his sudden miserliness. Hadn't she read that, in a single year—1973—he had cleared a cold profit of a hundred million dollars transporting oil to his supertankers? What she did not know was that, from a business standpoint, by the end of 1973 things were not quite that rosy. Flushed with his early profits that year, Onassis had ordered construction of a fleet of new supertankers—at a cost of more than a quarter of a billion dollars. But the Arab oil embargo of late 1973 caught him with construction of the new tankers under way. All at once there was nothing for his tankers to transport, no place for them to go. He had hastily had to order construction halted on at least two big ships. The losses had been enormous and, on paper at least, Onassis's worth had dropped from close to a billion dollars to something like half that amount. Typical of the Old World businessman, and of his personal penchant for secrecy, Onassis shared none of the details of these business reverses with his wife. He merely relayed orders to her to spend less.

The Onassis children did not help what was becoming a rocky marriage. Though Onassis's sister Artemis had openly approved of Jackie in the beginning, his son and daughter, Alexander and Christina, had openly disapproved. On the day of the wedding—while the press all over the world was berating Jackie for what she was doing—young Alexander Onassis had added his criticism when he told a group of reporters curtly, "My father needed a wife, but I certainly didn't need a stepmother." Later he said, "I do not understand my father's fascination with the Kennedy woman. He's been in love with her for ages. She's beautiful, intelligent, and quite formidable, in the best European sense. But she can be so alarmingly exigent. She could undermine everything. She could jeopardize a whole epoch." Christina Onassis, looking glum, had refused to speak to reporters at the wedding, but she had been overheard to refer to Jackie as "my father's unhappy compulsion." As for the Kennedy children, though John seemed to enjoy his new stepfather, Caroline continued to be hostile. And of course the differences in ages between the Onassis young and the Kennedy young meant that the two pairs of stepchildren had very little in common.

Nor did the Catholic Church help matters much. Would Jackie be excommunicated for marrying a divorced man out of the Church, the Vatican was asked. The Vatican replied with a rather stiff announcement to the effect that in the Church's eyes "Mrs. Kennedy"—as the Vatican pointedly referred to her—was considered to be living in a state of mortal sin. The sin could be expiated, of course, through confession and penance. Whether or not Jackie ever confessed her sin is unknown, but if she did she would have had to stop living with Onassis—since with confession is supposed to go the vow that the sin will not be repeated or continued. And yet, after her remarriage, Jackie continued to receive the sacraments of the Church, which is all very much against canon law, leaving the distinct impression that Jackie had never been a very pious or serious Catholic, or that she considered herself, as a Catholic, very much a special case.

Outside factors such as these would have plagued the most ordinary of marriages, which Jackie's and Ari's most certainly was not. But there were far worse disasters. On January 27, 1973, Alexander Onassis, who was then twenty-four—on whom his father doted and to whom he had planned to turn over his shipping empire—crashed in a light aircraft in which he was a passenger as it was taking off from Athens airport, and died the next day. Ari was crushed—so crushed that he could not bring himself to attend his son's funeral. The death of his only son seemed to unhinge him. He became convinced that the crash had not been caused by an accident and that the plane had been sabotaged, and offered a reward of $500,000 to anyone who could prove that his son had been murdered. No one with proof came forward. The air crash soured his feelings for Olympic Airways and for flying in general, and he began negotiations to sell Olympic to the Greek government. But he could not agree on a price, and his negotiations seemed uncharacteristically loose, vague, and imprecise. He seemed to have lost his business verve and to be falling apart, obsessed with violence, murder, death, and vengeance.

In October, 1974, his first wife, Tina, died suddenly in Paris. Tina had been married briefly after her divorce from Onassis, to the Marquess of Blandford, and then had married Onassis's arch-rival Stavros Niarchos. Niarchos had earlier been married to Tina's sister, Eugenie, who had also died under mysterious circumstances, apparently of an overdose of drugs. When Tina had married Niarchos, Onassis had been convinced that she had done it to spite him, and lately he had begun to speak mournfully of Tina as the only real love of his life and to confess that he should never have let her go. When Eugenie Niarchos had died, there were suspicions of foul play, though a lengthy and well-publicized trial turned up no evidence of this. Now that yet another Mrs. Niarchos—Eugenie's own sister—had died suddenly and unexpectedly, having appeared in rosy good health the day before, dark rumors began to spread throughout the international set that Stavros Niarchos—whose terrible temper was as well known as Onassis's—had somehow managed to dispatch both these wives to their Maker. Onassis himself encouraged and fed these rumors, and his daughter Christina, convinced of foul play, ordered an autopsy performed on her mother's body. Again, no evidence to incriminate anyone was found.

Jackie had for some time been trying to befriend Christina, and had had some success. But now some superstitious strain out of her Smyrna peasant past suggested to Christina that some sinister force had to be connected with all these deaths—first her aunt, then her brother, now her mother. It must be Jackie who was bringing all the bad luck to the family, "undermining everything," as her brother had predicted. To Christina it seemed as though Jackie killed every life she touched. She was the Angel of Death. This terrible conviction was all the more powerful because, by then, Christina could see that her father was also dying.

Earlier that year he had contracted a disease called myasthenia gravis, a progressive nerve disorder which induces fatigue, depression, and a gradual loss of muscle tone—most noticeably in the muscles that control the eyelids. Massive doses of cortisone were prescribed, but the disease progressed at alarming speed. His eyelids had to be taped to his forehead with transparent or adhesive tape, which gave him a grotesque, even frightening, appearance. He tried to hide it behind heavy glasses. When he appeared in public —he still endeavored to make his regular rounds of nightclubs—he looked suddenly old and tired and ill. His heavy body sagged, and his color was bad. His talk was slurred and rambling, and there were sudden lapses of memory—for names, for faces, for the point he was trying to make. Supported by the loyal members of his team, he continued to try to go about his businesses, but he seemed to have lost both his touch and his interest in it.

In the autumn of 1974, according to Frank Brady, he dispatched Johnny Meyer to New York on a secret mission, which was to meet with lawyer Roy Cohn to see whether a means could be devised to divorce Jackie. His choice of Cohn was an interesting one because Cohn's reputation was for toughness, and clearly Ari was in a tough mood. Meyer, says Brady, told Cohn that Onassis had "had it" with Jackie. In addition to her spendthrift ways, there were other minor complaints. Whereas Onassis admired punctuality, Jackie was often late. Once, at a Manhattan dinner party they had given, she had been too busy with her *toilette* to greet her guests, and had not put in an appearance until long after the last guest had arrived. Because of her tardiness she had even caused expensive delays on Olympic Airways flights which could not take off until the owner's wife had come aboard. Onassis objected to the sloppy way she allowed her children to dress and to the unruly length of her son's hair—the usual complaints of a disgruntled husband. She had, he said, "not kept up her end of the bargain," whatever that was, overlooking the fact that she had been the wife of a United States president and had grown accustomed to being treated like a queen, as he had once assured her that she always would be.

There were several meetings between Meyer and Cohn, and a number of telephone conferences. The stumbling block was the pre-marital agreement. The new Greek law that Onassis had got passed benefited him, and protected his fortune, only after he had died. Until his death, the agreement remained hopelessly binding and, under it, he had promised to pay Jackie $10,000,000 for each year of their marriage—or $60,000,000. The ironies of the situation did not escape Onassis. In order to be rid of a wife whom he considered inordinately extravagant he would have to make her an extraordinarily rich woman. She would cost him far less in death than she would in life. And so, with the grim resignation of a hero in a Greek tragedy, he decided to wait for that death.

It did not take long. In January, 1975, he took to his bed in his villa outside Athens for the first time. He rose a few days later to try to conclude the Olympic business in the capital, and returned from the city much worse. Jackie was summoned from New York, and Christina arrived from Paris. In February, his doctors advised that he be moved to a hospital and, at Jackie's insistence, he was flown to the American hospital in Paris where, she felt, he could get the best medical attention in Europe. Jackie and Christina accompanied him. In the hospital, his gall bladder was removed, and a severe kidney malfunction was also diagnosed. Little by little, more life-sustaining apparatus was applied. Throughout the next weeks, Jackie, Christina, and Onassis's sisters alternated sitting with him. Frequently Jackie spent the entire day with him, leaving only to have dinner, and returning in the evening. Though she played her role as the devoted wife of a dying husband, a noticeable chill had developed between Jackie and the other women, in whom Onassis had confided his plans for a divorce.

He was a difficult patient, often in pain. His disconnected thoughts wandered from Skorpios to his first wife to his problems with the Greek government over Olympic. He frequently spoke in Greek which only his sisters and daughter could understand, and at times even his Greek was unintelligible. His doctors advised the family that his condition could continue this way for weeks, even months, and so finally —weary of the animosity of the Onassis family and feeling that there was little more that she could do for him—Jackie flew home to New York and her children who she felt needed her presence more.

Thus it was that when Aristotle Socrates Onassis died on March 15, 1975, with only his daughter at his side, his wife was thousands of miles away—a fact that would again make her the object of sharp press and public criticism. "She *knew* he was dying," people said. "Couldn't she at least have *been* there?" At a husband's deathbed was the rightful, wifely place to be.

Of course it had never been intended as a conventional marriage in the first place. It had been more like a business merger between two important international talents. Jackie, no fool, had been quite aware that one of her functions as his wife would be decorative, to add luster and elegance to the image of a man who had been known as something of a roughneck. For this she had expected to be compensated, and he had promised her that she would be. Still, though it had been in many ways a marriage of convenience for both of them, there was no question that she had been fond of him as he—at least in the beginning—had been of her.

Jackie issued only two public statements about her marriage to Onassis. The first, to the horde of photographers that descended upon Skorpios at the time of the wedding and threatened to disrupt the ceremony, was: "We know you will understand that even though people may be well-known, they still hold in their hearts the emotions of a simple person for the moments that are the most important of those we know on earth—birth, marriage and death. We wish our wedding day to be a private moment in the little chapel among the cypresses of Skorpios with only members of the family present, five of them little children. If you will give us those moments, we will so gladly give you all the cooperation possible for you to take the pictures you need."

The second was the careful statement she gave to the press when she arrived at Orly Airport in Paris after her husband's death the day before: "Aristotle Onassis rescued me at a moment when my life was engulfed with shadows. He meant a lot to me. He brought me into a world where one could find both happiness and love. We lived through many beautiful experiences together which cannot be forgotten, and for which I will be eternally grateful."

The press was just as intrusive at Onassis's funeral at it had been at the wedding, and dealing with it was just as harrowing. Perhaps that was why, in the procession with Onassis's family to his grave, when the flashbulbs popped she smiled that enormous smile. Instinctively, automatically. When the photograph was published, the big smile seemed startlingly out of place. But it was her last and best defense.

25

New York

JACQUELINE ONASSIS HAD boarded a plane for Australia, where she would begin negotiations with the Earl of Snowdon for the publication rights to his memoirs. If he decided to "tell all," Snowdon had indicated, what he had to say would "blow the lid off the British Royal Family." These facts were announced on NBC's eleven o'clock news report.

Did Jacqueline Onassis receive free tickets from airline companies? A reader in a question-answer column of the *New York Daily News* wanted to know. Yes, the *News* replied confidently. In fact, the *News* went on to say, British Airways recently presented her with a gratis ticket from London to Athens so that she could visit the gravesite of her late husband.

Caroline Kennedy, as everybody knows, is a little "wild." In London, where she was studying art and art history for the better part of a year, she became even wilder. Jackie, furthermore, was furious with her daughter because Caroline wanted to take up photography. Jackie claimed photography would "damage the family image." So stated a national women's magazine.

Midnight, a notoriously unreliable gossip sheet that decorates the check-out counters of many supermarkets, reliably reported that Jackie had illegally made off with a number of precious art objects from Greece, and had stashed them in her New York apartment. "She could go to jail," *Midnight* added solemnly.

The only thing that any of the above stories had in common was that not a word of any of them was true. When NBC had Jackie in Australia, she was actually comfortably this side of the equator, in Round Hill, Jamaica, vacationing with her children. She had paid for her ticket, and neither British Airways nor any other airline company lets her ride for free. (With Onassis and Olympic, of course, it was another story.) Lord Snowdon had given no indication that he would, or would not write his memoirs. The assertion that Jackie feared that Caroline's alleged photographic ambitions would mar the family image was not only untrue but particularly farfetched, since Jackie herself had once worked as a photojournalist. And as for the stolen art objects, there weren't any. *Midnight* was simply up to its usual game of entertaining its readers by making up stories.

Would the barrage of publicity—true, false, exaggerated or indifferent—never end? Daily, it seemed, editors came up with more and increasingly fanciful Jackie stories to satisfy the insatiable curiosity of their readers about the most famous woman in the world— because, as has been proven, Jackie stories sold newspapers and magazines. On and on the stories went, and there seemed to be no end in sight. Even the Manhattan tour buses consistently pointed out the wrong apartment building for Jacqueline Onassis as they guided their passengers down Fifth Avenue.

Was it because, perhaps, after Onassis's death, the actual facts of Jacqueline Onassis's life became dull? Alone again in New York, she wasn't all that social, and spent many more evenings at home than she spent out—helping her son with his homework, or watching television while spooning yoghurt out of a paper container, or reading, reading, reading. (What startling things can be said about a woman who doesn't mind her own company and reads a lot?) She never went to cocktail parties and avoided most charity benefits. She didn't give grand entertainments, preferring occasional small dinners, sometimes black tie, sometimes not, usually for eight—for twenty-four at most, with guests seated at four round tables of six. Her old friend Nancy Tuckerman had become only a part-time secretary, devoting the balance of her days to a New York publishing company, and most of Nancy's time with Jackie was spent regretting invitations, including periodic requests to dine at the White House.

In New York her life settled into a pattern not all that different from any other well-to-do Manhattan housewife. She shopped—for bags at Art Bag on Madison Avenue, for shoes (size 10 medium, $55 to $88 a pair) at Lady Continental. She bought her groceries at the East 85th Street Gristede's, around the corner from her building, went to Miss Grimble's for cheesecake, bought brownies at William Greenberg's and chocolate truffles at $10 a pound from

Tom Kron's. Her flowers—she favored pink lilies, anemones, small bunches of violets—came from Flowers by Philip. She paid her bills promptly. She jogged in Central Park, in a bright red jump suit, visited her dentist on East 62nd Street, saw her woman analyst on Central Park West for one-hour sessions on Thursday afternoons. During non-rush hours she used ordinary taxis to get about the city. At busy times she used a radio-call cab service. On weekends, she got behind the wheel of her green BMW and drove to her country house in New Jersey, always careful to have the correct change for the "Exact Change" baskets at the George Washington Bridge toll stations (toll-takers in the manned booths tended to recognize her and to try to engage her in conversation.)

She said almost nothing, and did very little, that would seem newsworthy, much less make headline copy. Her public utterances, when they occurred, seemed almost deliberately calculated to be as bland and unquotable as possible, as in the following exchange on WNBC-TV's "Sunday" show, when she was being interviewed by reporter Ponchita Pierce at a museum opening:

Q: When you look at a painting, a photograph, a work of art, is that what's important, how it touches your spirit, what it says to you?
A: It depends. Painting and photography are different.

Could a banner heading be composed saying: JACKIE ONASSIS DECLARES PAINTING AND PHOTOGRAPHY ARE DIFFERENT? Steadfastly —politely but firmly—she refused to give newspaper or magazine interviews. She would "rather not," she said, and that was that. Even close friends in the media—Barbara Walters, for example—were unable to persuade her to alter this policy. If the details of her New York life—compared with the drama, glamour, and intrigue of her life with both Kennedy and Onassis—seemed a little bland and tame and ordinary, she has no comment on that. Still, ironically, the public speculation about her private life continued to build. Through it all—serene, smiling, aloof, mysterious, enigmatic and unapproachable—surrounded by a small but fiercely protective coterie of friends, Jacqueline Onassis remained sphinx-like, Garbo-like, our greatest, most tantalizing, most exasperating celebrity.

And yet, for all the aloofness and the mystery and speculation that continued to surround her, there was talk—in the months following Onassis's death when she came to settle, more or less permanently, into the New York scene—of a "new Jackie." It was said that she was consciously trying to cultivate a new "image" for herself, and it was certainly true that there were some interesting changes in her style of life. For one thing, there were noticeably fewer of those long, lingering lunches at expensive restaurants such as Orsini's, Lafayette, and La Côte Basque. Instead, she was seen popping in for a quick hamburger at P. J. Clarke's, where she preferred an inconspicuous table in the far corner of the back room. At the same time, there were more frequent public surfacings of the famous face with the enormous, photogenic smile—but not at parties, charity balls, or traditional society doings. She had begun to present a less frivolous face to the press and public. The surfacings tended to occur at cultural and intellectual affairs—a dinner honoring Lillian Hellman, concerts at Lincoln Center, museum and art gallery openings, and lectures at the International Center for Photography where, in sweater and slacks, she sat on the floor when the room ran out of seats.

Artists and writers, she had begun to reiterate, were the sorts of people whose company she enjoyed the most. Among the men who escorted her about town were Philip Roth, Pete Hamill, George Plimpton, Carl Killingworth of NBC, and Karl Katz, Chairman for

Special Projects at the Metropolitan Museum of Art,
who became known as "Jackie's intellectual boy-
friend." It seemed clear that if she was after a new
image it was that of a serious woman who would support only serious, worthwhile projects in the city.

In line with this, the professional Jackie-watchers
noticed that she no longer sported the expensive
clothes and jewelry that she once did. David Webb
seemed to have given way to Kenneth Jay Lane, and
not much of that either. Her style of dress, while
hardly mousey, had become distinctly more quiet,
simple, and understated. She appeared to be spending
less money on clothes than she once did (possibly because there was now somewhat less money to spend),
and to choose them with more care and thought. Designers like Halston pointed out that, as a customer,
she was far less lucrative than, say, Elizabeth Taylor.
Halston might make a hundred dresses a year for
Miss Taylor. But, for Jackie, it was one or two a season, always going over her choices carefully, and discussing price. Unlike Miss Taylor, she was not averse
to appearing in the same outfit more than once.

Her interests appeared to have turned to more interesting things than fashion. In 1975, for example,
she suddenly appeared at the South Street offices of
the *New York Post*—the celebrity coming to the press
instead of the other way around—where she was
taken on a tour of the city room. Why? "Just interested," she explained, "in seeing how a big-city newspaper works." In January of that year she had
delivered, unsolicited, a nicely written manuscript to
New Yorker editor William Shawn, in which she described the opening of the new International Center
for Photography, directed by her friend Cornell Capa.
The New Yorker published the piece, unsigned—as
is customary in the magazine's "Talk of the Town"
section—in its January 13 issue. For the nice plug it
gave to his museum, Mr. Capa is still overwhelmed
with gratitude. No, he had not asked her to do this

for him. It was entirely her own idea, and came as a complete surprise to him. Jackie had known that opening the new museum had involved tremendous expense, and that the museum sorely needed financial support. Her *New Yorker* piece was by way of a contribution.

One of the moving spirits behind the museum had been her friend Karl Katz and, no, he had not asked her to do it either—nor was it he who got her interested in the museum. "Nobody *gets* Jackie interested in anything," he said at the time. "She gets interested in things herself." At about the same time, she was asked by the Kennedy Center to be honorary chairman of a benefit for Roger Stevens. To everyone's astonishment, she volunteered to be *active* chairman. "This is the first time she's done anything for the Kennedy Center since she married Onassis," said one of the board members. Being active chairman of the event meant that Jackie put in many hours of work—telephoning, writing letters, setting up committees, and otherwise supervising the organization of the evening.

In other words, she seemed to be presenting herself in public in ways she never had before, and her friends began to feel that she was doing this quite deliberately to de-fuse the spendthrift impression the public had gotten of her, or to diffuse the publicity that followed her wherever she went. "If she keeps turning up at sober, worthy, intellectual and artistic affairs," said one friend, "she figures the press will eventually get bored with her and leave her alone."

It didn't happen, of course. In the autumn of 1975, Mr. Capa's museum mounted an exhibition of photographs by Ernst Haas, and Jackie had agreed to hostess a private fund-raising party to launch the show. The press had been invited for cocktails only and, though the occasion was decidedly a minor one in terms of newsworthiness, the press arrived in droves simply because *she* was coming. As usual, in any

Jackie appearance, there was a certain amount of suspense and doubt. Just as she occasionally appears at functions unannounced, she had been known to fail to appear when scheduled. As the cocktail guests wandered about, there was all at once a flurry of excitement. Her friend Mrs. Alexander Hillman, the art collector, had arrived. "That means *she'll* definitely be coming," one guest whispered. Then there was a sudden collective shout and push, a surge toward the door. It was, as one guest put it, as though the entire room had begun to list to one side as socially prominent and supposedly sophisticated New Yorkers shoved and jostled each other for front positions. Cameras clicked and flashbulbs popped, and there *she* was, with the smile, escorted by Karl Katz and accompanied by her friend Albina DeBoisrouvray. Immediately she was surrounded by a protective cluster of friends, including Mr. Capa, a phalanx she had learned to use to create a kind of buffer zone around her which keeps the photographers and the reporters at a comfortable distance. She was taken on a quick tour of the exhibit, smiled some more and posed for more photographs, murmured, "I want to do everything I can to help," shook a few hands, then disappeared upstairs and the non-event was over. But clearly the presence of Jacqueline Onassis had become an event in itself.

She proved that point again in the early spring of 1977. Her old friend, the former football star Roosevelt Grier, wondered if, as a favor, she would fly to Los Angeles to add her luster to a benefit show he was staging for Giant Step, a project to aid underprivileged children which Grier runs. Indeed she would, she replied. "I'll do what I can to help you, Rosey," she said. "I'm not a performer—I'm not going up on the stage—but I'll go into the community." No sooner had word of Jackie's impending appearance at the benefit got out than every ticket to the affair was sold. Hollywood, it might seem, would be blasé about stars in its midst. But Jackie was a different kind of star. Prior to the show, Grier took her on a riding and walking tour of the Watts section, and Jackie visited black families in their homes, chatted on a street corner with a group of black teen-agers—while Hollywood watched agog. Later, at the show, where she was technically just another member of the audience, there was no question that the dark-haired woman in the white strapless dress was the leading attraction of the gala.

She might not be succeeding in curbing the publicity about her, but she was certainly managing to control it. She was even, it began to seem, beginning to enjoy it. When Mr. and Mrs. Bertrand L. Taylor —he is a stockbroker, she the director of New York's Cooper-Hewitt Museum of Design—first encountered Jackie after Onassis's death, it was at a dinner party at the home of mutual friends. The Taylors live just a few blocks north of Jackie on Fifth Avenue and, at the end of the evening, asked her if they could give her a lift home. She accepted, and when Mr. Taylor stepped outside the building to get his car, while the ladies waited in the lobby, he noticed two men with cameras standing in the shadows. Stepping back inside, Taylor said to Jackie, "I think I'd better warn you that there are two photographers outside." With a look of mock anguish, Jackie replied, "Only *two*? I must be slipping!" Then, with a wink, she added, "Let's have some fun with them." Arranging her face in the smile, she put her hand in the crook of Taylor's elbow, and walked out onto the sidewalk with him, as if to say, "Here's my new beau."

In the fall of 1975, meanwhile, when Onassis had been dead for barely six months, Jackie made news of a new and different sort. She took a job—as consulting editor at The Viking Press, a properly small, select, and prestigious publishing house. Her wage was a scrivener's $10,000 a year but it was nonetheless sufficient to dispell the accusation that she was merely doing dilettantish volunteer work. Was this another attempt to assert the sense of purpose and seriousness of the new Jackie, and to bolster the "new image" which some of her friends said she wished to project? Partly, perhaps, but there were other reasons behind this move as well.

Over that past summer, friends had noticed that Jackie seemed bored, restless. The public airing of the details of Onassis's will—which, though it provided for her comfortably enough, had been something of an insult—had depressed her. She was sleeping late, and was spending longer hours than usual over her breakfast tray and the morning newspapers. When she telephoned friends to chat she seemed to have little to chat about. Her friends, meanwhile, could not help but feel their friendship somewhat compromised by her fame. She was no longer—no matter how good a friend—the kind of chum you could call and ask to a movie, or drop in on for a cup of coffee or a drink. She seemed isolated and a little lonely, but still one hesitated before dialing that private YUkon number.

To her old friend Letitia Baldridge, who had served as her social secretary in the White House, and who now operated a snappy East Side public relations agency, she seemed like a woman who needed something to do. "Who me—*work?*" was Jackie's first incredulous reaction to Tish Baldridge's suggestion. But, the more she thought about it, the more she warmed to the idea. "I believe work is good therapy for anybody," Tish Baldridge says. "I felt she needed something for her morale. I felt she really needed something to make her get up in the morning, get out in the world and meet interesting people who were doing interesting things, to use that energy and that good brain of hers. I suggested publishing. Viking was my publisher, and I said to her, 'Look, you know Tommy Guinzburg—why don't you talk to him?' "

Miss Baldridge went even further. She telephoned

Guinzburg, the head of Viking, told him of the conversation, and Guinzburg telephoned Jackie. A lunch was set up in June, 1975, at Le Perigord Park. This was followed by several more lunches and, by the end of the summer, the deal was set. "There was immediate understanding," Guinzburg said at the time. "I saw what she could bring to us. The wide range of her contacts and background and the world she moves in will result in all sorts of books—projects involving art and fashion and history, the things she's interested in. Book ideas don't just come out of editorial conferences. They come out of dinner parties, too. As for Jackie, publishing can offer her the kind of privacy and anonymity she wants. Editors aren't in the business of publicizing themselves. They're in the business of making *authors* famous."

Guinzburg admitted that his staff was "pretty stunned" when the Onassis hiring was announced. "Everyone wondered, 'What's this giant celebrity doing in our midst?' " he said, "and everybody assumed that she must be planning to write a book. She had no intention of ever writing a book. The biggest problem was how to get her started working here with the least amount of turmoil and public furor."

That, of course, turned out to be impossible. On her first day of work in September, the sidewalks outside Viking's offices were jammed with reporters, photographers, television news cameras, and ordinary gawkers as Jackie Onassis arrived at 625 Madison Avenue, made her smiling way into the building, and stepped into an elevator.

Soon, however, all that had changed, and the working editor was making her way between Viking and her apartment virtually unnoticed. At Viking, she was given a small, almost Spartan office with a single window, a desk, a typewriter, filing cabinets, and a couple of chairs. She started coming to work in sweaters and slacks, wearing no jewelry, "Dressed just like the rest of us," according to her assistant, Rebecca Singleton, "but always managing somehow to do it a little better." As she settled into the office routine, curiosity about her at Viking dwindled, and after a while no one looked up when the famous person walked down the halls—to the coffee machine for another cup, to the cigarette vendor for another pack of Salems (she smokes many), or to stand in line for her turn at the Xerox machine. From the beginning, Jackie worked with her office door open, did much of her own typing, placed her own telephone calls, and handled her own files—"which was terrific for me," says Miss Singleton, "because I'm terrible at that sort of thing."

Still, there were daily reminders that Jacqueline Onassis was no ordinary book person. There was the large volume of mail, for one thing. Fans from all over the country who did not know their heroine's address now had a published address and telephone number for her. There were many requests for autographed photographs, which were ignored. "Unfortunately, we've always had to ignore most of these," says Nancy Tuckerman. "We look at the postmarks. If a girl in the fifth grade at a school in Medford, Oregon, got an autographed picture of Mrs. Onassis, everybody in the school would want one. It would just get out of hand." There were also letters that asked for a lock of hair, which were also ignored. There were letters that began, "I love you. Please send me $10,000." Then there were the manuscipts that came in to her —"Mostly by little old ladies with new interpretations of the Psalms," according to Tom Guinzburg, "or with new theories about the Kennedy assassinations." These were politely returned, unread, to their authors.

Finally there were the telephone calls—from honest admirers, and from certifiable cranks. These, of course, were diligently screened. "I discovered that the crank calls had a lot to do with the weather," says Miss Singleton. "On rainy days the nuts stay home and use the telephone." When the cranks couldn't get through to Jackie Onassis, they tried to get Tom Guinzburg on the line. At one point Guinzburg's secretary had to deal with an irate lady from Texas who, marvelously confusing The Viking Press with a NASA project and Guinzburg himself with several other people with similar-sounding names, shouted, "Listen, I know all about this Guinzburg! He's that long-haired hippie homosexual who took drugs and wrote crazy poetry! Then he tried to publish that dirty magazine and they arrested him for it! Then he sent that Viking Mariner to the moon! Now he's hired Jackie Kennedy, and he's gone *too far!*"

There was hate mail too, and there were hate telephone calls. The letters were destroyed, and the calls disposed of as quickly as possible. Last but not least, there was the periodic pestering from the press. "Every time Caroline sneezed, twenty-five reporters called up," says Miss Singleton. "She learned long ago to ignore all this. She learned to not even look at the newsstands. All the Kennedys have." Of course working for Jackie Onassis managed to change Miss Singleton's life somewhat. "I tried not to tell people who I worked for," she says, "because the minute they found out they were full of questions—'What's she *really* like?' and so forth. If I said what she's really like—that she's terrific, great to work for, has tremendous energy and no airs whatever—people just weren't satisfied."

Perhaps the reason why people could not be satisfied with such an easy explanation was because Jackie's new life in New York as a single woman—and her new career—seemed so markedly in contrast with anything she had ever done before, from anything the public had been led to expect of her. If she had married another billionaire, or a prince from some exotic kingdom, that would have been understandable. But instead she showed no inclination to marry anyone, and had gone to work. Once again she had done the unpredictable.

Even more interesting was the fact that the public
adulation which she seemed to have lost so completely
when she married Onassis (JACKIE, HOW COULD
YOU? a Swedish newspaper had headlined at the
time) turned out not to have been lost at all. Or perhaps, by late 1975, she was being admired by a different type of public. A rural housewife in southern
Indiana might continue to view Jacqueline Onassis
as a kind of high-class prostitute, a bird in a gilded
cage who had sold her beauty for an old man's gold.
But to a more urbane, cynical, metropolitan mind of
the 1970's, she was a woman who had pulled through
very well. She had walked a tightrope between fame
and notoriety and made it—the successful aerialist—
beautifully to the other end of the wire. In New York,
that city of survivors, she was admired as a survivor
of a particularly tough game.

26

Working

WITHIN A FEW months after Jackie had gone to work
for Viking, Lee Radziwill announced that she, too,
was embarking on a new career—as an interior decora-
tor, a métier that had seemed to be in the Bouvier
blood since the first Michel Bouvier began "furnishing
cloth and silk for tables" in Philadelphia. Lee had
tried her hand at various other lines of work. In 1967,
she appeared briefly on the stage as the leading lady
in *The Philadelphia Story,* to generally unfavorable
critical reaction. The following winter, her friend Tru-

man Capote had persuaded her to take the title role in his television adaptation of the motion picture *Laura*. This time, the critics had been openly hostile, and had implied that she would never have been given the part at all if she had not happened to be Jacqueline Kennedy's sister. Following the collapse of her marriage to Radziwill, she had done some volunteer work. She had attempted to write her memoirs, and a brief episode from these—a somewhat breathless account of her happy girlhood—had appeared in *Ladies' Home Journal*. Nothing much more ever came of the memoirs.

To Lisa Taylor—offering to work for Mrs. Taylor's Cooper-Hewitt Museum of Design—Lee had said, "I need something to do. After all, I was a failure as an actress. I was a failure as a writer." And she had added ruefully, "I was even a failure as a princess." Now, however, she was determined to reverse this trend, and her first assignment was an ambitious one to supervise the redecoration of rooms for the Americana Hotel chain. Once again, what Lee was doing did not sound quite as interesting as what Jackie was doing—but it was something and, as Lee was quick to point out, her new job could in no way be considered "competition" with her sister.

In publishing, meanwhile, the job of "consulting editor" is somewhat loosely defined. Malcolm Cowley, a consulting editor for Viking for twenty-five years, has seldom ventured outside his Connecticut home in that capacity. Jackie Onassis chose to make more of the job than this. She arrived in her office between 9:30 and 10:00 in the morning, four days a week. She attended editorial meetings and conferences. On Mondays, her days off, she never failed to telephone in. One of her first projects at Viking was a book called *Remember the Ladies*, which celebrated American women between 1750 and 1815 and which, in addition to some 200 illustrations, contained essays by historians Linda Grant DePauw and Conover Hunt.

It was a book that combined both art and history—two of Jackie's enthusiasms—and was published in June, 1976, in conjunction with a Bicentennial exhibit at the Plymouth Historical Society in Massachusetts.

The book was not, however, Jackie's brainchild, as several accounts had it at the time. Credit for that belongs to Mrs. Henry Brandon, the wife of the Washington bureau chief for *Sunday Times* of London. Though the Brandons and the Kennedys had been friends during the White House days, Muffie Brandon and Jackie came together on the "Ladies" project almost by accident.

For several years, Muffie Brandon had been working to restore and preserve historic homes in Plymouth, where the Brandons spent their summers. One of these was the Mercy Otis Warren house, which had belonged to Abigail Adams's best friend. This gave Muffie Brandon the idea for a book and an exhibition on women of the Revolutionary period. "I had appointments to present the idea to Viking and to Random House," Muffie Brandon says. "My first appointment was at Viking, with Tom Guinzburg, and when I walked into the meeting I was quite surprised to see Jackie there—I hadn't seen her for some time, and she'd only been at Viking a few days. As I explained the idea, I saw her eyes begin to light up. She sat forward in her chair. She caught the idea immediately, and for the next two hours she asked the most penetrating questions. She wanted to know what proportion of the text would be devoted to black women—to working women, to Indian women. She wanted to know how the art would relate to the historical material, whether the book would be a catalogue or a history book. Finally, Tom Guinzburg turned to her and said, 'What do you think?' She said, 'Oh, let's do it!' I immediately telephoned and canceled the appointment with Random House. Later, she took me on a tour of Viking—showed me the art department, the marketing department, the paperback division. She was so proud, so professional."

At the time, Muffie Brandon was convinced that Jackie had found her niche in publishing, and at Viking. "It's obvious that she's made her peace, that she was born for this. As for what she's been through in the past—well, life is a river and one searches one's way. Now she's made the quantum leap," Mrs. Brandon said.

Jackie and Muffie Brandon spent long collaborative hours putting *Remember the Ladies* together, often spending "eight hours at a time, crawling around the floor, arranging picture layouts." When the two came upon an eighteenth-century sex manual, they roared over its various pronouncements and suggestions, wondering how to illustrate them. "We discovered that there was a root that women chewed to induce abortions," Muffie Brandon says. "Jackie said, 'Put that in —we want the book to be factual, and also earthy.' " Jackie's particular concern was a section treating the role of women in marriage. "We don't want the book to be a liberationist tract," she said. She insisted on the inclusion of such quaint bits of advice to parents as one which urged them to "rank their children in their early years among their cats and dogs." When the women came to a section on Presidential ladies, Muffie Brandon watched Jackie's face. "There wasn't a flicker—just interest and knowledge." When a letter from Martha Washington turned up which described Georgetown, where Jackie once lived, as "a dirty hole," Jackie roared with laughter and commented, "It still is." When Martha Washington added, "I lead a dull life—a state prisoner," Jackie laughed again.

Muffie Brandon says, "Even at Farmington we knew that she would go on to be outstanding at whatever she did, no matter whom she married." Others are less sure—among them Gloria Steinem, the feminist editor of *Ms.* magazine, who tends to feel that Guinzburg's hiring of Jackie was just another example of the way the male establishment tries to exploit women, that it was basically a public-relations trick. Jackie had at one point telephoned Miss Steinem and had asked her to lunch. Jackie's idea was that Gloria Steinem might have a book in mind that Viking might want to publish. Miss Steinem said that she had no plans to write a book, but offered to suggest other authors and ideas for books on feminist themes. In return, Miss Steinem asked Jackie whether she would be willing to issue a statement in favor of the Equal Rights Amendment. To this Jackie demurred, and the lunch ended on an unsatisfactory note. "I'm sure she's in favor of the ERA," Miss Steinem says today, "but she wouldn't make any statement. Of course I was disappointed—that she hasn't used, and won't use, the tremendous power that she has when it comes to backing important public issues. But I guess I can't criticize her. She didn't ask for that power. I'm convinced that she really is a private person. Also, though I questioned Viking's reasons for hiring her, I'm convinced that she was really trying to do the best possible job there that she could, and that that was really all she wanted at the moment."

"At the moment"—that is the key phrase, the skeptics say, to describe Jackie's behavior. Her detractors —and there are a number of these in the jealously competitive world of New York society—like to point out that Jackie Onassis has always been a woman who was primarily interested in doing what is currently in fashion. It is chic these days for a wealthy woman to have a job, and art and history are "in" at the moment. It was clever of Jackie to get involved in publishing an American history book during the year of the Bicentennial—and no coincidence. Next year, or the year after, when it becomes fashionable to crossbreed cattle in Vermont, say the skeptics, that's where Jackie will be. That's what her "new image" is all about.

In 1977, just two years after joining Viking, she

seemed to prove this thesis when she suddenly and angrily quit her job, and the quantum leap was—at least temporarily—aborted. At issue was a publishing matter which really did no credit to any of the people involved. Viking, it seemed, had earlier that year decided to publish a novel by a British author, Jeffrey Archer, called *Shall We Tell the President?* Set in 1983, it involved the fictional assassination of Edward Moore Kennedy who, by that year, had been placed by the author in the White House. As word of the Archer book began to appear in the press, various members of the Kennedy family expressed their distress and displeasure to their former in-law, the new Viking editor.

There are at least two versions of what happened. According to Tom Guinzburg, he had discussed Viking's plans to publish the Archer novel with Jackie prior to drawing the final contract and, at the time, she expressed no objections. It was only the later pressure from her Kennedy relatives that made her upset. At the time of her resignation, Guinzburg issued a statement to the press which said, "My own affection for the Kennedy family and the extremely effective and valued contribution which Mrs. Onassis has made to Viking over the past two years would obviously have been an overriding factor in the decision to publish any particular book which might cause her further anguish. Indeed, it is precisely because of the generous and understanding response of Mrs. Onassis at the time we discussed this book and before the contract was signed which gave me confidence to proceed with the novel's publication."

According to Samuel Vaughan at Doubleday, however, this is not quite true. Vaughan claims that Jackie first heard of Viking's plans from her friend Lisa Drew, also at Doubleday, sometime *after* the contract had been signed—that no prior discussion with Jackie had taken place and that Guinzburg had, in a sense, made his decision to publish behind her back.

In any case, the press, in reviews of *Shall We Tell the President?* took the opportunity to imply that Jacqueline Onassis had somehow been directly responsible for the book's publication. In his review for the *New York Times,* critic John Leonard called the book a "bad thriller," and said, "There is a word for such a book. The word is trash." Somewhat churlishly he added, "Anybody associated with its publication should be ashamed of herself." Though he did not say who "she" was, it was quite clear to whom he was referring. Following the lead of the *Times,* the *Boston Globe* also ran an article blaming Jackie for the book. Jackie was incensed. Although Tom Guinzburg's statement called the newspaper articles "grossly unfair," it was the end of a long friendship between himself and Jackie. He was particularly stung by the fact that Jackie had not discussed her resignation with him personally. She had simply cleaned out her desk and left him a curt, handwritten note. The romance with Viking was over.

What Jackie had discovered was that publishing is no longer the "occupation for gentlemen" that it once may have been, and that mixed with lofty aims to publish important literature are today's very real needs to make a buck. (*Remember the Ladies* had not been exactly a giant best-seller; *Shall We Tell the President?* has to date earned nearly a million dollars for its author.) Her brief statement to the press at the time of her resignation reflected her hurt at this discovery. "Last spring," she said through Nancy Tuckerman, "when told of the book, I tried to separate my lives as a Viking employee and a Kennedy relative. But this fall, when it was suggested that I had something to do with acquiring the book and that I was not distressed by its publication, I felt I had to resign." In New York, the literary and society worlds tended to take her side. After all, Viking had had a reputation of being a small, choosy "class" house. It did seem a little thoughtless—not to say tacky and tasteless—

for Viking to publish a book on a subject so sensitive to one of its consulting editors. It was widely rumored that Jackie would soon join another publishing house—Doubleday, perhaps, where she had many friends, though it was pointed out that John Sargent, Doubleday's chairman, was one of her frequent escorts. That a company head would hire a woman he was dating seemed unlikely. Still, unlikely things have a way of happening where Jackie is concerned and, in the early spring of 1978, it was announced that she would indeed be joining Doubleday's editorial staff. To put off the press and television cameras, she arrived at her new job a day later than had been announced, and soon everybody at Doubleday was saying the same nice things that had been said at Viking: that she was bright, efficient, undemanding and—well, just fitted right in.

She continued, meanwhile, to move in more or less literary circles in New York—turning up, for example, at a publication party for her friend Pete Hamill's new novel. At this occasion, a crowded roomful of supposedly sophisticated New Yorkers pushed, shoved, jostled and elbowed each other and stood on chairs to get a better look at her, offering such penetrating comments on her appearance as, "Her hands look old," and "Her feet *are* too big!" These semi-public surfacings of the face with the endless smile were, it was said, all a part of the "new image" Jackie was endeavoring to project.

But the close friends disagree. "She doesn't even think about projecting an image," her sister, and her friend George Plimpton both say. Plimpton says, "It's silly. One doesn't sit down one morning and say, 'I think I'll give myself a new image.' If she thought that way, she'd hire a public-relations agency." Another friend says, "Look, you've got to remember that she was married to not one but *two* of the most difficult men in the world. They were both ego-maniacs and bullies who treated women like chattel. Jackie was always somewhat diminished by them, dominated by them, and forced to live in their shadows. Jackie endured them both and outlived them both. Now she's on her own, as her own woman, and she seems to be finding it a thrilling experience. She doesn't want to be known as the wife of the President of the United States, or the wife of one of the richest men in the world. She wants to be known as *herself*. Of course she's ambitious, and wouldn't settle for being anything second-rate. She wants to be important—and in her own right."

She enjoys being important, her friends feel, and does not mind having become (to say the least) a public figure, but she is also determined to maintain a high degree of privacy. Doubleday, the friends feel, has helped provide this, and so has New York City. In the large, well-secured flat, decorated in sunny yellows, golds, and greens, she can spend quiet evenings alone with her children. In front of one living room window, overlooking the park and the lake and the Metropolitan Museum, stands an easel where she often sits and sketches. There is also a telescope through which she can study her West Side neighbors. (How many women on Central Park West, reading about Jacqueline Onassis in their magazines, realize that Jacqueline Onassis is watching them?)

Or, when she wishes, she can give one of her little dinners such as the one she gave for Sir Hugh Frazier, who had been Caroline's host in London. The guests —the George Plimptons, the Roger Mudds, the Stephen Smiths, the Arthur Schlesingers, Candace Bergen, Barbara Walters, the Peter Duchins, loyalists all—all offered lengthy and humorous toasts to their hostess, congratulating her on joining the ranks of the employed. She answered each toast with a bright smile, nothing more. And the make-up of the guest list guaranteed that the party would not make the papers.

Still, whenever she ventures out—an evening at the theater, for example, with Peter and Cheray Duchin, followed by a hamburger at P. J. Clarke's and a drink at Jimmy Weston's (where the party was joined by Frank Sinatra)—the photographers manage to find her, and her picture winds up in *Newsweek* and *Time*. Why, it is worth asking, do the public and, in turn, the press, remain so avidly interested in her every small move?

Photographer Cornell Capa thinks it is her physical beauty—"The excitement, elegance, and electricity she radiates." It lies in the wrap-around smile and the big, wide-set eyes. "She *projects*," Capa says. "She doesn't have to do much. Her face carries its own spotlight. She has the ability to be looked at, and to be one who *sees*. She always knows what she's saying, and to whom. She can fit in everywhere. She's absolutely unique. Throughout history, there's been no comparable figure—modern, a queen, but not living on a pedestal." Her friend Muffie Brandon thinks it's her combination of determination, spunk, and a certain daintiness. "She's a blend of iron and silk," Mrs. Brandon says. Karl Katz speaks of her sense of humor, "A wonderful way of seeing the funny side to even a serious situation. She loves to giggle. She's great fun to be with."

George Plimpton also talks of the giggle. "It's a very *intimate* giggle. She and her sister both have it, and a very soft, intimate speaking voice that completely absorbs you." Louis Auchincloss, a cousin by marriage, also speaks of that intense personal magnetism, the magic gaze: "When she talks to you she fixes those eyes on you, and you feel as though you're the only person in the world she's interested in or cares about. Then, when she turns to talk to someone else, it's as though you've been dropped off the planet." Others mention her considerateness. "I happen to have a bad back," Karl Katz says, "the way Jack Kennedy did, and Jackie knows this, and she's always making sure that I've got the most comfortable chair. She schleps

things around town that she thinks I shouldn't carry—
that sort of thing." Katz adds, "She's a wonderful
mother, silly as it sounds to say that. But all you have
to do is watch her with those kids—the way she laughs
and jokes with them—and you see they're more than
her children. They're her best pals."

Still, none of this explains why we, the public, remain so tantalized by her. Perhaps it is because, better
than any famous woman in history (including Garbo)
—tentatively at first, then with growing aplomb, and
finally with magnificent mastery—she has learned how
to play on her public, and to manage her celebrity.
Today, she is in utter control of it. She comes from a
family that has long had a streak of theatricality. There
was her grandfather Bouvier's dramatic courtroom
manner, her flashily handsome father who liked nothing better than to be mistaken for Clark Gable, her
sister, the actress *manquée,* and her aunt and cousin,
the two Edies, both of whom had dreamed of stage
careers. One has only to watch the Maysles Brothers
"direct cinema" film, *Grey Gardens,* to see how Jackie's Bouvier aunt and cousin relished displaying their
disheveled lives before the cameras, achieving a star-
dom they had always wanted but never before at-
tained. At the time of the film's release in 1974 it was
widely criticized as a cruel invasion into the privacy of
two defenseless eccentrics—it included a scene in
which one of "Big Edie" Beale's withered breasts
tumbled out of the top of her swimsuit. The Beales
themselves did not take that view at all. "They're very
nice people," Big Edie said of the film makers in 1976,
not long before her death. "It's the greatest thing that
ever happened to me in my old age. You know, I'll be
eighty-one in October. Nobody else wanted to take my
picture. I'm thrilled." Not long after her mother's
death, Little Edie made a long belated attempt at the
kind of career she had always wanted—the theater,
though her show-business debut was not all that auspicious. It consisted of a short engagement as a song-

and-dance act at a somewhat raffish New York night spot called Reno Sweeney's. People would come to see her, the club figured, out of sheer curiosity, and they were right. Before opening her act, Little Edie held a press conference in which she admitted that Jackie had been paying many of her bills, and added, "Jackie's sweet. I should write her a letter."

But Jackie's formula for dealing with her celebrity has been her own creation. She gives us that smiling face that beams from every newsstand. It is almost as though, in every American living room, a blowup of the face looks down on all of us. But behind that face we know almost nothing. Beauty is in the eye of the beholder, but what is in the eye that the beholder beholds? *Women's Wear Daily* will tell us where she ate lunch. But we know nothing of what she did for breakfast or dinner, which is exactly as she prefers it to be. Skillfully keeping the heavy smokescreen of publicity about her, she has managed to retreat behind it into an insulated and comfortable shelter. She has discovered the ironic fact that intense publicity can be a kind of protection against invasion of privacy. In this privacy, she is able to do the things she enjoys the most. She has achieved the best of both worlds: she's famous, which she likes, and she's little known, which she also likes. Her friends say that this cool management of her public image is completely unconscious and instinctive, a product of breeding, upper-class values, and Miss Porter's. Others say that it is shrewdly calculated. Whichever is the case—and it is probably a bit of both—it works.

But this still doesn't completely explain the public's continuing fascination with Jacqueline Kennedy Onassis. Perhaps it is because, in the public's mind, she embodies a kind of American storybook dream. Fiction and films have been filled with heroines who have risen to great heights, been struck down, and have risen again, and it is interesting that, as a girl, one of

Jackie Bouvier's favorite novels was *Gone With the Wind*. The parallels between Jackie and Scarlett O'Hara are interesting, too. Like Scarlett, Jackie grew up on plantation-like estates in Newport, East Hampton, and Virginia. Like Scarlett, Jackie had a father whom she adored, and who adored her, and who came to a bad end. There was the first love that ended tragically. Then, like Scarlett who also preferred older men, came the marriage to the swarthy entrepreneur from another part of the world—Onassis, her Rhett Butler. Like Scarlett, Jackie fascinated men not so much because she was pretty but because she was soft, feminine, and also tough-minded, determined—a combination of masculine and feminine traits, or what Jung called "competing tendencies." Today, we are watching Jackie Onassis's third Phoenix-like ascent from the ashes. In her new life in New York, we are witnessing what no doubt would have happened to Scarlett O'Hara after the novel ended.

Hammersmith Farm has now been sold, and its acreage will be subdivided but, for years, in the Deck Room of the house where Jackie spent her youthful summers, there were old family scrapbooks filled with her jottings—poems written in the round, schoolgirlish hand that has changed very little since she was ten or eleven, mostly about nature: the sea, the sunset, the changing seasons. The poems bear the signature "Me." Then there were the pencil sketches which she did of her mother, sister, and step-family—sketches labeled "Mummy," "Lee," "Uncle Hugh," "Yusha," and so on. One remarkable likeness is also labeled "Me." Her mother recalls how she sketched herself carefully in front of a mirror. Jackie Onassis, as any woman would who is approaching fifty, still spends a certain amount of time studying her reflection in a mirror—it is how she created that smile that is never less than perfect for the photographers when they appear. And —perhaps more industriously than ever before—she is working, with her new job, on becoming the sole proprietor of herself, and developing the potential of the "Me."

27

Search for
Tomorrow

TUCKED IN THE northwest corner of Somerset County, New Jersey, surrounded by green and rolling hills of woods and pasture and at the end of a bumpy road, stands a cluster of small and unprepossessing white frame buildings, rather in want of paint. A small stream winds in the distance through a grove of trees. A flock of wild geese paddles in a small pond at the foot of the hill. (The geese used to fly south in winter; lately, for some reason, they have chosen to make this pond their year-round address.) Approaching the white buildings, up a slight grade, there is a whiff of barnyard in the air. This is because, other than the manager William "Buster" Chadwell and his wife, the only other permanent residents of the place are a pack of brown and white American fox hounds some ninety strong who frolic or sun themselves in the grass in a large, well-fenced corral outside their kennel, and eleven horses, most of them boarding, in an adjoining stable. Still, unless one were alerted—no sign marks the entrance—one might suspect one was entering Hardscrabble Farm, instead of a private enclave of the very rich, the Essex Fox Hounds. This is where Jacqueline Onassis likes to hunt. Her weekend retreat where, with her friend and neighbor Murray McDonnell, she stables her horses, is in Bernardsville, a few miles down the road.

Though one rides to the hounds with a group, it is essentially a solitary, even contemplative sport, a contest between man and nature. There is little conversation during a fox hunt. Instead, each hunter is alone with his thoughts and the weather and the countryside —watching how the dogs pick up the scent, how the crafty and unpredictable fox, who knows the land better than anyone, evades and misleads the dogs, how the horse beneath one's seat responds to commands and takes the jumps over walls and fences. To those who love fox hunting, and Jackie is one, there is almost an element of mystery involved. One never knows where one is going, what tricks the fox will play, or how the day will end.

The only requirement for membership in the Essex Fox Hounds is that one must own land—preferably a large tract of land, say a thousand or so acres—in the area where the hunts take place. Among the nearby large landholders, and members of the hunt, are the Nicholas F. Bradys, the C. Douglas Dillons, and the George W. Mercks. Fox hunting requires space. It can also be hard on property, and having ninety hounds pursued by sixty horses tear through one's garden or across one's lawn can result in horticultural disaster. Jumping horses occasionally knock down fences. Fox hunting requires tolerant neighbors. If, the club decided, the members *are* the neighbors, the neighbors are more tolerant.

At the Essex Fox Hounds, however, the one exception to the property-owning rule—as she is an exception to most rules—is Jacqueline Onassis. Her Bernardsville land is not in hunt territory and, when she first began coming to the area, she rented. Still, she had become a member before the rule went into effect, and as Lewis Murdock, Master of the Hunt, says, "We couldn't go to her and say, 'Sorry, old cock, we've got this new rule and you're through.' That would be a pretty crappy thing to do, wouldn't it? So she stays on. She's never given us any trouble."

One of the oldest rules of fox hunting—and the club—is that privacy is respected, even revered. Business is never discussed, and gossip is frowned upon. The hunt is for hunting—nothing more. On her autumn and winter weekends during the hunting season with the Essex Fox Hounds, Jackie can find a kind of privacy that is available to her nowhere else. As Lew Murdock, a retired banker with a salty style of speech not usually associated with someone listed in the *Social Register* (which he is), says: "Hell, nobody here is impressed with who she is. Sometimes I take her and Caroline out alone. I say, 'Don't ask me any questions, just watch what I do and do the same thing.' She never said a damn word—just did what I showed her. She knows what she's doing, and she does it damn well. I never talk to her about anything else in her life except hunting, and neither does anybody else. Having her with us makes no damn difference to anybody. When we had to pass the hat for a new truck a while back, she gave us a hell of a nice check. She knows half the people in the field by name, and of course everybody knows who the hell she is. Hell, maybe she likes to hunt to get away from the kind of society life she lives in New York the rest of the time. But I know she hunts with us because she likes to hunt—just like the rest of us. When she's here, she's just one of us, having a hell of a lot of fun. Nobody here thinks anything else about her, one way or the other."

In the pastoral, moneyed reaches of the Essex Fox Hounds, no one may care, or think about, Jacqueline Onassis, but in the rest of America this would appear not to be the case and, in the end, it would be interesting to know just what Americans think of their enigmatic, many-sided former First Lady. When, in the fall of 1977, it was announced that Christina Onassis had agreed to settle something in excess of $20,000,000 on her stepmother, just to be rid of

Jackie's demands against the estate, a number of Americans concluded that she was simply greedy. After all, she had so much money already. When John F. Kennedy died, he left a trust fund of roughly $10,000,-000 to be shared by Jackie and their children. When she married Onassis, he had given her $3,000,000 outright, plus jewels and paintings. It had also been rumored for years, and never denied, that the late Joseph P. Kennedy gave her $1,000,000 to dissuade his daughter-in-law from divorcing his son during a rocky period in the marriage. She had the big house in New Jersey, the big apartment in New York. She had inherited $80,000 from her father, and her Grandfather Lee, when he died, had been generous to both his granddaughters in his will. Onassis had provided her a lifetime income of $200,000 a year, roughly half of it from tax-free bonds. How much money did the woman want? There wasn't enough in the world, it seemed, to slake her avarice.

Of course Jackie—abetted by her lawyers and by her brother-in-law, Ted Kennedy—had some justification for feeling cheated by Onassis's will. She had signed their pre-marital agreement in good faith. He apparently had not and, behind her back, had got Greek law changed in an attempt to nullify the document. He had misled her into signing a second agreement, and lied to her about its import. Surely he had not played fair with her and, through deviousness, had managed to trick her out of what would otherwise have been her legal widow's share of his estate. When Christina and her lawyers capitulated, it was obvious that they felt that Jackie and her lawyers would have, if it came to court, the stronger case. Jackie's lawyers had held a couple of other trump cards. In his will, Onassis had also rather unwisely left Jackie a share of the island of Skorpios and of the *Christina,* which would have left his daughter and his widow in unfriendly financial entanglement for years. In accepting the $20,000,000 settlement (some sources

245

placed the figure as high as $26,000,000), Jackie relinquished her shares of the island and the yacht to Christina. In New York legal circles it was felt that Jackie's lawyers had served her extremely well. They had served themselves well, too. Estimates on the legal bill for performing such a feat ran as high as $10,000,000.

In certain circles of New York society, meanwhile, Jackie is regarded as not only a money-grabber but also a man-snatcher. Helene Gaillet, a Manhattan photographer, claims, for example, that Jackie destroyed a "long-standing relationship" that Miss Gaillet had had with banker Felix Rohatyn, with whom Jackie was seen at the 1976 Democratic convention. "I thought she was my friend," Miss Gaillet says. "I'd even been her house guest on Skorpios. But men get bowled over by her. Felix and I had been together for years until he started taking her out, and they were seen together on national television. Felix kept saying to me that it was nothing, just a casual date, that it didn't change anything between us. It changed everything. Believe me, when every gossip columnist in the country began calling me to ask how I felt about it, everything was destroyed between Felix and me. Jackie runs through men the way she runs through clothes. All she wants, of course, are escorts. She did the same thing to Shirley MacLaine with Pete Hamill. Pete keeps saying that nothing has changed between him and Shirley. Ha! They should ask Shirley how *she* feels."

Miss Gaillet goes on to say, "To me, she's a very *insecure* person. She covers her insecurity by buying lots of things for herself. She's not even secure about clothes, or why would she buy so many of them? She's insecure, and she's insincere. I was going to have an exhibit of my photographs at a gallery on Madison Avenue, and she said to me, 'Oh, Helene, I do want to see it when it opens!' Well, as it happened, on the day of the opening I ran into Jackie on Madison Avenue right outside the gallery. I said, 'Come on in and see my show—it's just been hung.' She got all kind of nervous and said, 'Oh, I can't right now—I've got to go down to Art Bag and look at some handbags.' "

These views, of course, come from rather rarefied sources and special circumstances. What the vast general public feels about Jacqueline Onassis, from what they read about her, endlessly, in women's magazines and gossip sheets—is more difficult to pin down. Do they read about her merely because she is rich? There are a number of women—Doris Duke, Barbara Hutton, Marjorie Merriweather Post, Mary Lasker, to name a few—who are, or have been, far richer than Jackie, and who have stimulated far less public curiosity about their lives. Is it her beauty? At Madame Tussaud's Waxwork Museum in London, an annual poll is taken of whom visitors consider the world's most beautiful women. Jackie's name appeared on the list of winners only once, in 1972, and then in fifth place, behind Raquel Welch, Sophia Loren, Elizabeth Taylor, and Brigitte Bardot. In 1976, the *Ladies' Home Journal* conducted a poll of high school students all over the country in an attempt to determine who the "heroes and heroines" of today's youth might be. Interestingly, the boys' list of heroes turned out to consist mostly of males, and so did the girls'—supporting the theory in some psychological circles that women don't really like other women. Jackie Onassis did not emerge as a heroine to either sex. (O. J. Simpson turned out to be the top hero with both boys and girls.)

In a more recent survey, a group of American adults—both men and women—was presented with the following list of famous ladies, living and dead:

Elizabeth Taylor
Joan of Arc
Queen Elizabeth II
Eleanor Roosevelt
Raquel Welch

Cleopatra
The Virgin Mary
Marilyn Monroe
Bess Truman
Brigitte Bardot
Princess Grace of Monaco
Jacqueline Onassis
Grandma Moses
Greta Garbo
Billie Jean King
Katharine Hepburn
Bette Davis
Florence Nightingale
Marian Anderson
Anne Frank
Sarah Bernhardt
Barbara Walters
Catherine the Great
Ava Gardner
Rose Kennedy

The women were asked, first, which of these women they most admired and, second, which—given the time, place, and circumstances—they would most like to trade places with. The men were asked only which of the women they most admired. The results of this survey revealed that only four percent of the women polled admired Jackie Onassis. In terms of switching lives with her, Jackie fared somewhat better—six percent said they would like to do that. (Eleanor Roosevelt was the hands-down winner as most admired, and Katharine Hepburn led the would-most-like-to-be field.) Of the 250 men polled, not a single man said that he admired Jacqueline Onassis. Admiration and envy, then, must both be ruled out as reasons for the deep impression this woman has made on our national consciousness—the woman whose impact Cornell Capa calls "unique in history."

What in the world do we think of her? To begin

with, there is her enticing *Frenchness*. Americans have
long been intrigued by the French—who invented the
élan—who somehow seem to live better, and do things
better, than we do. We do not always like the French,
or find them particularly cordial company—they
rather look down their noses at us Anglo-Saxons—
but, as Oscar Wilde said, "when good Americans die
they go to Paris." Then there is the sympathetic version of the upper class that Jacqueline Onassis manages
to project. *Our Forebears* may have been a fiction, but
the sense of *noblesse oblige* that Grampy Jack Bouvier's little genealogy managed to inflict on the family
did not fail to rub off on her. Sincere or not, she can
be undeniably gracious. Friends speak of her warm,
personal letters—usually written in longhand in small,
rounded, boarding-school script—which often display
a charming, even poetic, turn of phrase. In the middle
of her acrimonious dispute with William Manchester,
when she heard that influenza—and a certain amount
of nervous exhaustion—had developed into pneu-
monia, and he had been taken to a hospital, she
quickly wrote him a kind, caring letter, wishing him a
quick recovery.

She also manages to convey an attractive human-
ness, and has made it clear that she is as capable of
vanity, cupidity, sloth, self-indulgence—or any other
Deadly Sin—as any of us. But she is indeed the
prototype of the successful American Woman: intelli-
ent, beguiling, adept at stroking the male ego. To this
extent, she has established a place among women as
the very essence of success. The detractors are merely
jealous. There, but for the grace of God, would they
go. Though men who know her do not tend to describe
her as sexy, all agree that she is exceptionally *female*.

Finally there is the fact that, more than a novel
(where, at least, one is permitted to peek ahead and
see how it turns out), her life—though not entirely at
her bidding—has had the quality of modern television

JACQUELINE BOUVIER KENNEDY ONASSIS

soap opera, with all the elements of one of Procter & Gamble's most ambitious afternoons. Think of it! The unfolding saga of Jacqueline Onassis has contained murder, betrayal, suspense, powerful men who have used and misused our beautiful heroine who, in the end, manages to triumph over them. There were money problems, infidelity, incurable illness, widowhood. We watch the progress of her life with the same distanced detachment with which we watch the doings on the little screen—not quite believing it all and yet, suspending disbelief for an hour or so, quite willing to succumb to the narcotic of what-happens-next. Like daytime television, we often deplore it, and yet we know that it can be quite habit-forming. Like addicts, we wait for each new episode. The most frequently asked question about Jackie Onassis today is, "Will she marry again?" Be sure to tune in tomorrow, when we will hear Jackie say, . . .

Before he married her, Aristotle Onassis said of his future wife, "She's a totally misunderstood woman. Perhaps she even misunderstands herself. She's being held up as a model of propriety, constancy, and so many of those boring American female virtues. She needs a small scandal to bring her alive. A peccadillo, an indiscretion. Something should happen to her to win our fresh compassion. The world loves to pity fallen grandeur."

That comment was made in 1967. Since then, we have seen the peccadillos, the indiscretion, the small scandals. We have witnessed the fall, and then watched her bounce back as vivid as before. She has always bounded back, with a fresh surprise, from the men who in one way or another failed her—back with that extraordinary flashy smile, the smile that has become a close-up in our minds and that has managed to keep her just one jump ahead of the game. And at each performance, from behind the wings we hear the voice of Black Jack Bouvier coaching her as he did from his

250

cluttered digs at the Westbury—Don't give too much of yourself, withhold a little, keep them guessing—They may not always understand you, but at least they'll come back for more—They may not always like you, but at least, darling, they'll never forget you.

Index